Reading Weber

Economy and Society

Edited by
Economy and Society **editorial board**
Talal Asad   New School for Social Research, New York
Beverley Brown   Edinburgh University
Mike Gane   Loughborough University
Terry Johnson   University of Leicester
Gary Littlejohn   University of Bradford
Maxine Molyneux   University of Essex
Ali Rattansi   Open University
Grahame Thompson   Open University
Harold Wolpe   University of Essex
Jonathan Zeitlin   Birkbeck College, University of London
Sami Zubaida   Birkbeck College, University of London

Economy and Society paperbacks

This new series focuses on major issues which have been the subject of debate in the journal *Economy and Society*. Books in the series include:

Economic Calculation and Policy Formation
Edited by Grahame Thompson

Soviet Industrialisation and Soviet Maturity
Edited by Keith Smith

Towards a Critique of Foucault
Edited by Mike Gane

The Value Dimension
Edited by Ben Fine

Ideological Representation and Power in Social Relations
Edited by Mike Gane

Ideology, Method and Marx
Edited by Ali Rattansi

Reading Weber

Edited by
Keith Tribe

R

Routledge
London and New York

First published 1989
by Routledge
11 New Fetter Lane, London EC4P 4EE
29 West 35th Street, New York, NY 10001

© 1989 Keith Tribe
Typesetting in Plantin 11 on 12pt by Columns of Reading
Printed by Mackays of Chatham PLC, Chatham, Kent

British Library Cataloguing in Publication Data

Reading Weber.
1. Sociology. Theories of Weber, Max
I. Title   II. Tribe, Keith, 1949–
301'.092'4

Library of Congress Cataloging in Publication Data
also available

ISBN 0–415–02890–6

Contents

Acknowledgements

I would like to thank Lawrence Scaff, Friedrich H. Tenbruck, and Martin Riesebrodt for their ready agreement to the reprinting of their articles in this collection. The original place of publication of essays and translations below is as follows:

Lawrence Scaff (1984) 'Weber before Weberian Sociology', *British Journal of Sociology* 35: 190–215.

Friedrich H. Tenbruck (1980) 'The Problem of Thematic Unity in the Works of Max Weber', *British Journal of Sociology* 31: 316–51.

Keith Tribe (1983) 'Prussian Agriculture – German Politics: Max Weber 1892–7', *Economy and Society* 12: 181–226.

Martin Riesebrodt (1986) 'From Patriarchalism to Capitalism', *Economy and Society* 15: 476–502.

Max Weber (1894) 'Entwickelungstendenzen in der Lage der ostelbischen Landarbeiter', *Preußische Jahrbücher* Bd. 77: 437–73. (Referred to below as DT.)

Max Weber (1895) *Der Nationalstaat und die Volkswirtschaftspolitik*, Tübingen: Mohr. (Referred to below as *NS*.)

Max Weber (1897) 'Über Deutschland als Industriestaat', *Verhandlungen des Achten Evangelisch-sozialen Kongresses*, Göttingen: Vandenhoeck und Ruprecht, pp. 105–13, 122–3. (Referred to below as IS.)

CHAPTER 1

Introduction

Keith Tribe

In the course of the last ten years the role of Max Weber as a founding father of 'sociology' has been thrown increasingly in doubt. His work (or rather, that portion of his work which was made accessible) had played an important part in the creation and legitimation of theoretical and empirical sociology as a viable academic proposition. But this sociology, as it developed in European and North American academic institutions from the 1950s, is now in serious disarray and the self-confident pose which it once struck with respect to its neighbours in the human sciences has dissolved. The discipline which in the later 1960s laid claim as a science of society (or in the 1970s as a science of social formations) to the domains of its neighbours has now ceded resources, personnel, and intellectual property to these neighbours, living on now as a collection of 'special sociologies' rather than as an identifiable intellectual endeavour.[1] While this process of fragmentation has left the work of professed 'theoretical sociologists' such as Parsons, Giddens, or Merton without a coherent intellectual constituency,[2] this same process has played a role in liberating the founding fathers from the discipline that had claimed them. The 'founding fathers' such as Weber and Durkheim have survived their progeny.

While this presents us with the opportunity of rediscovering them, it is not immediately self-evident that the effort will be generally worthwhile – there are any number of nineteenth-century European writers on social, cultural, and political issues who are today rightfully or wrongfully forgotten, when not ignored. For Max Weber, however, the shedding of a sociological legacy reveals a body of work which is at once diverse and stimulating. Far from being a 'founding father' of sociology, Weber has been shown to be a figure whose work belongs as much to classical political theory as to a more modern consideration of social and economic structures and processes.[3]

This collection of essays by and about Max Weber is intended to introduce the reader to some of the more neglected writings of Weber, while showing how our understanding of the work as a whole is enhanced by a confrontation with Weber's work as *writing*. The essays by Tribe and Riesebrodt, previously published

1

in *Economy and Society*, direct attention to the importance of
Weber's early agrarian writings, while the essay by Scaff provides
a long overdue consideration of those aspects of Weber's early
writings which have been overlooked by those who see in him
simply a 'founding father' of sociology. The essay by Tenbruck,
on the other hand, addresses itself to the issue of what might be
regarded as Weber's 'central work', and considers the problems
surrounding structure and composition of Weber's *Economy and
Society*. Unlike much Weberian commentary which organizes its
consideration of the writing in terms of contributions to modern
sociological theory, all of these essays take up a different task: the
reading of Weber's writings so that we might be able to discover
in them problems and themes disregarded or misunderstood by
modern social scientists.

The work of reading Max Weber is a task that has barely
begun, and which all the essays below seek, in their different
ways, to further. The propagation of Max Weber as a 'founding
father' is one that has for the most part taken place in the English
language, relying on translations of varying quality and commentaries written by readers of the translations and other English-
language commentaries.[4] In this way a corpus of received ideas
has been built up which bears a marked resemblance to the game
of Chinese Whispers, as Hennis has observed (1988: 60, 199). In
particular, it is the so-called 'early works', those written in the
years before the onset of his illness in 1897, that have been
neglected, a neglect no doubt in part prompted by the fact that no
translations were made available until the later 1970s.[5] Although
Bendix devoted a chapter to these writings almost thirty years ago
in his standard work on Weber (1959: Ch. 2), it is only in the last
few years that their existence, let alone significance, has been
generally acknowledged.

In some respects it is true that, superficially, the three pieces by
Weber published here – from 1894, 1895 and 1897 respectively –
lack the scholarly resonances of the later writings. It cannot be
claimed that they represent a key to the work hitherto concealed
from us. Nevertheless, they possess features which severely jolt
the received image of Max Weber. For those who have learnt that
Weber emphasized the development of capitalism as an 'intellectual' process (whether in terms of a 'protestant ethic' or of a spirit
of rationality) we have a detailed and thoroughly materialist
analysis of the development of capitalist enterprise in eastern
Germany and its socio-political effects – an analysis that
furthermore provides a coherent account of the absence of 'class
consciousness' (Weber's terminology) among eastern rural workers.
For those who believe that Weber was the bourgeois proponent of

value-free social science we see him in his Inaugural Address lambasting the bourgeoisie and proclaiming that economic science is a political science and, for him, one with German values at that. For those who have been raised on Weber the sociologist, we have Weber the economist demolishing the arguments of conservative agrarians and anti-capitalists. Moreover, the harsh and unrelenting tone (it is important to remember that this was a contribution to oral discussion) with which this is done will surprise many raised on an image of Weber as representative of a bourgeois moderation.

Precisely because these texts are relatively fresh for us their novel features are all the more striking, as is their lack of congruency with the apparent preoccupations and problems of the works 'after the break' – after 1903 and beginning with the first article on Roscher (Weber 1903). While a marked change of direction can be registered in the manner in which Weber resumed intensive work after a six-year interval, there are no grounds for arguing that his interests and preoccupations changed. Biographical and bibliographical knowledge is important in evaluating Weber's writing, as it is in the case of any writer. The chronology that is thereby established is not one of cumulative significance or progressive modification; the alterations which occur are far more the natural outcome of shifts in perspective brought about by external circumstances and the connections Weber was able to make over a wide range of material. In many ways his 'themes and problems' remain constant from first to last. It is because we cannot so easily fit the early writings into the conventional canon of Weberian writing that these 'themes and problems' become more evident; and so long as it is accepted that there is no radical change of line in Weber's thinking, we can with these rediscovered 'themes and problems' begin to make a new kind of sense of the 'mature' writings.

By way of demonstrating the thesis advanced above, that the work of reading Weber has barely begun, we can introduce two texts of quite varying nature and whose exposure has also been quite different. The first is an unpublished reading guide and partial summary of a lecture course in economics that Weber began to deliver in 1897–98 – an 'early work' and, on top of that, a text that relatively few people know of, let alone have ever seen. The second is the essay on 'Objectivity' dating from 1904 (Weber 1968). This is one of the foundation stones of Weberian methodology and as such is read as a normative text with respect to intellectual practices. What is rarely emphasized in considera- tion of this text is that it represented Weber's protocols for the running of an academic journal; a journal which rapidly became the most important German social science journal and remained so until its closure in 1933. If we read the text in these terms some features emerge that were hitherto obscure.

The 'Grundriss zu den Vorlesungen über Allgemeine ('theoretische') Nationalökonomie' (1898a) was the structured reading guide which Weber composed for his lectures on theoretical economics in the winter semester 1897–98 at Heidelberg. In addition to this 23-page text Weber also prepared a 34-page outline of the first major section ('Book 1') entitled 'The Conceptual Foundations of Economics' (1898b); in her biography Marianne Weber suggests that this outline represents the framework for a book that Weber intended to write (1926: 241). On the basis of these two printed guides we can begin to assess the work of Weber as a professional economist: what kind of economics did Weber represent as the successor to Knies at Heidelberg?

Weber had earlier described himself as an economist of the 'Younger Historical School', that is, in the tradition of Roscher and Knies but associated with the second generation of German economics. Foremost among this younger generation was Schmoller, and it is no surprise to discover on the first page of the reading guide, under the subheading 'Tasks and Methods of Theoretical *Nationalökonomie*' references to the dispute on method which took place in the 1880s between the 'historical economics' of Schmoller and the 'new Austrian' economics of Carl Menger.

It is sometimes supposed that this *Methodenstreit* involved the confrontation of a new analytical economics with an older descriptive tradition – Schmoller's writing itself is today hardly recognizable as 'economics' and would more usually be assigned to economic history. But in many respects Schmoller is unrepresentative of late nineteenth-century German economics. 'Historical economics' was not an enterprise that simply described the evolution of economic systems, in many respects it involved an evaluation of economic phenomena in terms of the varying conditions of economic life; it was thus more *descriptive* (or in our modern terminology, 'applied') than *historical* in the sense current today. The theoretical tradition of *Nationalökonomie* in which Weber stood, unlike the Anglo-French tradition of political economy, turned on the concept of 'human need', its variations and the modes in which it could be satisfied. Thus Menger's *Grundsätze* of 1871 begins from the nature of utilities which, when embodied in a manner related to the satisfaction of need are called 'economic goods' (1968: 2). In establishing this point Menger appends a lengthy footnote which begins with a definition drawn from Aristotle and, via physiocratic literature, works its way towards earlier nineteenth century writers such as Soden,

Hufeland, and Jacob. Likewise in his later discussion of value, this is constantly related to the question of the satisfaction of needs. If we compare this approach with the contemporary work of Jevons we can immediately note some differences: here the calculus of pleasure and pain is employed so that the value of a good in exchange might be related to the optimization of utility with respect to quantity of a good. This theory of economics is, as Jevons states, 'purely mathematical in character' (1879: 3). The new economics of later nineteenth-century Britain carries over from Smith and Ricardo a concern with value, but formulated in a mathematical fashion first by Jevons, and then by Marshall.

This departure did not go unchallenged, and in the 'Preface to the Second Edition' of Jevons's *Theory of Political Economy* he notes first Cliffe Leslie's inductive reconstruction of economic science, and then Cairnes's deductive but anti-mathematical approach in his *Character and Logical Method of Political Economy* (1875: vi–vii). At the very least this serves to remind us that Jevons's economics does not confront a unitary 'traditional' classical economics in Britain, and that it was not until the beginning of the twentieth century that economics began to assume the shape of a self-conscious and united 'academic discipline' with theoretical protocols dictating what was acceptable as 'real economics'.[6] But it is also of interest to us that Weber's reading guide, beginning with the main works of the 'Older Historical School' (Roscher's *Grundriss* of 1843, Hildebrand's *Nationalökonomie* of 1848, and Knies's *Politische Ökonomie* of 1853) and covering the main writings of the *Methodenstreit*, also includes works by Cairnes and Cliffe Leslie. These are the only English-language texts among a list of sixteen; and although it is the second edition of Cairnes's *Logical Method* which is cited, containing the pointed critique of Jevons's 'mathematical' economics, Jevons does not figure elsewhere in the list (although Walras does). More importantly perhaps for Weber's position in the emergent profession of economics is his neglect, in this first section, of J. N. Keynes's *Scope and Method of Political Economy* (1891). Keynes's basic distinction between 'abstract, theoretical and deductive political economy' on the one hand and 'ethical, realistic and inductive political economy' on the other gained rapid acceptance in the discussions of the methods proper to economics and formed the methodological counterpart to Marshall's *Principles* (which does find a place among the foreign textbooks and compendia cited by Weber) in the development of economics teaching in Britain.

The importance of this 'omission' is not that it indicates Weber's lack of awareness of recent developments in economics;

as we have seen, in citing Cairnes Weber is citing a book which
takes issue with Jevons, a figure who is today regarded as one of
the most significant in the development of modern economics.
The fact that Weber does not introduce Jevons or Keynes at an
appropriate point into his survey of relevant literature is more
likely an indicator that he thought them irrelevant for his
purposes. Why should this be so?

If Weber's 'historical economics' were simply a systematization
of economic history in the manner of Schmoller then we should
not expect his central course to begin with methodological issues.
Neither should we expect this to be followed by a section entitled
'The conceptual foundations of economics' in which the list of
books is headed by those of Menger, Böhm-Bawerk, and Pierson.
In the related outline Weber defines 'abstract theory' as based
upon 'modern occidental Man and his activity. It strives initially
to disclose the most elementary life-phenomena of the *fully mature
person*' (1898b: 1). The focus is thus upon the conditions of
modern economic activity, and not an attempt to grasp the nature
of economic life as the outcome of a long process of historical
development. 'Abstract theory' ignores this and places at the
centre of its analysis an artificial economic subject which with
respect to real, empirical men:

a. *ignores*, treats as if *not present* all those motives which have an
influence on real men which are specifically *non-economic*, i.e.
all those motives not arising from the satisfaction of material
needs;
b. *imputes* as actually present in men particular qualities which
are either *not* present or only incompletely, namely
a) complete *insight* into the given *situation* – perfect economic
knowledge;
b) exclusive selection of the *most appropriate means* for a given
end – absolute 'economic rationality';
c) exclusive devotion of one's own powers to the attainment
of economic goods – tireless economic endeavour.
It therefore argues on the basis of *unrealistic* men, analogous to
a mathematical ideal.

(1898b: 2)

The contrast which is at work here is not one which turns on an
opposition of historical to analytical method, nor one which turns
on the deductive-inductive opposition emphasized by Keynes.
Weber has no time for a mathematical apprehension of economic
phenomena as practised by Jevons and as developed by Marshall
because he believed that this left to one side a considerable

proportion of the subject matter proper to economics. If we are to identify a relevant contrast separating the economics of Weber from that of Marshall or J. B. Clark then the distinction would perhaps turn on his opposition to the development of a mathematically-based science of economic behaviour and his belief in the material variety of economic life. This is evident in the second section of his lecture course, entitled 'The natural foundations of the economy'. Here we find reference to literature on communication in its widest sense, political geography, population, and racial characteristics – the material foundations of economic activity. There then follows 'The historical foundations of the economy' which covers primitive peoples, theories of the family, settlement, and the development of property, the development of commerce, the nature of ancient economy, the agrarian foundations of medieval economies and the emergence of the modern enterprise, completing the eight-page section with a sub-section entitled 'The emergence of the economy'. If we look at the reading here we find that, far from a simply historising account of economic processes, Weber covers under this heading the development of contemporary economic institutions such as the factory, the banks, the stock exchange, and the institutions of trade (1898b: 12–14).

There are three more sections of unequal length in the course. 'Book 4. The stages of development of economic theory', is divided into pre-Smithian, classical and socialist economics, in which the latter interestingly enough contains 23 references including *Capital* and Engels's *Anti-Dühring*. The fifth 'book' is longer, being devoted to a 'theoretical analysis of the modern economy (*Verkehrswirtschaft*)'. '*Verkehr*', literally 'intercourse, traffic, communication' was a central term of the German economics of the time and is the mode in which production and distribution are integrated into the subject at both theoretical and practical levels. The organizing concept of *Verkehr* does however make for some strange combinations for those used to the regularities of classical political economy with its emphasis on value forms. While the reading begins conventionally enough with Cannan's *History of the Theory of Production and Distribution in English Political Economy*, the following sections on industrial and agricultural enterprises emphasize the fact that production and distribution are understood as material processes, and not exclusively as moments in the valorisation process. The sub-section '*Verkehr* and its theoretical problems' includes means of transport, the telegraph, shipping, currency, the organization of credit, banking, and foreign exchange, followed by markets, exchanges, and the institutions of trade. Only then does Weber arrive at price formation and income distribution, devoting most attention to the 'typical categories of income in the *Verkehrswirtschaft*' – profit, rent, and wages. Finally Book 6 covers the development of social and economic ideals in an extremely cursory manner, adding texts by Stammler and Sombart to literature already cited and concluding the reading guide with Weber's own Inaugural Address.

In the absence of an adequate understanding of the diversity of later nineteenth-century Political Economy (i.e. the economics practised in Britain, France, and the United States), and in our almost complete ignorance of the German tradition of economics as it developed from mid-century, it is difficult to arrive at a rounded assessment of the manner in which Weber apprehended and related to the economics of his time. The sheer range of the literature with which he deals is immediately impressive, and testifies to a comprehensive grounding in the (German) literature of the day. It is also quite obviously not simply a 'historical economics' of the kind that one might be led to expect from some of his writings on antiquity, for example – his apprehension of ancient economy was driven far more by his interest in property and law. Weber's exclusion of the new economics practised by Jevons, Marshall, Menger, and Walras among others can also be demonstrated to be a conscious exclusion – while aware of the economics which they were developing he set himself against it, arguing for a more extensive definition of the scope of economic science than they were prepared to allow. The fact that this position was shortly to be eclipsed in the hierarchies promoted by the professionalization of economics is no reason to dismiss Weber's economics as dated. What does clearly emerge from the above is the degree to which, in 1898, Weber had an excellent working knowledge of the economics of his day; a fact which has gone largely unnoticed in the vast bulk of the commentaries. Professionally, Weber was at this time an economist, and it was as such that he embarked in 1904 on the editing of a journal with two other prominent economists – Edgar Jaffé and Werner Sombart. We can now turn to the second example to be discussed here.

The *Archiv für soziale Gesetzgebung und Statistik* had been founded in 1888 as a journal dedicated to the 'labour question'. Emphasis was placed on the 'cultural significance' of this question, and in this respect the journal represented a new type of specialized literature. The new editors summarized and confirmed their agreement with the posture of the established journal in an introductory note, in which the phrasing is again of interest for those who have assumed Weber to be a proponent of capitalism's rationality as against Marx's critical option. Capitalism is here described as an irreversible result of historical development which had irrevocably displaced the social order of ancient society; henceforth a leading concern of state politics must be the social and cultural assimilation of the proletariat which capitalism had created as a class and which was also conscious of its historical uniqueness. The transformation of society was however a gradual process, to be achieved step-by-step through the organic reconstruction of 'historically transmitted conditions and circumstances' (Jaffé, Sombart, and Weber 1904: iv). This was essentially a process of legislative change, and in so far as the journal pursued social-political objectives, these were in future to be founded upon a *Realpolitik* confronting the world as it actually was.

This general project had the agreement of the editors; what did they wish to alter? First, the scope of the journal had to be drastically extended:

Our journal will today treat the historical and theoretical knowledge of the *general cultural significance of capitalist development* as that particular scientific problem with which it concerns itself. And because it does and must proceed on the basis of a quite specific perspective – that of the economic determination (*Bedingtheit*) of cultural phenomena – it cannot avoid close contact with neighbouring disciplines such as general *Staatslehre*, philosophy of law, social ethics, social psychology and those investigations usually brought together under the name of sociology.

(Jaffé, Sombart, and Weber 1904: v)

Second, the manner in which these subjects were to be treated would alter. Whereas the journal had initially devoted a great deal of space to the presentation of relevant data, a number of new journals had been founded since the 1880s which devoted themselves to the collection and recording of data. In future, argued the editors, the simple replication of legislative material would be displaced by a critical work of review; what was needed now was a work of synthesis.

The *Archiv für Sozialwissenschaft und Sozialpolitik* thus began publication as a journal that would further the development of the social sciences as sciences relating to problems arising from the conditions of capitalist development. This dictate presented the editors with the task of synthesizing material from a number of related disciplines – and it was in fact Weber who in the early years bore much of the editorial responsibility for the journal. He wrote the protocols for his editorship himself, and they were published in the first number of the new journal under the title

'The "Objectivity" of Knowledge in Social Policy and the Social Sciences' (Weber 1968). In many respects this represents a set of rules for the commissioning, acceptance, and rejection of articles for the new journal.

When a new journal appears, begins Weber, the first question asked concerns the 'tendency' that it represents.[7] The *Archiv* in its previous incarnation had published material on 'social conditions in all countries' combined with the adoption of a critical stance on related legislation. As a 'scientific' journal, however, it was bound by academic conventions regarding truth and objectivity. But how were these conventions to be made congruent with the stated purpose of the journal? What norms were applied, and how did this in turn affect the production of scientific truth? Given that today 'value-judgements are made everywhere in a nonchalant and spontaneous manner' (this volume: 200, if the new journal was to be anything other than merely modish it had to clearly state its position on this question: 'in what sense are there "objectively valid truths" in the domain of the sciences of cultural life?' (1968: 147).

Such truths could not simply be discovered 'in history', whether this ethic was located with respect to historical evolutionism or to a historical relativism, thereby lending 'our science' (*National-ökonomie*) generally valid norms which it was its business to produce.

> Our journal, as the representative of a specialised empirical discipline has to *completely reject* this view, as we wished to establish above from the outset; for we believe that it can never be the task of an empirical science to establish binding norms and ideals so that practical recipes can then be deduced from them.
>
> (1968: 149)

This does not mean however that a value-free science is to be constructed; the important point is instead to establish what relation the science has to identifiable value judgements. At a general level this means that the values embodied in scientific discourse must be 'declared' if, in the 'cultural' sciences, a science is to avoid the risk of 'discovering' these values as truth. But it also presents a useful standard for the acceptance and rejection of manuscripts; and the remarks which Weber proceeds to make on the 'evaluation' of values underline this point (1968: 151).

Partisanship exists, of course, and it would be foolish to ignore it; but Weber emphasizes that the journal cannot hope to deal with the problems that it presents simply by striking a cross-

section or synthesizing diverging perspectives on a subject. This
kind of 'balance' is no path to 'objectivity' in the social sciences,
argues Weber (1968: 155).[8] It has to be made clear to the reader
that values and standards are being employed, particularly where a
confrontation of values occurs. It was not possible to retreat to a
'neutral' position from which values could be judged independently
of a 'world view'. When such 'world views' clashed it had to be
made clear to the reader where the 'thinking researcher stopped
speaking and the feeling man began' (1968: 157). Accordingly, the
Archiv should be a place where political opponents found
themselves practising scientific work. However, there was a
problem with the present character of the journal; concerned as it
was with workers' conditions and aspirations, a constituency of
writers had formed around the *Archiv* which gave it a certain
image for the readership (1968: 159–60). This again is an editorial
problem, and one which Weber appears to have confronted by
deliberately commissioning new writers and, it must be said,
filling many of the pages himself.

In the first volume of the new series of the *Archiv* there are 725
pages, 136 of which are accounted for by Weber (the essay on
'Objectivity' and the essay on entailment in Prussia). The first
major piece is by Sombart, 'Towards a Systematization of
Economic Crises'; the 'Objectivity' essay is followed by Tönnies
on Ammon's social theory, Eduard Bernstein on the British
worker and tariff imperialism, an essay by Bonn on the Irish
agrarian question, Tugan-Baranovsky on the breakdown of
capitalist economy, Kestner on household budgets and their
significance in the assessment of nutrition, and finally a piece
entitled 'Thirteen Years of Social Progress in New Zealand'. In
addition there are sections on legislative material, social science
bibliographies, and reviews. This is clearly a mixed bag politically
as well as substantively; and in the next few volumes we find, for
example, contributions from Radbruch, Simmel, Michels,
Bortkiewicz, Gottl, Grünberg, Hasbach, and Lederer. In 1905 the
section on legislation is dropped, making way for more articles
and reviews, while there is a slow expansion to around 900 pages
in 1909. By this time the content has settled in each number to
200–250 pages of articles, 20 pages of surveys of literature, and 50
pages of reviews.

There is not space here to do anything more than suggest the
range of material published by the *Archiv*, and in the absence of
the journal's archives and without ready access to Weber's
correspondence it is difficult to establish the scope of this more
'managerial' aspect of Weber's work. But anyone who leafs
through the *Archiv* – as anyone can do who cares to visit the

British Library for Political and Economic Science, where it is on open stacks – cannot but be impressed by the consistency in quality and relevance of the contributions to the journal. When Weber resumed his work in 1903–4 he began a phase of his life in which his political activity centred chiefly on the university. But another aspect of his activity at this time not directly devoted to scholarly study was his editorial work for the *Archiv*, and the degree to which this gave him an opportunity to assess the nature of contemporary German 'cultural sciences' should not be under-estimated. A more adequate assessment of Weber's work must take account of the social sciences of his time and his quite practical engagement with it, as the editor of the *Archiv* and then later as the editor of the *Foundations of Social Economy*, in which series *Economy and Society* appeared.

This approach to the re-reading of Weber could be extended through the writings, emphasizing the *occasional* nature of their composition and the consequences for our appreciation of their significance. In some respects this project might recall the methodology preached for the history of political thought by Quentin Skinner, in which the 'intentions' of an author are assigned paramount importance in the understanding of the development of political argument. While this approach has the virtue of establishing a standard for historical argument and evidence founded upon what a particular theorist *could have* known and what would have been taken for granted (thus ruling out the imposition of retrospective judgements), it does bring with it a subjectivism in the evaluation of discourse – 'language' is considered as the expression of a subject, rather than as a discursive complex which 'speaks through' the subject and in so doing creates subjectivity. Furthermore, the recovery of an 'original intention' is rendered problematic by the interposition of a reception process which has shaped our perceptions of Weber: his work has been reconstituted by the readings of others, and there is a limited value in counterposing the 'original intention' (whatever that might be) to what this 'intention' has come to mean.

But here our interest is different. The work of Max Weber has suffered greatly in its transmission – by translation, neglect, and fragmentation.[9] It might reasonably be doubted whether there is today much to be learnt from considering the reasons for this; what 'Weber' has come to mean in the sociological tradition is often of dubious value. A reconstruction of Weber should therefore return to his writings and seek to read them in a new way: as interventions in contemporary debates (here then we must understand these debates and their conditions); as the product of particular lines of argument (grounded individually and institutionally); as continuous with, and at times departing from, the intellectual environment surrounding the figure 'Max Weber'. In so far as we would thereby approach the original 'intentions' of Weber's work, this would involve a conception of 'intentionality' which was freed of some of the more restrictive subjectivist features inherent in the concept. We should read Weber as a writer trained in specific scientific traditions, whose interventions in contemporary issues were conditioned both by his preoccupations and the possibilities embodied in definite institutional forms. This requires a deeper knowledge of the texts than we have hitherto acquired, and also a more comprehensive knowledge of the contemporary state of the 'human sciences' as developing knowledges and practices. As we are beginning to improve our understanding of Weber, so there is gradually revealed to us a figure whose questioning of modernity, both as a realized future and as a mode of apprehending the present, still has something to say to us.

Notes

1. As much a symptom as an outline of this problem is Geoffrey Hawthorn's response to the appointment of Giddens to the Cambridge chair in sociology (1986).
2. These general remarks refer of course to emergent trends and do not pretend to a characterisation of the sociological enterprise as embodied in an educational apparatus ranging from schools to research institutes, in which the institutional function and practice of 'academic' sociological discourse varies greatly.
3. See in particular the work of Wilhelm Hennis (1988) and the collection edited by Mommsen and Osterhammel (1987).
4. Apart from individual disputes over the proper translation into English of some of Weber's key terms – for an accessible example see Mommsen's sketch of the problems associated with the translation of *Herrschaft* (1974: 74) – texts in English such as the *Protestant Ethic* suffer from the suppression of cognate terms central to the argument through the selection of dissociated English terms. Another problem is the obscuring of thematic continuities: would it strike the averagely attentive reader that the word used by Weber for 'calling' in *Protestant Ethic* is the same as that for 'vocation' in 'Politics as a Vocation' – *Beruf*? And that in both cases the translation misses the more 'occupational' sense of the German term? It must be said that, for its time, the translation of *Protestant Ethic* is solid and reliable, given a then-common practice of producing 'readable' translations which were more a smooth precis than an accurate translation. However, contemporary understanding of many of Weber's texts is altered by retranslation according to modern principles.
5. In the bibliography of Weber's work issued by the publishers of the *Gesamtausgabe* five closely printed pages cover the work up to 1899. To my knowledge, the first piece translated from this was the (partial) translation of the 1895 Inaugural Address which appears in Runciman's collection (1978: 263–8).

6.   For a lucid discussion of the process by which economic argument became conventionalised see Maloney (1985).
7.   This essay has been translated as ' "Objectivity" in Social Science and Social Policy' in Weber (1949). Since this translation is in some respects deficient I cite here from the German version.
8.   In the early years of the journal Weber adopted the practice of appending critical editorial comment to some articles which were published in the *Archiv*; a more detailed analysis of the issues touched on here would need to examine the incidence and substance of such remarks.
9.   For a brief outline of the reception of Weber's work up to the later 1940s see my introduction to Hennis (1988).

References

Bendix, R. (1966) *Max Weber*, London: Methuen (first published in USA, 1959).
Cairnes, J. E. (1875) *The Character and Logical Method of Political Economy*, 2nd edn, London: Macmillan.
Hawthorn, G. (1986) 'Sociology in Cambridge', *London Review of Books* 8, 19 (6 November) 14–15.
Hennis, W. (1988) *Max Weber: Essays in Reconstruction*, London: Allen & Unwin.
Jaffé, E., Sombart, W., and Weber, M. (1904) 'Geleitwort', *Archiv für Sozialwissenschaft und Sozialpolitik*, N. F. Bd. 1: i–vii.
Jevons, W. S. (1879) *The Theory of Political Economy*, 2nd edn, London: Macmillan.
Keynes, J. N. (1891) *The Scope and Method of Political Economy*, London: Macmillan.
Maloney, J. (1985) *Marshall, Orthodoxy and the Professionalisation of Economics*, Cambridge: Cambridge University Press.
Menger, C. (1968) *Grundsätze der Volkswirtschaftslehre* (1871), Gesammelte Werke Bd. 1, Tübingen: Mohr.
Mommsen, W. J. (1974) *The Age of Bureaucracy*, Oxford: Basil Blackwell.

Mommsen, W. J. and Osterhammel, J. (eds) (1987) *Max Weber and his Contemporaries*, London: Allen & Unwin.
Runciman, W. G. (ed.) (1978) *Weber. Selections in Translation*, Cambridge: Cambridge University Press.
Weber, Marianne (1926) *Max Weber. Ein Lebensbild*, Tübingen: Mohr.
Weber, Max (1898a) 'Grundriss zu den Vorlesungen über Allgemeine ("theoretische") Nationalökonomie', unpublished.
Weber, Max (1898b) 'Erstes Buch. Die begrifflichen Grundlagen der Volkswirtschaftslehre', unpublished.
Weber, Max (1903) 'Roscher und Knies und die logischen Probleme der historischen Nationalökonomie', *Jahrbuch für Gesetzgebung, Verwaltung und Volkwirtschaft*, Bd. 27 H.4: 1–41.
Weber, Max (1949) *Methodology of the Social Sciences*, New York: Free Press.
Weber, Max (1968) 'Die "Objektivität" sozialwissenschaftlicher und sozialpolitischer Erkenntnis', *Gesammelte Aufsätze zur Wissenschaftslehre*, 3rd edn, Tübingen: Mohr, 146–214.

CHAPTER 2

Weber before Weberian sociology*

Lawrence Scaff

From its earliest reception Max Weber's work has been closely associated with the idea of a *verstehende* sociology that defines its subject matter as 'social action' and its methodology as the postulate of the 'subjective interpretation of action'. But in a recent study Bryan Turner has sought to undermine this received view, arguing for a fundamental incompatibility between Weber's 'substantive studies' and his 'methodological principles', an incompatibility revealed by the way in which those studies 'adhere far more closely to a Marxist structuralism than they do to *verstehen* principles'.[1] The intention behind Turner's invention of a 'structuralist' Weber is to show, first, that 'meaningful social action' for Weber is always subjected to 'structural' or 'objective' constraints; second, that Weber's sociology shares with Marxism a 'deterministic perspective' having an internal logic independent of individual consciousness; and third, that *this* sociology is philosophically – ontologically and epistemologically – 'autonomous'. Such Weberian revisionism may be new, contentious, or both. It is important in any case as part of the struggle for the mastery of Weber, a struggle that is important since Weber is thought to occupy a central terrain in the social sciences. Whoever controls the interpretation of Weber can entertain hopes of also governing scientific activity.

It must be said, however, that Turner's argument puts us on precisely the wrong ground. We are compelled to choose between two allegedly divergent strains in Weber's thought, strains that Weber himself somehow failed to conceptualize in terms adequate to our present understanding. The basis of the choice is uncertain: is it textual, theoretical, polemical, or political? In addition, the choice is not attuned to the dynamics of Weber's entire sociology, but to Turner's partial instrumentation of its modes, splitting Weber's voice into two dissonant lines, pitting Weber against Weber. To choose *for* Weber is also to choose *against* him; to accept a 'structuralist' Weber is to reject the sociology that typically bears his name. The paradox will merely mislead instead of yielding a more fruitful orientation. The question to ask is not,

15

which is the true Weber, but rather, what assumptions must be present in order for this kind of choice to be possible at all?

For Turner two assumptions are essential: first, what Weber really means can be separated from and substituted for what he only says. In Turner's words, 'Weber did not adhere to his own interpretative principles.'[2] Second, genuine meaning can then be extracted by squeezing Weber's thought into pre-formed categories of the interpreter's own making. Thus, Weber can be imagined to play 'the Jeremiah of modern capitalism'[3] – in conjunction, one supposes, with Marx's Isaiah. Unfortunately, both assumptions must be rejected. Nevertheless, I do not wish to take away everything from Turner's efforts, for there is a serious problem concealed in his approach. The problem can be restated in the following way. There are two analytically distinguishable tendencies in Weber's substantive thought: one in which status groups, social classes, patterns of domination, and material interests define the analytic core; and a second in which religious ethics, normative orders, patterns of legitimation, and ideal interests define a rather different set of core notions. This distinction is present *within* the substantive sociology itself, not between that sociology and any set of methodological principles. It has to do with the very content of Weber's work, not with oppositions between substance and form, rhetoric and meaning, structuralism and subjectivism, materialism and idealism. The problem is not to find a point of leverage from which Weber can be catapulted either closer to 'Marxist structuralism' or further away from it, but rather to discover what the relationship is between these two tendencies in Weber's thought, why that relationship is important, and what consequences it can have for social theory.

This is the first of my themes. In developing it I want to suggest that there is a distinctively Weberian 'structuralism' which can be established well before Weber's methodological reflections, that Weber's mode of analysis employs a special conceptual terminology, and that any alleged 'determinism' in Weber's thought needs to be reformulated in terms of a 'developmental history' which assumes 'reciprocal causality' and a plurality of institutionalized spheres of action. Far from establishing the 'autonomy' of sociology, Weber's approach seems to be self-consciously embedded within a set of assumptions about the nature of history, society, and human understanding. In order to recover these points I propose to place Weber in his intellectual milieu and to look closely at what he actually says and why he says it.

I also want to suggest as a secondary theme that Weber's approach was intended in large part to counter the achievements

of two predecessors: Marx and Nietzsche. Weber himself raises
the possibility of such a view, remarking in 1920 that a scholar's
integrity can be judged

> according to how he takes a stand in relation to Nietzsche and
> Marx. Whoever denies that he could not have accomplished the
> most important parts of his own work without the work done
> by both of them deceives himself and others. The world in
> which we live as intellectual beings is largely a world bearing
> the imprint of Marx and Nietzsche.[4]

The 'philosopher of history' against whom these remarks were
directed, Oswald Spengler, had failed the test by claiming to
'refute' Nietzsche's philosophy and Marx's historical predictions
through a stylish and misguided 'academic prophecy' of his own.
Weber could not restrain his scorn: confronted with such
alternatives, he retorted, our allegiance should be commanded not
by someone like Spengler, but by his opponents. As for Marx,

> Should he arise from his grave today and look around, despite
> several important deviations working against his prophecies, he
> would have every reason to say, truly this is flesh of my flesh
> and bone of my bones.[5]

The same could have been said for Nietzsche.

The story may be apocryphal, but it is certainly allegorical: as a
reflection on modernity, a claim that we moderns live in a post-
Marxian and post-Nietzschean world, it can become a parable of
Weber's own intellectual genesis. The brief confrontation with the
philosophy of history succeeds in illuminating an essential part of
the substructure of Weber's thought, without which his contributions would not have been possible at all. Omissions are important
in these self-reflections: Kant and Hegel remain in the shadows.
There appears to be a special connection to Marx and Nietzsche,
for it is only with them that we move to the centre of Weber's
world, a world presupposed at the beginning of his intellectual
journey. I want to ask what Weber could have owed to an
encounter with *both* of these antagonistic spirits, to the master of
dialectic *and* the dialectician of mastery.

The two themes I am proposing to consider appear at the
foundations, so to speak, 'before' Weberian sociology. They
suggest the problem in the Weberian terminology, derived from
Kant and Nietzsche's critique of the Kantian philosophy, of a
science 'with presuppositions' – historical and philosophical,
practical and theoretical.[6] I mean to invoke this language in a

double sense: logically and textually my themes precede the work
for which Weber has become famous. Weber's sociology of
legitimate domination and sociology of religion, for example, can
be seen as responses to the crisis of western thought occasioned by
Marx's critique of capitalist production and Nietzsche's critique of
the philosophical foundations of knowledge. Political-ethical
correlates can be found for both critiques: revolution and nihilism.
Weber's self-defined vocation, we might say, was to see whether
any meaning at all could be wrested from the post-critical,
disenchanted world, the 'age of subjectivist culture'.[7] I propose to
consider this project in relation to the work before *The Protestant
Ethic and the Spirit of Capitalism* (1904–5), for I think the essential
design of it is to be seen there. The later texts are a reflection of
the formative ideas, according to the view taken here. Thus, what
I shall say is less about any aspects of Weber's later substantive
sociology than about the groundwork of that sociology, the
preparation for it. I intend in this way to push Weber's analysis
back to its practical and theoretical sources, to judge its breadth
and depth, not by neatly separating the 'history' from the
'systematics' of theory, but by seeing how the one can instruct the
other.

   Is it possible, then, that when brought before the bar of
judgment Weber may appear to stand in a different relation to
Weberian sociology than we have come to expect?

I

Max Weber's intellectual and political environment was dominated
by four critical issues: the end of liberalism, the growth of
socialism, the spread of economic perspectives in the social
sciences, and the propagation of cultural pessimism. It was above
all these issues, both historical and theoretical, that shaped his
thinking from beginning to end. One might say that they provided
the framework within which his scientific contribution evolved.

   The theme of liberalism's demise has several dimensions to it,
many of which are political and specific to the German situation
after 1878: the alliance between industrial capital and semi-feudal
agrarian interests, the impotence of the old middle-class liberal
parties, and the authoritarian 'revolution from above' in social
policy. But the more fundamental shift occurred in thought as a
movement not so much from history to sociology, as Antoni would
have it,[8] as from the liberal historiography of a Ranke or Roscher
to the political economy of figures like Rodbertus, Bücher and
Knapp. This meant a rather startling shift in the most funda-

mental categories of analysis: from *Rechtstaat* to *Machtstaat*, from Manchesterism to *Volkswirtschaft*, from a concern with civilizational progress to a critique of developmental sequences. Weber had started at the liberal end of this continuum, as a student of Roscher and careful applicant of historical method, but through the 1880s and 1890s his imagination was attracted to the newer modes of post-liberal, economic thought. The tasks in politics and science were different now, 'not to be understood with the means of our science', he once complained as a Berlin doctoral candidate, and they therefore called for different modes of analysis and different analytic vocabularies.[9]

The obverse and complementary theme was in many ways the growth of socialism as a political movement, a cultural doctrine and belief system, and a system of thought claiming scientific status. Weber's acute awareness of these factors cannot be exaggerated. Stated in rather schematic terms, this can be demonstrated in two spheres: Weber's political and scholarly involvements with Naumann's Protestant reform movement (the *Evangelisch-soziale Kongress*) and with the *Verein für Sozialpolitik* in the 1890s, and his stance with respect to the reception of Marx's work during the same decade. In the case of the Protestant movement, it was clear from the start that Naumann conceived his agitation as an alternative to organized socialism, as a haven for social reform on the left, and as a force for overcoming divisions between middle and working classes.[10] Activist members like Weber and his friend Paul Göhre (who later joined the SPD) – 'radicals' as they were called – typified the combative reformist stance, at least prior to 1897.[11] As for the *Verein*, its research projects and debates through the 1890s, including Weber's own work on agrarian relations in East Elbia, were also typically motivated by a concern with socialism and general questions of 'social policy'. In fact the *Verein*'s activities were largely defined by 'conservative' academic socialists (*Kathedersozialisten*) favouring a kind of state-sponsored 'socialism from above', but the Association was still sufficiently eclectic to include Socialist Party members like Max Quarck and Bruno Schönlank, as well as a number of nonconformists like Lujo Brentano and Weber. As would be expected, the *Verein* became the leading forum for wide-ranging political and social-scientific controversy.

A simultaneous reception of Marx occurred in two phases: in 1891 at the Erfurt Congress German socialism abandoned the moderating emphases of the Gotha Programme (1875) in favour of Marx's critique and revolutionary ideology. And in 1894, with publication of volume three of *Capital*, Marx's thought began to penetrate academic circles and scientific discourse. The historical connections to Weber are complex, as Roth has shown,[12] but they can be summarized in the following way: Weber had numerous opportunities to know about practical developments in Socialist Party politics, and there is every indication that he followed these developments closely.[13] In addition, according to Sombart, whose association with Weber dates from the 1890s, Marx was really 'discovered' as a theorist when *Capital III* became available.[14] Weber participated in this discovery: for instance, when compiling the reading bibliography for his Heidelberg seminar of 1898, he included not only the works of Bernstein, Engels, Kautsky, Lassalle, Proudhon, and other socialists, but also the three volumes of *Capital*.[15] In other words, considerable evidence supports the conclusion that Weber's knowledge of Marx and his quarrel with Marxist socialism's claims as a science found its first expression in the studies written from 1894 to 1898, roughly from the 'Developmental Tendencies' essay to the second version of 'Agrarverhältnisse im Altertum'.

The third critical issue – the growing attraction of economic categories and explanations in the social sciences – follows from the first two. Here it was a matter of the convergence of a number of lines of thought, not only Marxism, around a single insight. According to Weber's observations, 'We find the economic mode of thought advancing in all spheres: social policy [Sozialpolitik] in place of politics, economic power-relations in place of legal relations, cultural and economic history in place of political history.'[16] But while the new orientation represented an advance in the sciences, it also suggested a danger: the 'economic point of view' was capable of 'overestimating' the significance of its achievements, Weber argued, by postulating an autonomous, self-evident sphere of economic 'ideals' according to which policy could be judged and corrected. This could be seen as the familiar Platonic ambition to secure the foundations of knowledge, only now separated from philosophy and reinstated in the socio-cultural sciences. Like the earlier attempt in philosophy, as Nietzsche had shown, the newer variant would run headlong into 'a chaos of value-standards' that could not be organized using its own tools, the tools of economic analysis.[17]

Finally, to mention Nietzsche is to remind ourselves of the undercurrent of 'cultural pessimism' that gained force through the 1890s, a force that was surely strong enough to capture Weber's attention. Unfortunately, the probable connections between Weber and the reception of Nietzsche have remained quite obscure; there is still no adequate account of the important historical relationships.[18] Nevertheless, one can briefly suggest that the effects of Nietzsche's work would have been felt by

Weber in two spheres: the *Evangelisch-soziale Kongress* and the university community. The 'cult of Nietzsche', as Tönnies called it, became a controversial topic for the Congress after 1892, the year in which Weber became active in its forums and publications. It was primarily Nietzsche as 'moralist', as 'the Copernicus of the moral world' in the words of one reviewer, that sparked this critical debate.[19] In academia, on the other hand, the critical response took different forms: Alois Riehl, Weber's Freiburg colleague, claimed Nietzsche's 'aristocratic radicalism' for the canon of philosophical reflection, while in sociology Tönnies, an early devotee, now turned against the 'aristocratic and androcratic' social implications of the Nietzsche legacy.[20] Given Weber's well-known passion for public and cultural affairs, it is certainly no exaggeration to see the burgeoning Nietzsche-movement and the critical responses provoked by it as an important part of his intellectual horizon.

Of course, indirect evidence of this kind cannot be construed to mean that Weber adopted Nietzschean philosophy, any more than he accepted Marxist theory. On the contrary, unlike Tönnies or Simmel, his writing did not traverse the Nietzschean terrain. But one can say, nevertheless, that Nietzsche's arrival as a serious critic brought before Weber the problematic character of the meaning of culture and the moral ideals by which a particular culture is justified. If Weber's early attacks on a 'eudaemonian' ethics and politics could appear 'Nietzschean', it was not so much because of a direct borrowing of substantive ideas, but rather because of a similarity in the form of his questioning.

II

How did Weber respond to these four issues? What path did his thought follow as he worked through the configuration of problems confronting the political and scientific communities? What were the original elements in his theoretical contribution? The answers must be sought, I think, in what might be called Weber's first analysis of capitalist development and in his writings on antiquity. There was in fact a close relationship between the two, for both contained an analysis of the conditions and origins of capitalism and an analysis of the 'developmental history' of social and economic forms in the west.[21] The discussion was initiated with the two 'dissertations' (1889, 1891) and it ended with the work on agrarian sociology in 1897–8.

The important starting points for Weber's early work on capitalism can be found in two places: the studies of G. F. Knapp, the doyen of agrarian economists and the authority on East Elbia prior to Weber's studies; and the evolutionary schema of theorists like Rodbertus and Bücher, who had aimed for sweeping reconceptualizations of history in terms of material production.

Knapp was important because he had asked Marx's old question about the essential characteristics of capitalism, but then instead of pursuing a formalistic analysis of economic 'laws' had sought an answer in historical relations. The answer to the question, according to this view, could best be grasped when one asked, when and where did capitalism *begin*? Knapp's thesis (which has been popularized once again) placed those origins in sixteenth-century agriculture, especially the *Gutswirtschaft* of East Germany, where one could observe production for a market and accumulation of profits by an entrepreneurial class, both necessary conditions for capitalist development, whether agrarian or industrial.[22]

On the other hand, Rodbertus and later Bücher had attempted to address the problem of evolutionary stages and sequences, a problem that had also taken shape in Marx's writings, and one that was acknowledged and emphasized in Weber's own time by Engels. We know from Weber's early reading and correspondence with Brentano that he was familiar with Engels's 1884 study, *The Origin of the Family, Private Property and the State*, and that he credited Rodbertus' reconstruction of 'oikos economy' as a type of productive system with stimulating his own work on antiquity.[23] The same can be said for Weber's interpretation of Bücher's three-fold typology – household economy, city economy, and national economy (*Volkswirtschaft*) – and its evolutionary historical application, a terminology that Weber also borrowed and regarded as a fruitful starting point, even though it was eventually criticized, altered, and discarded.

What Weber retained from these beginnings is a complex matter. In his early work on the East Elbian territories, for instance, he largely accepted Knapp's views about the sixteenth-century transformation and the basic characteristics of capitalist production, but he also sought to reconceptualize the problem of capitalism's development in terms that would make sense out of the economic *and* political demise of the traditional patriarchal system of domination in the East. In order to accomplish this project Weber had to look more closely than did Knapp and others at the systematic relationships connecting the system of economic production, social stratification, and political power. Also, Weber came to reject any ordering of these relations in a mechanistic or dialectical 'stage theory', whether espoused by Rodbertus, Bücher, Marx, or Engels. The questions raised in these controversies were partly historical, partly theoretical. Thus, Weber rejected Rodbertus's thesis of the 'autarchy of the oikos' on historical grounds, as Eduard Meyer acknowledged,[24] but he also reworked the entire idea of a necessary progression through step-like stages, an evolutionary theory, while retaining the developmental perspective in historical studies through elaboration of type concepts. The shift from 'real' historical stages (i.e. thought to be real), as found in Bücher and Engels, to hypothetical and heuristic types was Weber's solution *in nuce* to the theoretical dilemma presented by a naive superimposition of historical and conceptual forms.

It is in light of these starting points that we should understand Weber's self-proclaimed reputation as the younger generation's 'enfant terrible'.[25] The epithet is thought usually to derive from Weber's sharp and unconventional practical-political views, but there is in fact a significant theoretical-scientific source for it as well. Knapp himself recognized the extent of Weber's innovations at an early stage: commenting on Weber's lengthy study for the *Verein für Sozialpolitik*, Knapp declared that 'this work above all has led to the perception that our expertise has been surpassed, that we must start to learn all over again'.[26] The factual details amassed by Weber in his systematic analysis of the *Verein's* questionnaires would not have surprised Knapp, for such facts were well-known to those who had studied the problem, but the interpretive perspective according to which Weber ordered his observations would have provoked surprise and controversy. Indeed, it continued to provoke controversy; as Weber said of the polemical Freiburg Inaugural Address three years later, 'not agreement, but opposition' encouraged the resolve to publish his views.[27] The 'oppositional' element was also remarkably evident in most of his scientific work during these years and stimulated the controversial response to its publication.

Knapp's unusually generous praise can be attributed specifically to two novel aspects of Weber's theoretical contributions: first, formation of a new analytical language which recombined elements from diverse sources in the historical school, classical and Marxist political economy, and political sociology; and second, the attempt to conceptualize a 'developmental history' (to use the terminology employed by Roth and Schluchter),[28] starting with nineteenth-century Germany, but in the end including all of antiquity. Finally, Weber's 'developmentalism' (in contrast to Marx's evolutionism) also led to a frank assessment of political ends and the limits of science, combined with what might be termed a 'pessimistic' appraisal of the course of history. Each of these innovations invites close consideration.

III

The analytic language Weber employs in his early studies contains some intriguing and problematic features. Turning to the 1892 text to which Knapp referred, one finds Weber opening the study with a statement about the problem of 'social class formation', class conflict, and competing 'material interests'.[29] The introductory chapter is a sophisticated class analysis of the agrarian social structure of the eastern territories, one that exposes the morphology of relations (*Verhältnisse*) and oppositions (*Gegensätze*) among the economically and politically relevant strata. The emphasis is upon relationships, conflicts, and dynamic processes. The concepts Weber uses might therefore be designated 'relational', for they either connect one social unit with another or refer to patterned social interactions. This level of language is then continued and augmented through subsequent texts: we hear of labour-power and capital, production and exchange, material interests and ideal interests, division of labour and relations of domination. The terminology of superstructure (*Ueberbau*) and base (*Unterbau*, *Basis*) also makes an appearance, although always in a critical context.

Of course it is this kind of conceptual terminology that has led some writers to see the not-so-invisible hand of Marx in Weber's earliest studies. Thus Löwith has suggested that some evidence points toward Weber's predilection for 'a free application of the method of historical materialism' taking 'the contradiction between relations of production and forces of production as a guide for explanation'.[30] Or Fleischmann even goes so far as to say (although Löwith refrains from doing so) that Weber grasped for Marx's guidance early, ' "verifying" the correctness of the Marxist theory', only to turn away from it later, presumably under Nietzsche's aegis.[31] However, Weber was emphatically not Sombart, the 'proteus of German social scientists', who as a young socialist and scholar received Engels's grudging praise as a 'somewhat eclectic Marxist'.[32] Unlike some of his contemporaries, Weber was not weaned on the Marxist dialectic.

We see the distance between Weber and the Marxism of his day most clearly by raising two questions: (1) Is there a central concept, nodal point or idea – such as 'equality' in Tocqueville, 'alienation' in Marx, 'anomie' in Durkheim, the 'unconscious' in Freud – around which Weber's thought develops? Is there anything in Weber's early writing that would qualify as a conceptual breakthrough? (2) What is Weber's understanding of social and historical explanation? Can it be said that he accepts the basic form of 'Marxist structuralism' (to use Turner's phrase) and works within the limits of its assumptions?

The first question appears more difficult to answer for Weber than for other major nineteenth-century social theorists. Concepts like rationalization, bureaucratization, and domination come to mind. However, none of these are satisfactory as starting points, even though all become prominent after 1905. Instead, another concept seems an attractive candidate: *Arbeitsverfassung*, the key theoretical term in Weber's major writings from 1892 to 1894. This term, which resists precise translation, was common among political economists, Weber included, as a shorthand way of characterizing the historically-given 'constitution', 'condition', or 'organization' of labour, or labour-relations.[33] It was not a purely formal category like those used in classical economics and for this reason found favour in the 'historical school'. In its most general usage the concept was unusual because of a double origin and meaning. Combining both social and juridical connotations, political-economic and Aristotelian languages, it could refer to 'environmental' conditions (including legal norms) acting on the individual conceived as a 'unit of labour' and to the 'material' and 'mental' state of labour in the abstract. Thus, one could speak of 'labour' as both concrete activity and abstract potential, and of the 'constitution of labour' as a summation of a given configuration of material conditions, social structure, legal principles, and even psychological or ethical motivations.

Weber did employ the concept in this general sense, but he also modified the standard connotation in two important ways. First, he sought to give *'Arbeitsverfassung'* a particular meaning that would render it useful for causal explanations. This required postulating a distinction among different kinds of explanatory factors: for example, in the East Elbia studies labour's situation was said to be 'determined' variously by economic forces, such as the 'mode of enterprise' (*Betriebsweise*); by political considerations, such as the workers' 'desire for freedom', an 'ideal interest' that was quite 'irrational' from a 'materialist' standpoint, as Weber remarked; and by the existing system of social stratification. Weber's most novel suggestion was then to identify the *Arbeitsverfassung* specifically with 'relations' of social stratification within the larger socio-economic system, as appears repeatedly in passages in which he weighs the significance of multiple causal factors:

Thus, for the factors discussed so far – size of the enterprise [Betriebsgrösse] and intensity of cultivation [Wirtschaftsintensität] – we found that in their significance for the workers' situation they were less influential than the

inherited *Arbeitsverfassung* (which at the same time includes
the social stratification of all the inhabitants of the large estates,
or rather is identical to it) and less influential than the
traditional living standard of the workers, which is based upon
this *Arbeitsverfassung*.[34]

For, as we see again and again, it is the *kind of
Arbeitsverfassung*, therefore the kind of social stratification and
grouping of the rural workers, that is decisive for the workers'
material situation, and if it further appears that with current
power-relations [*Machtverhältnisse*] in rural areas the monetary
reorganization of the *Arbeitsverfassung* seriously endangers the
workers' material situation, then a change in the mode of
enterprise [*Betriebsweise*] (which has the tendency to bring
about this monetary reorganization) carries the same dangers
within itself. Indeed this is the case with the intensive mode of
enterprise.[35]

These are difficult passages, part of an argument in which
Weber attempts convincingly to demonstrate the relative explanatory autonomy of the *Arbeitsverfassung*, now sociologically defined,
in relation to economic factors (e.g., *Betriebsgrösse*, *Betriebsweise*)
and political factors (e.g., *Machtverhältnisse*) in determining the
contemporary 'material situation' of agrarian labour. Briefly his
argument seeks to show that none of the economic variables can in
themselves account for workers' material situation; the *Arbeitsverfassung* (i.e. system of social stratification) and its 'developmental tendencies' must always be included as an 'independent
variable', a viewpoint lost on even some of Weber's most
knowledgeable colleagues.[36]
The second innovative modification appears at this point as
well, for clearly Weber proposed that the *Arbeitsverfassung* be
viewed as a 'type', that is, a logically coherent statement of the
characteristic properties of a particular social stratification system.
Underlying Weber's argumentation is a fundamental opposition
between 'patriarchal' and 'capitalist' types of *Arbeitsverfassung*, the
former characterized by numerous strata of dependent labour, the
latter by 'proletarianization' of agrarian labour and polarization of
class conflict. Methodologically, such 'real' consequences of
capitalist 'rationalization' can be clarified, Weber argues, only on
the basis of a specification and comparison of heuristic types. In
fact, the later methodological commentary on types is a reflection
on Weber's early practice, not the reverse. Substantively, the
historic shift from patriarchal to capitalist types, an inevitable
process of change, is responsible for restructuring the stratification

system, generating for instance a new stratum of migrant labourer who is 'torn out of the collective unity of his family and familiar surroundings and is *only* labour-power for the owner as well as in his own eyes'.[37] The status of the formally free labourer, emancipated from dependencies, contains a deep paradox: for him 'homelessness and freedom are one and the same'.[38]

Weber's critique of agrarian labour's 'exploitation', a term appearing only occasionally,[39] or (as he preferred to say) 'material situation', can remind us of Marx's early discussions of 'alienated labor' or Tocqueville's disturbing passages on the degradation of workers under conditions of an increasingly rationalized division of labour.[40] But for Weber it is a case of the old struggle for 'emancipation of labour from property', first acted out in antiquity and repeating itself in new circumstances.[41] From Weber's perspective there are no philosophical forms for describing the constitution and reconstitution of labour in the course of these struggles, but rather sociological and logical 'types' that characterize entire systems of stratification (and production). Unlike Marx's view, there is no ontology or teleology of labour in this analysis, only a sociology, a 'developmental history'. Weber does not defend a standpoint from which to condemn the separation between social forms and authentic human nature. In his critical view, one that emerges in Nietzsche's writings as well, the latter can never be more than a philosophical fiction.

Here, then, is a Weberian structuralism. It is a kind of 'structuralism' because Weber conceives of action as partially a result of material (economic) forces external to the individual, and it is Weberian because it refuses to concede a monopoly either to economic rationality or to what one might call foundational ontology. Be this as it may, one still wonders whether it is possible to be more specific about Weber's causal model. Does Weber work within the boundaries of a world conceived as forces of production, relations of production, and superstructure; or does he propose modifications in the 'materialist' terminology?

The language Weber employs suggests a fundamental modification. For one thing, he avoids the requisite terminology of forces and relations of production (*Produktivkräfte*, *Produktionsverhältnisse*); his early analysis of capitalism is centred much more on labour, interest, and social structure or stratification (*soziale Struktur, soziale Schichtung*). Moreover, when he speaks directly to the issue, he advocates what can be designated 'reciprocal causality'. One representative passage, again summarizing results from the East Elbia research, bears quoting in full:

The causal relationship is at least partially reversed here. With our modern scientific method we have become used to viewing technical-economic conditions [Bedingungen] and interests [Interessen] basically as primary, from which a people's social structure and political formation [Gestaltung] are derived . . . but here we see quite clearly that it is a matter of reciprocal effects in which the purely economic factor does not by any means play the leading role. Population distribution, division of trades, division of land, the legal forms of the organization of labor [Arbeitsverfassung] within individual districts have a much more decisive significance for the material and social-ethical condition of the agricultural worker, for his total standard of living, than do possible differences between favourable or unfavourable economic conditions for agricultural enterprise in certain areas, or than the relationship of profits from one form of production to profits from another form. It is those relations of social stratification [soziale Schichtungsverhältnisse] which almost entirely determine the workers' standard of living, and as a result of this standard of living – not the reverse – almost entirely determine their wages, their total economic condition.[42]

Once again the relations of social stratification, the *Arbeitsverfassung* in its particular sense, receive primary emphasis and reveal Weber's reliance upon sociological categories. In addition, by speaking of 'reversal' and 'reciprocity' Weber signals the revision of a dominant causal model; yet his alternative is far from self-evident.

The surface clarity of Weber's undogmatic understanding of 'cause' and 'effect' in the above passage masks a complex line of reasoning, beginning with an apparently commonplace distinction between 'technical-economic conditions and interests' on the one side, and 'social structure and political organization' on the other, the former viewed as 'primary' by Marxist science, the latter as epiphenomenal. Such a separation of causal factors implies that for Weber, as for G. A. Cohen and William Shaw recently, Marx was a determinist in the strong sense: that is, 'productive forces' (technological, economic) were taken to be 'the determining factor in historical development'.[43] But for his own purposes Weber deliberately separates 'social stratification' as relations (*Schichtungsverhältnisse*) from the productive 'base' of society and ascribes independent causal significance to such *social* relations. Thus, in this revised model there are three kinds of relations – economic, social, and political – and Weber is free to use each as independent causal agents. It must be stressed that 'relations of production' in Marx are redefined as 'relations of social stratification' by Weber;

in other words, economic content as 'production' is excluded from the conceptualization of the social sphere.

In addition, we must see that Weber abandons the idea of a level-structure causal model, ordered from the foundation upward, in favour of what should be understood as a network model of causality. Put another way, the hierarchical metaphor dominating Marx's writing is replaced by a cyclical one. The network or cycle imagery contains the symbolization that permits Weber later on to speak of 'causal chains' or to deride the 'theorists of the super-structure' for their belief in an 'ultimate' or 'essential' cause in which a secular theory of history can be grounded.[44]

Thus, it will not prove adequate (and not only because of Hegelian innuendoes) to suppose that Weber wanted either to join with Marx in standing right side up, or to change the intellectual environment by having Marx's followers learn the mysteries of Althusserian consciousness-raising. Weber attempted rather to alter the terms of discourse, not simply by reconstructing 'Marx's shattered system' (as he called it) from its original pieces, but by substituting new conceptual blocks of his own.[45]

IV

Returning to G. F. Knapp's assessment, let us consider the second dimension of Weber's theoretical contribution: the conception of 'developmental history'. Building on the preceding discussion, it is important to acknowledge that Weber proposed the use of types not only as a way of settling the *Methodenstreit* between 'historical' and 'theoretical' economics, but also as a strategy for fighting clear of the Hegelian legacy (inherited by Marx) of an objectivist philosophy of history with its assumption of necessary, law-like progression through universal stages. Weber seemed to have this in mind when he once remarked, 'There are only two ways: Hegel's or our own approach.'[46] As is well-known, he also thought clarity could be brought to the interpretation of Marx's historical generalizations if his concepts and 'develop-mental laws' were treated as contingent 'tendencies' and 'ideal types' rather than as 'necessary' and 'real' entities. Consequently, when employing the language of development, Weber spoke of 'developmental tendencies' and of 'developmental stages' or 'phases' (*Entwicklungsstufe, Entwicklungsstadium*) merely as hypo-thetical, heuristic constructions useful for understanding processes of historical change.

There is ample evidence for Weber's strategy in texts leading to the 'Agrarverhältnisse' essay of 1898, not only in his application of the '*Arbeitsverfassung*', but also in a general typology of agrarian economies throughout history; in a scheme for clarifying types of agrarian relations west of the Elbe, ranging from small-holdings in the south-west to large peasant enterprises in the north-west; and in a set of analytic types like *oikos* and *polis*, city economy and market economy in the writings on antiquity.[47] What is most interesting about these various, overlapping schemes is not their systematic logical coherence – they remain suggestive only – but the connection they reveal in Weber's mind between antiquity and modernity. It turns out that a single question orders the diversity in Weber's earliest version of developmental history: how have societies organized labour-intensive agricultural production, especially in the face of inevitable seasonal fluctuations in labour requirements? Weber's types, composing a kind of 'genealogy of labour', can be seen as containing possible and actual answers to this central question. But there was a further important question: antiquity entered Weber's field of vision because, like East Elbia in the nineteenth century, it also raised questions about the transformation of agrarian economies under conditions of mixed socio-economic and political forms, sharing features of dependent-feudal relations and capitalist appropriation. Yet outcomes were radically different in the two historical cases. To ask why this was so was to push the analysis beyond a *histoire événémentielle* to the higher plane of theoretical conceptualization.

Now Weber was careful to deny any direct lessons from the study of history, either for comforting theories of progress or for strategies of political action. In his words, a study of antiquity could be expected to have only 'historical interest', for 'a modern proletarian and a Roman slave would be as unable to understand one another as a European and a Chinese. Our problems are of a completely different character'.[48] It can hardly be accidental that in this same introductory passage from 'The Social Causes of the Decline of Ancient Civilization' Weber reproduces Marx's epigram from the first German Preface to *Capital I* – 'This story is about you' (*de te narratur fabula*) – in an identical context, but with a precisely opposed meaning.[49] For Weber history issues a harder lesson: it is never simply a story about ourselves, but rather a record of differences, contingencies, unanticipated consequences, and paradoxical meanings. The rhetoric of difference can function to create a necessary distance between past and present, antiquity and modernity, text and audience, Marx and Weber himself – distance that is necessary as a precondition for judgments of meaning.

Yet the exercise of judgment raises the possibility of exploring certain suggestive historical analogies. As Weber notes, to study

ancient civilization is to observe a process of 'internal self-
dissolution' (*innere Selbstauflösung*), and to study the patriarchal
system in nineteenth-century Germany is to observe a repetition of
that process. Weber says as much at the very end of the East Elbia
report, 'now we stand once again before the old problem', namely,
the 'emancipation of the lowest stratum of the old society' and the
consequences of that emancipation. In Greek and Roman
antiquity the struggle for emancipation took the form of a clash
between slave and market economies, unfree and free labour.
Ancient civilization experienced a nascent 'agrarian capitalism', an
'exchange economy', even what Weber calls a '*grossbürgerliche
Politik*' combining commercial and landed interests, but the
ancient *polis* remained a centre of consumption, not production,
and it was eventually subordinated to the 'base of an economy
without exchange'. In the case of Rome, Weber contends, the *polis*
even finally transformed itself into 'an enormous *oikos*'. This
transformation marked a victory of economic over political forces,
a victory that would spell the end of the civilization of antiquity
and the gradual emergence of conditions that Weber foresaw as 'a
new basis for agrarian society'.[50]

What I am suggesting, therefore, is that in this part of his work,
particularly the first versions of the *Agrarian Sociology*, Weber's
theme is defined by the double interplay between *polis* and *oikos* in
antiquity, polity and economy in the modern age. In both Greek
and Roman antiquity the theme is emphasized by an argument
that is designed to document the way in which the *oikos* came to
obscure and replace the *polis* in the west, and with ambivalent
consequences for ancient civilization: on the one hand a decline
into feudalism, on the other the restoration of the family as a
viable social and productive unit.[51] At the end of this historical
process stands the patriarchal 'organization of labour' with its
forms of socio-economic dependency and political domination,
confronted once again by the corrosive, yet revolutionizing forces
of capitalist production and exchange, the 'most fateful force in
our modern life'.[52] In the modern age of western civilization the
question then became, could it be possible to say along which
developmental path the clash of dynamic forces would move
modern society?

As a philosophical aside, one might add that this last way of
posing the 'developmental' problem for Weber finds a parallel in
Nietzsche's short essay, 'The Use and Abuse of History', at the
end of which a rationale emerges for Nietzsche's own speculations
on antiquity. Like Weber, he understands the Greeks' cultural
achievements as presupposing a reinterpretation of 'history'. The
Greeks too, Nietzsche writes, were in 'danger of being over-

whelmed by what was past and foreign, and perishing on the rock of "history" '. But they 'gradually learned to organize the chaos by . . . thinking back to themselves, to their own true necessities . . . and did not remain long the epigoni of the whole East, burdened with their inheritance'.[53] In Nietzsche's symbolic language what they overcame was the stance of those 'historical men' who champion an ethics of happiness and who 'believe that the meaning of existence will become ever clearer in the course of its evolution'.[54] Recalling Weber's critique of 'eudaemonian' ethics and 'ethical culture', we see here the beginnings of his scathing repudiation of those 'last men who invented happiness', confronted in the pages of 'Science as a Vocation'.[55] For one problem in Weber's thought, as in Nietzsche's, was the 'chaos' of value and existential conflict, the probability that nothing would be clarified in the course of historical 'evolution', indeed the questioning of the Enlightenment faith that could presuppose a 'progressive' world of rosy hues and laughing voices. Surely this questioning defines a limit to Weber's neo-Kantian attachments, the point at which Nietzsche's presence can be felt.

V

The parallel with Nietzsche is itself limited, however, by Weber's explicit political argumentation. For in the first place Weber did not doubt the long-term strength of either capitalist developmental tendencies or pressures for increasing 'democratization'. As the most political of scholars, he was therefore deeply worried about developmental effects on class structure and leadership in the new industrial state. In some respects his orientation was shared by a select number of like-minded social scientists. For instance, Schulze-Gävernitz, the Freiburg colleague with whom Weber had collaborated in seminars on political economy, had asked how the position of labour could be strengthened in politics. Previous radical thought provided little guidance for an answer: 'Marx's great mistake', Schulze-Gävernitz had written, was to assume the emergence of 'class domination by the bourgeoisie' in Germany equivalent to that in England; but the German state instead produced 'a Junker-feudal superstructure much more than a bourgeois-liberal one'.[56] Given such a retrograde class structure, in comparison with England's, the most adequate *Sozialpolitik* revolved around promotion of industrialization, an alliance between working and middle classes, and certain legal reforms (e.g. freedom of association) and legislative enactments (e.g. use of state lands for resettlement in the east). We find Weber's position here too, but it is accompanied by a more radical scepticism about the probable future of labour-relations and class leadership in the new state.[57]

Second, in Weber's thought this scepticism assumes a theoretical form and argument. It can be summarized in the following way as a series of statements about the contradiction between 'economic' and 'political' domination: (1) In contemporary Germany political power, consolidated through the Junkers and their control of the state bureaucracy, is used to maintain the economic supremacy of the same aristocratic class. Or as Weber wrote, 'Instead of being able to base itself on a secure material foundation, political power must now be placed conversely in the service of economic interests'.[58] Thus, there is a kind of 'political determinism'. (2) But in the face of contemporary developmental tendencies, the real decline in the economic strength of the eastern estates will undermine and eventually destroy their assumed political jurisdictions, national power, and leadership position in the state; thus, a case can be made for an 'economic determinism'. (3) Nevertheless, it is in the 'ideal interest' of all strata in society for natural political power and leadership to be restructured in accordance with long-term transformations in economic strength or the 'material situation' of different classes; thus, there is a 'co-determinism' of political and economic factors. (4) And how is such restructuring to be accomplished? Short of revolution, it must come about through political initiative and education, as Weber argued in the Freiburg Address. Of course, this is an explicitly value-laden political argument and can be seen as a plea for the 'relative autonomy of politics'.

This is a remarkable pattern of reasoning, and it is scattered in its different parts throughout Weber's early writings. Nowhere is the force of the argument more obvious than in the 1897 debate with Karl Oldenberg, a representative of the opposite view, the incurable romantic proponent of the distinctive moral achievements, solidarity, and productivity of agrarian society. Oldenberg foresaw a choice between a 'cosmopolitan' and adventurous export policy or a policy of autarchic agrarian development and national independence, between 'industrialization and extreme individualism' or 'agrarian civilization, the age-old master'. Embracing the latter alternative, he expounded an early version of 'dependency theory', but in defence of agrarian conservatism or the 'feudal-Junker superstructure'.[59] In Weber's eyes this analysis was noteworthy as a 'Philippic' against industrialization and capitalism, a mythical picture presupposing the actuality of an 'idyllic politics' of precapitalist, patriarchal solidarity.[60]

Weber's 'Jeremiad' contained all of the necessary and contrary

elements: capitalist development, like political struggle, was
'inescapable for us' and a matter of 'our fate'; 'only the path
within which it moves can be economically influenced'. In the
German case attempts at resistance resulted in oddly distorted
manifestations: 'bureaucratic religiosity' in the middle class,
'feudalization of bourgeois capital', a philistine politics and
political environment.[61] In one of his most revealing perorations,
Weber added,

> There are optimists and pessimists in the consideration of the
> future of German development. Now I don't belong to the
> optimists. I also recognize the enormous risk which the
> inevitable outward economic expansion of Germany places upon
> us. But I consider this risk inevitable, and therefore I say, 'So
> must you be, you will not escape from yourself.'[62]

This is passionate and perhaps exaggerated rhetoric, to be sure,
but its meaning is hardly self-evident. Given Weber's well-known,
vigorous commitment to a national *Machtpolitik* of new tasks and
grand horizons, a politics in the mode of Gaullist *grandeur*, so to
speak, one may well wonder at the collision of identifications with
'fate', 'inevitability', 'pessimism', and 'development' against the
epigoni. What, precisely, did Weber have in mind?

Few passages in Weber's early writings are more significant or
complicated, for they are passages reverberating with the echo of
ideas from Nietzsche back to Burckhardt and Goethe. Weber was
prepared to go part way with Nietzsche, to side with 'pessimism'
against the naive evolutionists, those 'historical men' who
'invented happiness'. But what kind of pessimism was it? In this
symbolic and surprisingly differentiated language to affirm the
'risk' accompanying 'historical inevitability' was intended by
Weber as a way of repudiating the 'romantic pessimism' of
Oldenberg, just as Nietzsche had cast off Schopenhauer in favour
of a 'pessimism of strength'.[63] For Weber, however, the turn away
from the literati's grey, retrospective romanticism led not to
Nietzsche's Dionysian *force majeure*, but rather, as was so often
the case for Weber, to the classical brilliance of Goethe's
Olympian *force d'âme*. In fact the key to an understanding of
Weber's stance is found in his last sentence – 'So must you be,
you will not escape from yourself' – a line borrowed appropriately
from the stanza on the 'Δαιμων' in Goethe's 'Urworte. Orphische',
a quotation from a famous cycle immediately recognizable to
Weber's audience, and a line that introduces one of the great and
problematic *leitmotifs* in Weber's thought.[64]

For Goethe as for Weber the 'daemon' was present as 'fate', as the characteristic and pre-formed essence of individual identity, the unchanging and self-directive 'law' of destiny. As in Greek tragedy, the individual was seen to be propelled forward according to its own internal developmental 'forms', 'stamped' on it for eternity, thus paradoxically present as both limitation and infinitude, actuality and possibility. By invoking Goethe's prophetic imagination and disclosing it within the unanticipated context of 'developmental history', Weber chose to emphasize the conjunctive formation of these paradoxes in their historical bearing: risk was accompanied by certainty, the agonistic by the necessary.[65] In the terms of this discussion 'fate' became symbolic for the sense in which history could be said to be constrained by 'structure', yet open to 'living' (as opposed to mechanical, stage-like) development. Put somewhat differently, if there could ever be any meaning to declaring with Marx that humans 'make their own history', for Weber it would be because 'the possible is often reached only by striving to attain the impossible that lies beyond it'.[66] However, on this view 'fate' and not simply 'will' governed the painfully 'indifferent' results of history.

By invoking Goethe's 'daemon' did Weber cast his lot with the forces of irrationalism and hopelessness in history? Was his a counsel of despair? The short answer is, 'I think not.' But the long answer admits that with this question we are led beyond the limits of the present study – and back to its beginnings. For Weber the 'fateful' source of pessimism lay not in cultural decadence, as Spengler believed, nor even in the 'paradox of unanticipated consequences', as Turner suggests, but rather in the deeper perspective of 'historical inevitability', in the assumption of a displacement of human action and meaning between infinite possibility and finite (im)possibility.[67] Weber may have adapted the thought from Goethe, but among contemporaries he shared it most closely not with Nietzsche but with Burckhardt, for like Burckhardt, Weber's pessimism was classical and 'Hellenic', if not cast in the 'heroic' or 'realistic' mould of Thucydidean politics.[68] 'It seems to me', Weber once wrote in comments on Burckhardt's *Griechische Kulturgeschichte*,

> that the struggle of all against all in the sphere of *foreign* policy was the unalterable primary factor for the Hellenic states. (Burckhardt understands it as the outwardly-directed agon.) And I think the atmosphere that produced this condition of permanent threat to all of existence ('in the midst of life we are overtaken by death') sounds its strongest note in the specific Hellenic pessimism that Burckhardt depicts so well.[69]

What Weber attributed to Burckhardt could have applied with equal ease to his own position on the 'mutability of fortune', only with the qualification, as Bendix has acknowledged, that 'he did not achieve the personal serenity that Burckhardt did'.[70] But this was partly because for Weber's agonistic drive the aim would be 'to protect and sustain that which appears *valuable* in people – self-responsibility, the deep impulse toward achievement, toward the intellectual and moral excellence of mankind'.[71] Weber could say this – and continued to do so – *against* the lessons of history, *despite* the 'fate of our times'; it was, after all, the starting point for his public vocation, for his declaration that 'we individualists and partisans of democratic institutions are swimming against the stream of material constellations'.[72] This was a statement of purpose that could never have been uttered by Marx or Nietzsche.

The 'permanent threat to all of existence', a phrase with a peculiarly sobering effect in the nuclear age, returned in Weber's concluding reflections on modernity, now cast against the growing murmurs of 'disenchantment'. The old analogy with antiquity still prevailed: 'We live as did the ancients', Weber remarked, 'only we live in a different sense.' 'Many old gods ascend from their graves; they are disenchanted and hence take the form of impersonal forces. They strive to gain power over our lives.'[73] If that power cannot be fully abolished, then to recognize it and see it face to face is in itself a minor triumph, a step toward converting impossibility into possibility, and possibility into actuality.

VI

In this paper I have sought to recover and clarify the basis for a Weberian sociology, freed from the usual systematizing ambitions of the 'theory of social action'. By considering the work before *The Protestant Ethic and the Spirit of Capitalism* I have attempted to demonstrate the sense in which we can speak of Weber's 'structuralism' and 'developmental history' in connection with his critical stance *vis-à-vis* Marx and Nietzsche, his conceptual terminology, and his overall theoretical project. Although the results achieved here cannot yet boast completion, they should assist in the effort to clear away some interpretative misunder-standings, to show what Schluchter has characterized as the 'continuity' in Weber's work,[74] and to prepare the way for both a reinterpretation of Weber's contributions and a reformulation of social theory. I take it that in the present state of theoretical proliferation (and confusion) to engage at this level with Weber is to engage with theoretical issues as well. But a precise and critical demonstration of the way in which such an engagement could in fact live up to a promised rescue from our present discontents cannot be taken up in this investigation. It is a problem that lies beyond Weber before Weberian sociology.

Notes

* In revising this essay I have benefited from thoughtful comments by Robert J. Antonio and Guenther Roth.
1. Bryan Turner, *For Weber, Essays on the Sociology of Fate*, London: Routledge & Kegan Paul, 1981, p. 9; see also his earlier paper, 'The Structuralist Critique of Weber's Sociology', *British Journal of Sociology*: 28, 1, March 1974, pp. 1–16.
2. Ibid., p. 352.
3. Ibid., p. 354.
4. Cited in Eduard Baumgarten, *Max Weber, Werk und Person*, Tübingen: Mohr, 1964, pp. 554–5.
5. Ibid., p. 554, referring to *Genesis* 2: 23.
6. See Weber, ' "Objectivity" in Social Science and Social Policy', *Methodology of the Social Sciences*, New York: Free Press, 1949, pp. 76–84; 'Science as a Vocation', *From Max Weber: Essays in Sociology*, New York: Oxford, 1946, pp. 143–7; and compare Nietzsche, *On the Genealogy of Morals*, New York: Vintage, 1967, p. 151, and sections 24 and 25 generally.
7. From a statement in 1909, in Weber, *Gesammelte Aufsätze zur Soziologie und Sozialpolitik*, Tübingen: Mohr, 1924, p. 420 (hereinafter *GASS*).
8. Carlo Antoni, *From History to Sociology*, London: Merlin, 1959, ch. 4.
9. Letter to his uncle, Hermann Baumgarten, 30 September 1887, in *Jugendbriefe*, Tübingen: Mohr, 1936, pp. 270–3; Weber later reported that he had 'become approximately one-third political economist', 3 January 1891, p. 327.
10. See Naumann, 'Unsere Stellung zur Sozialdemokratie', *Die Christliche Welt*, vol. 7, 1893, 904–10, 938–41, 958–63.
11. See the accounts of the Weber-Göhre position in Göhre's own history, *Die Evangelisch-soziale Bewegung, Ihre Geschichte und ihre Ziele*, Leipzig: Grunow, 1896, esp. pp. 161–3; M. A. Nobbe, *Der Evangelisch-soziale Kongress und seine Gegner*, Göttingen: Vandenhoeck, 1897, pp. 23–4; Georg Wermert, *Ueber den christlichen Sozialismus und seine wirtschaftliche Bedeutung*, Halle: Kaemmerer, 1897, p. 34; and Martin Rade, 'Die unfreiwillige Bedeutung des Evangelisch-sozialen Kongresses', *Die Christliche Welt*, vol. 11, 1897, 521–4; also Weber's defence of Göhre, 'Zur Rechtfertigung Göhres', *Die Christliche Welt*, vol. 6, 1892, 1104–9, and his review of Naumann, 'Was heisst Christlich-Sozial'? *Die Christliche Welt*, vol. 8, 1894, 472–7.
12. Guenther Roth, 'The Historical Relationship to Marxism', in Bendix and Roth, *Scholarship and Partisanship: Essays on Max Weber*, Berkeley: University of California Press, 1971, pp. 227–52.
13. Weber had direct knowledge of two influential studies: Karl Oldenberg, *Die Ziele der deutschen Sozialdemokratie*, Leipzig: Grunow, 1891; and Adolf Wagner, *Das neue Sozialdemokratische Program*, Berlin: Rehtwisch, 1892. Insight into the level of the discussions in Weber's circle can be gleaned from his report, 'Die Evangelisch-sozialen Kurse in Berlin im Herbst dieses Jahres', *Die Christliche Welt*, vol. 7, 1893, 766–8.

14. Werner Sombart, *Das Lebenswerk von Karl Marx*, Jena: Fischer, 1909, pp. 7–9. Sombart reviewed *Capital III* in the same issue of the *Archiv für soziale Gesetzgebung und Statistik* in which Weber published 'Developmental Tendencies in the Situation of East Elbian Rural Labourers'.

15. *Grundriss zu den Vorlesungen über Allgemeine ('theoretische') Nationalökonomie*, as discussed in Wilhelm Hennis, *Max Weber: Essays in Reconstruction*, London: Allen & Unwin, 1988, pp. 207–8, n. 99.

16. From Weber's Freiburg Inaugural Address, 'The National State and Economic Policy', this volume, p. 199.

17. Ibid., p. 200.

18. The most ambitious attempt is Eugène Fleischmann, 'De Weber à Nietzsche', *Archives europ. sociol.*, vol. 5, 1964, pp. 190–238, who attempts to trace a parallel shift in culture and in Weber's thought from Marx to Nietzsche, from a concern with 'economic forces' to an interest in 'cultural norms', suggesting Simmel as the intermediary. Unfortunately neither the historical evidence nor the textual evidence can support such a thesis.

19. E. W. Mayer, 'Jenseits von Gut und Böse', *Die Christliche Welt*, vol. 6, 1892, 685–9, who comments further, 'Today the name of this remarkably original thinker is mentioned almost daily'; also P. Schubring, 'Friedrich Nietzsche', *Die Christliche Welt*, vol. 9, 1895, 959–62, 987–90.

20. Riehl, *Friedrich Nietzsche, Der Künstler und der Denker*, Stuttgart: Frommann, 1897; Tönnies, *Der Nietzsche Kultus, Eine Kritik*, Leipzig: Reisland, 1897. On Riehl's relationship with Weber in Freiburg see Marianne Weber, *Max Weber, A Biography*, tr. Zohn, New York: Wiley, 1975, p. 204.

21. The developmental theme is also addressed in Wolfgang Schluchter, 'Der autoritär verfasste Kapitalismus, Max Webers Kritik am Kaiserreich', *Rationalismus der Weltbeherrschung, Studien zu Max Weber*, Frankfurt: Suhrkamp, 1980, pp. 134–69.

22. Knapp, *Die Bauern-Befreiung und der Ursprung der Landarbeiter*, Leipzig: Duncker & Humblot, 1887; and 'Die Erbuntertänigkeit und die kapitalistische Wirtschaft', 1891, in *Die Landarbeiter in Knechtschaft und Freiheit, Gesammelte Vorträge*, Leipzig: Duncker & Humblot, 1909, pp. 45–64.

23. Lujo Brentano, 'Die Volkswirthschaft und ihre konkreten Grundbedingungen', *Zeitschrift für Sozial- und Wirthschaftsgeschichte*, vol. 1, 1893, pp. 77–146; Weber to Brentano, 20 February 1893, in *Jugendbriefe*, Tübingen: Mohr, 1936, pp. 363–5.

24. 'Die wirtschaftliche Entwicklung des Altertums' (1895), in *Kleine Schriften*, Halle: Niemeyer, 1924, vol. 1, p. 83. On Weber, Meyer, Bücher and their generation's scholarship on antiquity generally see M. I. Finley, *Economy and Society in Ancient Greece*, London: Chatto & Windus, 1981, pp. 3–23.

25. Weber, 'Referat [über "Die ländliche Arbeitsverfassung"]', *Schriften des Vereins für Sozialpolitik*, vol. 58, 1893, p. 62.

26. Knapp, 'Referat', in ibid., p. 7.

27. Weber, *GPS*, p. 1.

28. Wolfgang Schluchter, *The Rise of Western Rationalism, Max Weber's Developmental History* (introduction by Guenther Roth), Berkeley: University of California Press, 1981.

29. *Verhältnisse der Landarbeiter im ostelbischen Deutschland*, Leipzig: Duncker & Humblot, 1892, pp. 3–8.

30. Karl Löwith, 'Die Entzauberung der Welt durch Wissenschaft', *Merkur*, vol. 18, 1964, p. 504.

31. Fleischmann, op. cit., p. 194.

32. Paul Honigsheim, *On Max Weber*, New York: Free Press, 1968, p. 9; Engels, in Marx and Engels, *Werke*, Berlin: Dietz, 1973, p. 414; Roth, 'The

Historical Relationship', op. cit., pp. 239–40.

33. For the problems of translation see Keith Tribe's note to Max Weber, 'Developmental Tendencies in the Situation of East Elbian Rural Labourers', below p. 185.

34. 'Entwickelungstendenzen in der Lage der ostelbischen Landarbeiter', *Archiv für soziale Gesetzgebung und Statistik*, vol. 7, 1894, p. 28, the original version of the text cited in notes 33 (a translation) and 35.

35. 'Entwickelungstendenzen in der Lage der ostelbischen Landarbeiter', *Preusssische Jahrbücher*, vol. 77, 1894, reprinted in *Gesammelte Aufsätze zur Sozial- und Wirtschaftsgeschichte*, Tübingen: Mohr, 1924, p. 498 (hereinafter *GASW*). I have translated the passage rather literally (cf. Tribe, op. cit., p. 178) in order to stay as close as possible to Weber's own terminology and causal imputations.

36. See Weber's corrections to Kaerger's misinterpretation of these points in 'Entwickelungstendenzen', *Archiv*, op. cit., pp. 33–6.

37. Ibid., p. 23; Weber continues by asserting that 'the migrant workers' barracks function as the money-economy's analog to the slave barracks of antiquity'.

38. Ibid., p. 41.

39. Ibid., p. 18.

40. In Marx's familiar *Economic and Philosophical Manuscripts* (1844), and Tocqueville's *Democracy in America*, vol. II, part 2, ch. 20.

41. 'Agrarverhältnisse im Altertum', *Handwörterbuch der Staatswissenschaften*, Jena: Fischer, 1897, p. 1 (the first version of this text on agrarian relations in antiquity.)

42. 'Die deutschen Landarbeiter', *Bericht über die Verhandlungen des 5. Evangelisch-sozialen Kongresses*, Berlin: Rehtwisch & Langewort, p. 66.

43. Shaw, *Marx's Theory of History*, Stanford: Stanford University Press, 1978, p. 53; and Cohen's 'primacy thesis' in *Karl Marx's Theory of History, A Defence*, Princeton: Princeton University Press, 1978, esp. p. 134.

44. See the 1910 statement in *GASS*, op. cit., p. 456.

45. 'Zur Gründung', 1896, *GPS*, op. cit., p. 26.

46. Quoted in Schluchter, *Rise of Western Rationalism*, op. cit., p. 21, from a letter of 1909.

47. See especially 'Die Erhebung des Vereins für Sozialpolitik über die Lage der Landarbeiter', *Das Land*, vol. 1, 1893, pp. 8–9, 24–6, 43–5, 58–9, 129–30, 147–8; and 'Referat [über "Die ländliche Arbeitsverfassung"]', op. cit.

48. 'Die sozialen Gründe des Untergangs der antiken Kultur', 1896, in *GASW*, op. cit., p. 291; imprecisely translated in Weber, *The Agrarian Sociology of Ancient Civilizations*, London: NLB, 1976, pp. 389–411.

49. From Horace, *Satires*, I, i, 69–70.

50. For these quotations see Weber, *Verhältnisse der Landarbeiter*, op. cit., p. 800; 'Sozialen Gründe des Untergangs', op. cit., pp. 291, 294; 'Agrarverhältnisse', 1897, op. cit., pp. 7–10, 16.

51. Weber, *Die römische Agrargeschichte*, Stuttgart: Enke, 1891, p. 275, with the ensuing comment that 'Bebel's ideal of the proper construction of marriage' was realized de facto in the upper classes, de jure among commoners at the beginning of the Empire.

52. *The Protestant Ethic and the Spirit of Capitalism*, trans. Parsons, New York: Scribner's, 1958, p. 17.

53. Nietzsche, *The Use and Abuse of History*, 1874, New York: Bobbs-Merrill, 1957, p. 72, from *Unzeitgemässe Betrachtungen*.

54. Ibid., p. 10.

55. 'Science as a Vocation', op. cit., p. 143; quoted from *Thus Spoke*

Zarathustra, Part 1, sec. 5.

56. Gerhard von Schulze-Gävernitz, 'Die gegenwärtigen Mittel zur Hebung der Arbeiterklasse in Deutschland', *Ethische Kultur*, vol. 3, 1895, p. 151.

57. In this connection there is a surprising similarity between Weber's 1895 Antrittsrede and Marx's 'Kritik der Hegelschen Rechtsphilosophie', 1844, where Marx writes, 'But every class in Germany lacks the logic, insight, courage and clarity . . . which identifies itself, if only for a moment, with the popular mind; that genius which pushes material force to political power . . .' (*The Marx-Engels Reader*, ed. Tucker, New York: Norton, 2nd edn, 1978, p. 63).

58. 'Entwicklungstendenzen', *Archiv*, op. cit., p. 4.

59. Karl Oldenberg, *Deutschland als Industriestaat*, Göttingen: Vandenhoeck, 1897, esp. p. 41, a speech to the annual meeting of the *Evangelisch-soziale Kongress*, followed immediately by Weber's reply, this volume, pp. 210–20.

60. Weber, 'Germany as an Industrial State', this volume, pp. 211–12.

61. Ibid., pp. 216–18, because of Nietzsche's apotheosis of the 'will to power' Weber included him in the charge of 'philistinism', as noted in marginalia in Weber's copy of Simmel, *Nietzsche und Schopenhauer*: see Wolfgang J. Mommsen, *Max Weber, Gesellschaft, Politik und Geschichte*, Frankfurt: Suhrkamp, 1974, p. 261, n. 125.

62. Ibid., p. 220.

63. For this language see the 1886 preface to *The Birth of Tragedy, or Hellenism and Pessimism*, and *Die fröhliche Wissenschaft*, sec. 370, in Nietzsche's *Werke in drei Bänden*, ed. Schlechta, Munich: Hanser, 1955, vol. 1, pp. 9–10; vol. 2, pp. 244–6.

64. Goethe, *Werke*, Hamburg: Wegner, 1949, vol. 1, p. 359; Weber's memory was a bit faulty, for he rendered the relevant line, 'So musst du sein, du wirst dir nicht entrinnen', instead of 'So musst du sein, dir kannst du nicht entfliehen'. (Freud would no doubt have exulted in the possibilities buried within this parapraxis.) The category 'das Dämonische' becomes central for Weber, as in 'Science as a Vocation' with its final appeal to the notion of each person finding and obeying 'the demon who holds the fibers of his very life'.

65. For these ideas see also Georg Lukács, *The Theory of the Novel*, Cambridge: MIT Press, 1971, pp. 86–93, written in 1914 when Lukács was still under Weber's spell.

66. Weber, *Methodology*, op. cit., p. 24; Marx's line begins the second paragraph of *The Eighteenth Brumaire of Louis Bonaparte*.

67. Turner, *For Weber*, op. cit., p. 178.

68. Mommsen speaks of 'heroic pessimism' in *The Age of Bureaucracy, Perspectives on the Political Sociology of Max Weber*, Oxford: Blackwell, 1974, p. 112; and Bendix prefers 'pessimistic realism' in *Scholarship and Partisanship*, op. cit., p. 270.

69. Letter to Carl Neumann, 11 November 1900, in the Zentrales Staatsarchiv Merseburg, Nachlass Weber, 30/4, 82–3. Weber and Burckhardt shared with Nietzsche an admiration for the political 'culture of realism' from Thucydides to Machiavelli, from the *polis* to the urban *coniuratio*, but for them 'realism only meant opposition to illusions, not, as for Nietzsche, anti-idealism and immoralism', in the words of Alfred von Martin, *Nietzsche und Burckhardt*, Munich: Reinhardt, 1942, p. 92. For Nietzsche's unsettled views on Burckhardt, his Basel colleague, and on Goethe, see *Werke*, op. cit., vol. 2, pp. 1024–6, 1030–2.

70. Bendix, *Scholarship and Partisanship*, op. cit., p. 271.

71. Weber, 'Die deutschen Landarbeiter [Korreferat und Schlusswort]', in *Bericht über die Verhandlungen des 5. Evangelisch-sozialen Kongresses*, Berlin: Rehtwisch, 1894, p. 80.

72.   Weber, in *Gesammelte Politische Schriften*, 2nd edn, Tübingen: Mohr, 1958, p. 61; cf. G. Roth and W. Schluchter, *Max Weber's Vision of History*, Berkeley: University of California Press, 1979, pp. 201–6. The relationship Weber forms between 'individualism' and 'democracy' suggests that his political values are not to be understood simply as a species of 'aristocratic individualism' derived from Nietzsche, but instead have sources in Protestant theology, Kant, and Goethe.
73.   'Science as a Vocation', op. cit., pp. 148–9.
74.   Schluchter, *Rise of Western Rationalism*, op. cit., p. 7, n. 3.

CHAPTER 3

The problem of thematic unity in the works of Max Weber*

Friedrich H. Tenbruck
translated by Dr M. S. Whimster

Prefatory Remarks (1987)

I would like to thank the editor for reprinting the following article which, I believe, is still worth a hearing after twelve years, although some commentary is necessary.

I have to start on the biographical note that, over the past forty years, I have become involved in new approaches to Max Weber, at first only with a sense that Weber dealt with problems that shattered the concepts of accepted sociology. The fascination of something I could not comprehend led me to ever new studies and seminar courses, occasionally to publications, among which I can mention here: 'Die Genesis der Methodologie Max Webers', *Kölner Zeitschrift für Soziologie und Sozialpsychologie* (1959); 'Wie gut kennen wir Max Weber? Über Maßstäbe der Weber-Forschung im Spiegel der Weber-Ausgaben', *Zeitschrift für die gesamte Staatswissenschaft* (1975); 'Abschied von "Wirtschaft und Gesellschaft" ', *Zeitschrift für die gesamte Staatswissenschaft* (1977); 'Das Werk Max Webers: Methodologie und Sozialwissenschaften', *Kölner Zeitschrift für Soziologie und Sozialpsychologie* (1986); and 'Max Weber and Eduard Meyer', in W. J. Mommsen and J. Osterhammel (eds), *Max Weber and his Contemporaries*, London 1987 (a fuller version in Italian, *Comunità* 39 (1985)). Among these is placed the following article which originally appeared in the *Kölner Zeitschrift für Soziologie und Sozialpsychologie* in 1975, and which, like all the rest, represents a step towards the understanding of Max Weber but which does not pretend to be a final interpretation of his sociology. In this sense I still subscribe to the intentions of the earlier publications, although I later expressly revised some of their arguments.

Every contribution on the question of thematic unity in Weber's writings remains a makeshift so long as it cannot deliver an interpretation of the sociology which Weber wished to present in *Economy and Society*. When I wrote the articles noted above I was convinced of the fact that *Economy and Society* was not only unfinished, but had been artificially and forcibly assembled by the editor into a single text out of diverse manuscripts. The thesis which I put forward in 1977 has in the meantime been confirmed. At that time I concluded that we could not decipher the conception and construction of *Economy and Society* – one can try to detect in the list of contents an obvious and logical construction deriving from a unitary conception! – and that we would have therefore to keep to the other writings and to Weber's 'theme'. Moreover, more recent work that I have done has demonstrated to me that we can indeed reconstruct the theoretical construction underlying *Economy and Society*, although this work will never lie before us as a single text. In this respect *Economy and Society* has again assumed for me a central place in the interpretation of Max Weber. Work on the 'theme' has shown us the evaluative perspectives which conditioned his selection of questions and facts, but it does not reveal to us the methods, concepts, and theories which constitute his sociology as conception and going concern. This has to be emphasized today, when discussion of Weber's theme has happily become more lively.

Aside from that, my essay is exposed to the positive or negative misunderstanding of presenting an evolutionary reading of Weber when all that it sought to demonstrate was that 'the rational in the sense of a logical or teleological "consistency" of a theoretical-intellectual or a practical-ethical standpoint . . . exercises power over men' (Weber, *GARS* I: 537). [Translator's note: the German acronym is retained since there is no equivalent English language edition. *GARS* stands for *Gesammelte Aufsätze zur Religions-soziologie*, 1st edn, 1920–1. Listed at the conclusion of the article are the contents of this collection with the dates of their first appearance.] The extent of this power in history, and its simultaneous limitation by 'irrational' presuppositions and cultural, historical, and social circumstance, is shown in the 'sociology of religion'. The misunderstanding that Weber was concerned with an unconditioned and unstoppable 'rationalization process' terminating inevitably in the sole domination of modern western purposive rationality appears quite ineradicable, even though Weber repeatedly referred to the ambiguity of 'rationality'. It cannot be emphasized too often that there are different modes and tendencies of rationalization which are, in a quite different manner, also at work in East Asian culture.

But one also needs to remember that Weber's investigations are made with ideal-typical constructions which cannot, and are not intended to, exhaust historical reality. His remarks on the 'anethical' market deliver an 'ideal type' that here as elsewhere immediately raises the question of where reality diverges from it.

Whoever overlooks that point falls straight into those basic mistakes from which Weber wished to save sociology; Weber's 'ideal types' are thus mistaken for 'theories' by means of which sociology should comprehend and reproduce the whole of reality. Whoever reflects upon Weber's statements on the four 'forms' of action should know that, however things are placed, traditional, affective, and value-rational action does not simply disappear, nor does charisma simply belong to the past. Weber understood the modern nation as a new *Vergemeinschaftung*. He recognized the ceaseless formation of new groups and sociation in modern society which have been evident to us for decades; later in his political sociology he pursued the value-rational and charismatic forces, which had both originated in religion, into parties and the socialist movement. Even the society organized along 'purposive-rational' lines cannot simply close off other inclinations of its people, and in this way it mobilizes its own opposition.

I have unswervingly argued that Weber had men and women in view as 'cultural beings' and that his sociology possesses an 'anthropological' dimension; and I am glad that these ideas are being increasingly taken up in interpretations. The scientific justification for this perspective was however explicitly supplied by Weber in his conception of a science of reality which obliged researcher, discipline, and the time to become conscious of their ultimate values, and direct their gaze to specific elements of reality instead of becoming entrenched behind a Naturalism which imagines that it can grasp 'society' itself. But even here Weber's 'theme' does not lead us to the conception of his sociology.

Finally, in its urge to write pure 'social history' sociology repeatedly forgets the role of 'intellectuals' (and 'ideas'), or restricts them to periods in which religions were dominant social forces. It is not possible to understand Weber if one transforms the process of rationalization, which without the continued efforts of 'intellectuals' would not occur, into laws of social development. Weber has demonstrated how 'ideas' have selected the track along which interests proceed. But even today men and women do not simply confront their conditions of existence as individuals, they are rather to a great extent dependent upon others for interpretations of their situations. The fact that this work of 'interpretation' is no longer to be found in the older religions renders even more urgent the question of who then are these 'intellectuals' who as ever command the selection of the course along which things move. As long as this always partial, but all the same significant, power of 'intellectuals' (and therefore of 'ideas') is overlooked, its realistic recognition decried as 'idealistic' sociology, then we cannot gain sight of Weber's sociology with its facts and problems.

It must suffice to close with the comment that the task and significance of Weber-research has only grown. Despite the important advances that have been made, other developments become ever more depressing. It augurs ill if in America those Weberian scholars who still can read German texts, and wish to do so, become ever rarer; and that publications there degenerate into an American, or at any rate English-language citation community unwilling to take the slightest note of current research in European languages. A sociology which seeks only to function in one language no longer fulfils the idea of a science as an international intellectual endeavour and community.

Economy and Society – the assumption that it was Weber's principal work

When Marianne Weber brought out *Economy and Society* (*ES*) in 1921, she described it in the first sentence of her preface as Weber's posthumous and principal work (*Hauptwerk*). Even without this label, the scientific world would have been persuaded of this designation. Whenever a solid work of this extent appears in the literary legacy of a scholar (*Gelehrter*), it is taken to be his life's work and this was even more so in the case of Weber whose earlier writings had only been submitted as essays. Here was the product of a lifetime's labour and hence the principal work. This ambiguous designation attained a deeper significance when it appeared that *ES* provided a *summa* of the discipline, and undertook to cover and make accessible all areas of sociology. Thus *ES* was taken to be Weber's comprehensive and authentic testament to which he had given everything. When, in the opening sentence of the preface of Johannes Winckelmann's studious edition, the contemporary reader is again told that he is in receipt of the posthumous and principal work, there seems little else to do than treat the statement as indubitable.

Accordingly, one might have expected that interest in Weber's works would have centred on *ES*. That, however, has not been the case. The best known and most widely read text was, instead, the *Protestant Ethic and the Spirit of Capitalism* (*PE*), an early work, which in spite of its peculiar importance cannot be counted as his major work. In contrast, *ES* is very rarely read as a whole and at no time has it, *in toto*, been the subject of interpretation.[1] Certainly many sociologists have concerned themselves with chapters of this mammoth work, especially with those on domination, stratification, and bureaucracy. A complete interpretation though, has never seriously been attempted. Given the

absence of any convincing substantive problematic that could
unlock *ES* and show how all the parts are interlinked and relate to
the whole in keeping with a reliable criterion, parts were extracted
and ranked in relation to one another according to personal
interpretation. To a large extent the parts have been freely used
without regard to an overall understanding.[2]

In fact the presentation of Weber's sociology has not been the
outcome of a debate with his major work but rather has followed
other lines. For many sociologists – for example, the neo-positivist
school – his main achievement lies in the field of methodology.
This school views him as a prophet of a methodology which finds
a path through the morass of uncertainties of the human sciences.
Uninterested in Weber's substantive researches, they make him
the advocate of a future sociology that would proceed strictly
according to the model of the natural sciences. The principal work
is not taken into account and the methodology is so imperfectly
summarized as to become rather inverted. Small wonder then that
it is often doubted whether Weber's substantive research conforms
with his own methodology.[3]

Another reading has confined itself to the conceptualization of
an interpretive (*verstehende*) sociology and has tied itself to the
opening paragraphs of *ES*, the explication of basic concepts, and
at best reckons itself to be concerned with the architectonic
structure of *ES*. However persuasive such analyses might be, they
have not been able to explain how the parts of *ES* are linked to a
theme or where the centre of the structure is to be located. As
soon as one has passed beyond the basic concepts, one is assailed
by an impenetrable diversity of themes and theses which blend to
form an infinite net, in which one knot leads on to another
without any notion of priority. The basic concepts are unable to
uncover a thematic unity within *ES*, so that any one substantive
chapter could be tied in with either a theoretical or a methodological conceptualization.

Thus, in 1949, J. Winckelmann summed up the position as
follows: 'It may be established without exaggeration as *communis
opinio doctorum* that, in its present form, the work is an *irregulare
aliquid corpus*.'[4] In a way he adhered to the view that, since Weber
had not been able to complete the masterwork, it must,
ultimately, be beyond comprehension. However, unlike others,
Winckelmann had not given up on the problem of reconstructing
ES in the image of its author. As the new editor he has tried ever
since, by transposing and adding material, to create an edition in
which 'ES becomes less fragmentary and a significant degree of
completeness and accessibility is established that would bring out
Max Weber's scientific knowledge as well as providing a definitive

expression to his intellectual conception'.[5] However one values his
several editions (1956, 1964, 1972, 1976), they have not made the
work as a whole readable and intelligible, and indeed they could
not; for the major difficulties lie not in the small number of gaps
and uncompleted sections but in the unresolved question of the
unity of this mammoth work.[6]

From the first publication of ES, opinion has diverged as to
whether Weber actually sought a substantive unity for the work,
or whether he was unable or unwilling to provide such a unity.
With no resolution of this divergence, ES has, for some, been
reduced to a posthumous work of reference[7] and, for others, its
author a critic. Belonging to the latter group is Jaspers, who
writes, 'in spite of their span, the massive fragments remain the
unused building blocks of a titan'; somewhat obscurely, he locates
Weber's completeness and integrity in terms of his failure.[8]
Neither characterization is satisfactory. Weber's intellectual
passion excludes the possibility that his life's work should lie
buried in a reference work, his intellectual decisiveness must place
him beyond the critic, and his intellectual consistency rules out
the possibility of a collection of fragments lacking any conscious
notion of design.

Given the absence of a key to ES, it has been impossible to
complete an exposition of Weber's sociology in terms of this major
work and the way out of this dilemma was to opt for
methodological and theoretical conceptualizations. Those who
remained dissatisfied with these conceptualizations felt compelled
to replace the writings with the man. For no other sociologist has
biography played such an extensive and commanding role in
interpretation. Those who knew him all report coming under the
force of his authority by virtue of his personality rather than his
writings.[9] With regularity later analyses too have sought the unity
of the *oeuvre* in terms of the man, his fundamental outlook, and
his attitudes, so as to tie together the otherwise unrelated texts and
to serve as a substitute for the indecipherable major work. Even
Bendix in his search for a meaningful interpretation has entitled
his book *An Intellectual Portrait*.

More than half a century of commentary confirms the
paradoxical conclusion that the interpretation of Weber's sociology
is not based upon the work that is commonly regarded to be his
major work. This applies equally to current interpretations. By
alternating between the man and his work, Bendix's reading has
improved upon the numerous shortcomings of previous interpretations and has brought to light a unity within Weber's sociology,
though not without incurring a cost. Bendix has eschewed
reductionism to either methodological or theoretical conceptualiza-

tion and has boldly grasped the substantive research work. The unification he seeks is accomplished by resurrecting from an old supposition the question: 'What were the origins of rational culture in the west?' which he treats as the central theme of Weber's work. However, an important consequence of this is that *ES* and the *GARS* collection are merged together to establish a new direction. The price may appear small in relation to the gains. But a conscientious interpretation poses the inescapable question that, had Weber wished to explain the origin of occidental rationality, why didn't he make it the central theme of his principal work. For it is obvious that he did not do so. Certainly within *ES* there are significant fragments and observations, and the question often remains just below the surface, but the work exhibits no compulsion to acknowledge or develop the question. No interpretation, therefore, can adopt this position. If *ES* is Weber's principal work and if *ES* like the *Economic Ethic of World Religions (WEWR)* [translator's note: again to avoid confusion the German acronym is retained, see previous translators' note, p. 43] can stand alone by itself, then it is unsatisfactory to produce a new work out of two already existing – particularly as only a few segments are crucial to the rationalization thesis – and thereby reduce the major part of *ES* and *WEWR* to merely contrasting studies. Bendix's interpretation, in other words, still cannot be considered the last word.

No one, since the publication of Bendix's text, has managed to extract more from *ES* other than additional contributions to specialist areas of sociology. Given the acceptance of its status as the principal work, the question then arises as to whether *ES* has been pushed into a blind alley. What is a principal work (*Hauptwerk*)? Perhaps this ambiguous term has so prejudiced interpretation that an impartial view of the work is almost unobtainable. It is time to return to the sources, to read the texts without preconceived ideas and intentions, so that a fresh light may be cast on the individual works and their relation to the whole.

The historico-religious process of disenchantment (*Entzauberung*)

[Translator's note: the term disenchantment should be read not so much as the final state of a world purged of illusion, but as an actual process, literally, or dis-enchantment.]

In an attempt to locate the *PE* within the system of Weber's writing, W. M. Sprondel uses the following quote: 'That great religious historical process of disenchantment of the world, which disavows all magical ways to salvation as a superstition and sacrilege, found its conclusion here.'[10] However, if one turns to the 1904 publication of the *PE* one will not find the cited passage, which Weber inserted in 1919/1920 when he was preparing *PE* for the *GARS* collection.

Considering its scope and radicalness, the bold insertion clearly goes beyond the original thesis, and anyone familiar with the *PE* could not fail to notice this. Since the *PE* is exclusively concerned with the origin of the spirit of capitalism, where in this work does he refer to the historico-religious process of disenchantment, and how could Calvinism be represented as the concluding stage of a process when only its particularity and effects were being debated? And on the authority of what argument could Weber have referred the reader of the *PE* to the further propositions that the disenchantment of the world 'commenced with ancient Judaic prophecy' and that it terminated 'in association with Greek scientific thought' in the inner-worldly asceticism of Protestantism?[11] There is no mention of this in the *PE*, and Weber's insertion, taken solely in the context of the *PE*, must have appeared as some amazing personal brainwave which far exceeds the permissible limits of scientific statements. One thing is clear: the section is completely alien to the rest of the *PE*. The insertion was not part of the original and it never could have been, as it breaks loose from the initial format and surveys completely new dimensions.

First let us establish that the *GARS* collection reproduced neither the original text of the *PE*, nor that of the *WEWR* essays. In the 'Author's Introduction' (*Vorbemerkung*) Weber had deliberately spoken of 'the following collected and enlarged essays',[12] a statement which has never received serious attention by commentators. All the editions have simply printed the final versions of the *PE* and *WEWR*; despite an otherwise lavish commentary they did not mention, let alone draw attention to, the changes.[13] For 55 years we have been reading and interpreting the *GARS* under the erroneous assumption that it reproduced the original texts of the *PE* and *WEWR*. Under this deception a satisfactory exegesis is scarcely possible, since no clean demarcation has been established between the earlier and later versions; nor has it been possible to relate the separate works to each other, nor to reliably gauge the progress of ideas.[14]

The passage quoted above belongs to the enlargements that Weber made and it clearly goes beyond the boundaries of the *PE*; therefore greater importance should be attached to it. These additions provide the reader with an adumbrated version of a

more extensive process, the historico-religious process of disenchantment, in which the *PE* is to be understood as the final act.
Since this idea was not even hinted at in the original text, it
follows that it must have been conceived at a later date. But this
then prompts the question: when and where did Weber develop
this idea? Furthermore, why did he introduce the additions at a
later date, despite the fact that even the later edition of the *PE* is
not concerned with the historico-religious process?

Now it is known that similar passages can be found scattered in
Weber's later works, that is, in both *ES* and *WEWR*. All these
passages are in agreement that the process starts with Judaism and
terminates in the inner-worldly asceticism of Puritanism. The
intermediary stages remain relatively undefined. They are, for
instance, referred to in the essay on Ancient Judaism, (there,
Roman law stands alongside Hellenic intellectual culture (*Geistes-
kultur*) and, through the agency of the Roman concept of office,
led to the institution of the Christian Church),[15] and in *ES* (where
Weber records the circumstance that occidental religion was not
created by intellectuals).[16] In other places the intermediary stages
are described only in the most general terms, instanced by the fact
that occidental rationality is to be explained predominantly by
religion when political factors do not intervene.[17]

These remarks may have been influenced by the fashionable
belief of that time which Weber could have included in the text
without further evidence. Modern civilization was referred to as
having a threefold origin in Judaism, Christianity, and Antiquity,
though not without making the usual reference to the Germanic
legacy; however, these views were much too unspecific in their
speculations to serve as an adequate model for Weber's quite
different stipulation of the historical origins in the construction of
the historico-religious process of rationalization. Here is a theory
both completely novel and unique whose originality is presaged in
its terminology. The possibility must be ruled out that Weber
could have repeatedly, yet casually, inserted such a sweeping view
in the course of his work, had he not been convinced that he had
elsewhere submitted the proof for this process. This in turn raises
the question: where and when had Weber presented and worked
out his conceptualization of a historico-religious process of
rationalization extending from ancient Judaism to the Protestant
ethic?

Occidental rationalization, and historico-religious disenchantment

This takes us to the centre of Weber's sociology, beyond the basic concepts and methodology which were for him a means to enable research in historical sociology. From Bendix we know that the kernel of these researches is the process of rationalization whose outcome is the modern world. It should be noted, however, that the term 'rationalization process' was hardly ever employed by Weber,[18] who alternated between the more general concepts of rationality, instrumental rationality, rationalization, and disenchantment. The problem of interpretation is how to decide whether the changes in the use of these terms involve more than stylistic variation; in particular, whether the processes of rationalization and disenchantment are equivalent. There has been a tacit acceptance that they are equivalent. However, leaving aside the fact that disenchantment in many instances amounts to the same thing as rationalization, and that the term 'rationalization' is wide enough to include disenchantment, Weber did actually make a distinction between religious disenchantment and occidental rationalization.

If the central features of Weber's writings are to be comprehended, we have to be quite clear as to the specific meaning of terms in particular texts. Here one is confronted with a major difficulty, the multiple usages of the concept rationalization. This is an oversight on Weber's part; indeed he constantly impresses on the reader these multiple meanings of the term.[19] As we shall see below, he acknowledged different forms of rationalization which had occurred not only in the west but in quite different ways in other civilizations (*Kulturen*), too. Today 'rationalization process' is taken to be synonymous with occidental development but, for Weber, this was a particular case of a more general class of events.

Even if we limit ourselves to the course of occidental history, further differences in the usage of rationalization become apparent, for Weber did not use the same term in the same way throughout his life. Considering that Weber shifted his ground on this issue several times, an interpretation which adheres to one concept of rationalization across the length of Weber's works is more likely to cover up rather than expose these shifts.

There are two main shifts involved. First, Weber belonged to an age which took for granted the rational character of its civilization. He did not doubt that European history exhibited a development of increasing rationality. He was not content, though, with contemporary explanations which referred to the legacy of Greece and the progress of modern science. Weber was

to discover the specific process of rationalization only in the course
of his research, and this discovery was not a matter of description
but of explanation: an explanation, moreover, that was only
gradually developed. This development is marked in his writings
by a transition from accounts of the historical facts to a
sociologically explained process.

The second shift concerns the historical periodization of the
process of rationalization. In the *PE* Weber's purpose was to
explain the late phase of capitalism, and only afterwards were the
earlier phases gradually included. That is why the idea of a
process of rationalization, extending throughout the whole of
European history, is a later product of his thinking. Rationalization (as well as the process of rationalization) can, therefore, mean
the process as a whole, but it could also mean its various parts.
The historico-religious process of disenchantment, displaying its
own course of rationalization, is clearly one such part of the
overall process of rationalization in Europe. Religious disenchantment terminates in the Protestant ethic, at the point at which
other specific forms of rationalization are only just beginning. The
conclusion of the process of religious disenchantment provides the
spirit from which capitalism unfolds in its role as the rationalizing
force of modernity. The emergence of the last stage of rationality
is carried forward by new agents – science, economics, politics.
Inner-worldly asceticism not only marks the end-point but also the
internal limits of religious disenchantment.

Weber's terminology obscures these distinctions and here the
following usage is proposed to enable, somewhat arbitrarily, the
intended characteristics to be specified. The rationalization
process will refer to the overall sequence, the development up to
the Protestant ethic will be known as disenchantment, and the
condensation and continuation of disenchantment will be called
modernization.

Weber could only conceive of the rationalization process after
he had uncovered the process of disenchantment. When and
where this occurred takes us to the centre of Weber's sociology
and to questions about the unity, origins, and coherence of his
writings. It also leads to the central difficulty of comprehending
the *oeuvre*, because the process of disenchantment (like that of
rationalization) does not receive a complete and comprehensive
treatment in his writings.

We know that in 1903 Weber recovered from his illness and
embarked on a double sociological enterprise: methodologically,
the essay on 'Objectivity' and, substantively, the *PE*.[20] By 1904
Weber was already examining the beginnings of modernization,
that is, the inner-worldly asceticism of Protestantism. However,

the shaping of the capitalist spirit from the Protestant ethic is considered in itself and not as the end of a much larger process.[21]

About ten years later in his work on the sociology of religion Weber fastened upon ancient Judaism, and thus came upon the initial term of the process: it was 'the highly religious ethic of conduct, one that was free of magic and the search for irrational forms of salvation'.[22] But when and where did Weber develop the concept of the historico-religious *process* of disenchantment which in a subsequent phase led to modernization? Obviously separate inspection of Judaic rationality and Protestantism is not sufficient to form the idea of a process linking them together. The crucial task was to show how the rational Judaic ethic could produce inner-worldly asceticism that was the driving force behind modernization in the west.

Weber had handled modernization, from different standpoints, in the *PE* and certain sections of *ES*, and had devoted a part of *WEWR* to the study of Judaism. Yet he had to link both together in a historico-religious process of disenchantment in order to arrive at the conceptualization of the rationalization process. Therefore a central question in the comprehension of Weber is: where had he presented the process of disenchantment which, from the legacy of Judaism via the conduit of Christianity, results in the inner-worldly asceticism of Protestantism?

The rationalization thesis

Bendix is the author who has turned attention away from methodological and theoretical questions to the substantive researches, in particular the process of rationalization which he sees 'as a thread running through Weber's life work'.[23] Bendix has convinced sociologists that if we are to comprehend Weber, then we have to grasp the design of the rationalization process. He has, therefore, undertaken to reconstruct this process from Weber's writings. While his portrait of Max Weber has been eminently successful, the same cannot be said for the rationalization thesis (this term will denote his reconstruction of the rationalization process), since it contradicts the texts in a number of elementary ways and is in itself contradictory.

Bendix fails to tell us where Weber addressed the theme which was the predominating issue in his life's work. He elevates the rationalization theme to an ubiquitous topic without specifying a text that is exclusively and thematically concerned with the process. Bendix can only reconstruct the theme by dismantling the separate texts in order to utilize specific parts from them. Roughly it goes like this: from the *PE* Weber turns back to 'Ancient Judaism' (a chapter belonging to the *WEWR*) and fills in the necessary intermediary and final stages of the process with selected passages taken from *ES* – the sociology of law, the city and the state. Abramowski's reconstruction, though more historically descriptive, is not much different.[24]

Bendix and others have only been able to reconstruct the process of rationalization by assuming and imposing a thematic unity upon Weber's researches. The price of attaining this understanding is a contradiction between the reconstruction and Weber's works, and a loss of identity of the separate texts. It is hard to assess an interpretation that remains indifferent to the subject, purpose, and outcome of specific works.

One of the drawbacks of Bendix's reading is a disregard for the chronological sequence of Weber's writings. While, on the whole, adhering to the chronological sequence in the attempt to decode the process of rationalization, at the decisive point Bendix reverses the sequence, placing *WEWR* prior to *ES*. This is consistent with the publication dates but inconsistent with the dates of their composition. All the sections of *ES*, from which Bendix fashions his reconstruction, belong to Part II which Weber had written in the period 1911–13, and so, before *WEWR*.[25]

This reversal of chronology is consistent with Bendix's rationalization thesis which stipulates that *ES* was designed to present the final crowning stages of the process of rationalization. This presupposes, however, that Weber was at least clear in his mind as to the earlier preceding stages; without such a conceptualization how could he have conceived of the process in its entirety? Weber must have – and Bendix recognizes that this is essential to his argument[26] – recognized the cultural uniqueness and historical significance of ancient Judaism. Without this presupposition it might still be possible to read the central chapters of *ES* on the city, state and law in the light of the rationalization thesis, but it would be impossible to view them as the crowning stages. Whatever one finds in these chapters, it is not a mature and comprehensive expression of Weber's ideas on the process of rationalization, for he had not yet reached such a conceptualization. *ES* cannot, therefore, be regarded as the final and conclusive presentation of the process.

The rationalization thesis stands, and so falls, because it is assumed that *WEWR* was written before *ES*. Since Bendix accepts that *ES* is the final presentation of the process, it is perfectly consistent for him to argue that all the essays on the sociology of religion are 'a mere preface to what he had not yet explained for the West',[27] and that the relevant parts of *ES* are

'continuations of the sociology of religion'.[28] If the references used
by Bendix are scrutinized with regard to chronology, it is hard to
avoid the conclusion that Bendix has erroneously supposed that
Weber had written *WEWR* before *ES*.[29] This mistake is in line
with the traditional acceptance that *ES* is both a late work and the
principal work that brings together all of Weber's answers and
solutions. While Bendix might have allowed himself considerable
latitude to range over the output of Weber's lifetime in the
presentation of *An Intellectual Portrait*, he clearly has exceeded the
boundaries of this licence.

Furthermore the rationalization process is, for Bendix, the
outcome of an aggregation of historical events and factors which
all must be taken into account; as such the outcome of the process
is essentially fortuitous. Thus a further price has to be paid for
subverting the rationalization thesis to the identification of a
collection of heterogeneous historical factors.

Bendix is able to utilize only a few passages from the alleged
principal work as direct contributions to Weber's major preoccupation, and the vast bulk of the remainder is explained away
as 'contrasting material' or simply ignored. The same fate awaits
WEWR. Although this collection takes as its theme the role of
religious ethics and their consequences for orientations toward the
economic and, indeed, concerns the subject of rationality, the
direction of this work is not aimed exclusively at the process of
rationality in the west. Characteristically Bendix writes, on the one
hand, that Weber had wound up his sociology of religion with the
chapter on 'Ancient Judaism', and, on the other hand, that the
chapter should be seen simply as the opening phase of the
following stages of the rationalization process, the chapters of *ES*
on law, state, and domination being the concluding phase. The
long expositions on China and India are seen as non-essential to
Weber's true intentions and are devalued to a kind of experi-
mental control to the Protestant ethic thesis and simply serve to
justify the generality that religious ethics are an important
influence on orientations towards the economic. *WEWR*, however, cannot be understood solely within the framework of the
process of rationalization in the west.

If it was Weber's intention to trace out the whole process after
the publication of the *PE* and, strangely, if he intended to do this
in two very different works, he didn't actually carry out his plan.
Although *WEWR* does analyse ancient Judaism, it contains no
general conceptualization of occidental development, and *ES*, in
so far as it admits to a general theme, is almost exclusively
concerned with modernization; it has little to offer on the
extensive periods of religious disenchantment and nowhere does it

conduct a comprehensive exposition of occidental development. If Weber was pursuing the theme of rationalization in the west, why did he disperse the subject in an athematic way between two works, *WEWR* and *ES*, and, in particular, why is the process of disenchantment, which is the central strand of occidental development, ignored?

Given this situation it has to be asked whether Weber planned to trace out and substantiate the essential stages in the rationalization process. And if it wasn't Weber's intention, Bendix's interpretation has to be rejected. For Bendix rationalization remains a historically fortuitous occurrence, the result of a series of particular events that consecutively have produced a specific outcome. Between the rationalism of Judaism and the inner-worldly asceticism of Protestantism no process of religious disenchantment is discerned. Instead, the legacy of Judaic rationalism is transposed by purely secular forces to become a prevailing world view. The significance of religious ethics is restricted to the demonstration of 'how some had an accelerating and others a retarding effect upon the rationality of economic life'.[30]

Weber's important discovery, however, lay in the knowledge that rationalization in all its historical fragility was born from the compulsion of an inherent logic, which was situated in the irresistible drive towards the rationalization of religious ideas. Therefore, the process of rationalization is at heart an historico-religious process of disenchantment, and the stages and moments in the history of rationalization derive their unity from the process of disenchantment. Weber's discovery was not the identification of the separate events but a logic, the internal drive behind the whole sequence. The key to this view of Weber is to be found in the work that, in spite of some progress, has resisted interpretation in its central part, namely in *WEWR*.

The Economic Ethics of World Religions (*WEWR*): its place in Weber's *oeuvre*

Given a situation in which Weber's works possess a fragmentary character lacking form and have such broad objectives, how those works relate to one another and what their positional significance is within the overall output can scarcely be gathered from the intellectual contents alone. Exterior criteria such as the origin of the work, the dates of composition, and stylistic comparison could be an important aid to interpretation. This holds above all for *WEWR*, whose outer form as well as its internal construction conceals its central position within Weber's work.

For a long time the *WEWR* collection played almost no part in the interpretation of the Weberian *œuvre*. As long as attention had been focused on theory and methodology, these essays have seemed an incidental research interest, and some have gone so far to regard them as a regrettable waste of energy on a peripheral subject. Those who did establish an interest in the *PE* were sometimes ignorant even of the existence of the *WEWR* essays,[31] which otherwise were held to be a form of control evidence to the Protestant ethic hypothesis containing no independent thesis of their own: the *PE* establishes the force of ideas over interests, i.e. how the spirit of capitalism originated from Protestant asceticism, whereas *WEWR* demonstrates the obverse: in those situations where the spirit of capitalism did not materialize the conviction of an inner-worldly asceticism was also absent. Yet anyone who is familiar with the 'Author's Introduction' (*Vorbemerkung*) to *GARS* will realize how untenable such a methodological reading is. At no time was *WEWR* meant to be a counterpart to the *PE*, for it presents and establishes its own major thesis. As we will see, the work is linked to the *PE* but at the same time it transcends that context. To see it as a mere counterpart to the *PE* is a lamentable blindspot in Weberian research. Since Bendix, *WEWR* has been regarded as a preliminary study to those chapters of *ES* in which Weber wished to give the explanation, still outstanding, of the process of western rationalization, so that the only directly relevant chapter has to be 'Ancient Judaism'. This fundamentally misconstrues the nature and position of *WEWR*.

In this collection Weber adopts a specific and unique position. Unlike *ES*, which was written under a contractual obligation, Weber is free in this work to pursue his own interests. In terms of periodization of Weber's life and work this collection has a predominant position in that it has to be valued as the last of the major substantive researches and so as his final explicit conceptualization (*Erkenntnisstand*).

Moreover *WEWR* is the work on which Weber laboured most persistently. The substantive material for the chapters on China, India, and Israel – after several years work – were, in essentials, prepared and more or less finished as provisional manuscripts by towards the beginning of the war. This was not the case with the chapters planned on Islam and Christianity. Convinced that he would not be able to return to this enterprise after the end of the war, Weber decided on a serialized publication in the *Archiv für Sozialwissenschaft*; however the manuscripts were neither fully prepared, worked through or completed.[32] How much work he expended on seeing the three chapters into print is unknown. But publication meant that he had to prepare hurriedly a general conclusion based on the trunk of the three special studies. The concluding statements, which one would expect at the end of a book and which Weber would have certainly placed as the conclusion to the final planned volume on Christianity, were brought forward to provide the 'Introduction' (*Einleitung*), probably written in 1915. It is clear that the results of his studies, which he saw himself forced to bring to a hasty and premature fruition, could not very well be included in the already finished substantive chapters of *ES* or *WEWR*.[33] Moreover, since the 'Introduction' and the chapter on China were probably already in print, Weber saw reason to correct and further extend the introductory resumée with the hastily inserted 'Intermediate Reflections' (*Zwischerbetrachtungen*).[34] [Translator's note: I have restored the main title to this essay. Gerth and Mills adopted the sub-title in their translation (p. 323) which entirely ignores the positional significance of the essay.]

The reader of the *WEWR* collection should be aware that the hurried and opaque propositions of the 'Introduction' and 'Intermediate Reflections' do not relate to the main body of the text as introductory comments and additional remarks, but represent the first systematic, though highly enigmatic, *summa* of his long term historico-sociological researches. They contain the final account and the last stage attained of the torso that is *WEWR*.

The specific and, in terms of chronology, the authoritative position of *WEWR* can be brought into sharper focus if its relation to the *PE* is considered. With the *PE*, Weber had commenced his own sociology and it comes as no surprise when, at the end of this work, he projects a research programme that reads almost like a life-time's work: an inquiry into the significance of ascetic rationalism for practical social ethics (*sozialpolitische Ethik*) and social groups, and the tracing of inner-worldly asceticism back into the middle ages. This programme remains wholly within the framework of the *PE* in that it limits itself to an inquiry into the immediate origins of European modernization, and seeks to research the role of ascetic rationalism on a broader front.

In the later revision of the *PE* for *GARS*, Weber explained in the final footnote why he had not undertaken the programme at the time. Aside from external factors, Weber expressed the wish to set the problem 'within the totality of cultural development'.[35] The theme of the *PE*, the dependence of the capitalist spirit upon the religious notions of asceticism, is now broadened in scope and elevated to a universal subject: what is the role of ideas and interests (or, what amounts to the same thing for Weber, religion and society) for long run developments, and how are such forceful and enduring settings formed which determine the course of history, as did the Protestant ethic? The *PE* is an example of one of those determining religious ideas which, through the mediation of economic ethics, define the long run development of civilizations. This clearly goes beyond the question whether those civilizations that lacked inner-worldly asceticism also failed to adopt a rational economic orientation, and instead confronts the more general question of how rationality in conjunction with ideas and interests is produced and comes into effect. In the planned volume on Christianity, this problem must perforce have appeared as the question whether the momentous Protestant ethic was a fortuitous historical circumstance or whether it was the outcome of long term forces, either of ideas or interests. Notwithstanding the particular interest Weber took in European development, he had to count both projects equally. They led him, as we shall see more precisely, to place the *PE* thesis within a general inquiry into the role of rationality in history, in order to discover the rationalization process. He did this in *WEWR*.

The *PE* and *WEWR* do not belong together as hypothesis and control evidence. *WEWR* is the legitimate consolidation and extension of the path Weber had started with the *PE*. Through a consideration of Christianity the series would examine European rationalization prior to the Protestant ethic, and through a consideration of the remaining world religions would be able to overview the course of rationalization in other civilizations; and finally Weber would seek a general solution to it by generalizing the question as to the direction of rationality linking ideas and interests.

The *GARS* collection spanned the entire creative period of Weber's life from the *PE* onwards till his death; it, and not *ES*, was the work that had occupied him continuously.[36] The *PE* is the vehicle which provides the first clear but limited expression of this profound question. The *WEWR* documents how this problem was extended to a higher level of thinking: first, the evidence brought together in the substantive chapters, and then the theoretical summary of the 'Introduction' and the 'Intermediate Reflections'.

Weber's development displays the clear stages of the rationalization problem. The starting point is his acute interest in western capitalist rationality. In the *PE* Weber uncovered some immediate origins of economic rationalism. From there he developed (at the end of the *PE*) a programme that would research, on the one side, the significance of ascetic Protestantism for the modernization of society (the state, practical social ethics, and social groups); on the other, some other origins of modern rationalism (humanistic rationalism, scientific empiricism, medieval forerunners of asceticism). This inquiry was transformed in the course of the following work, *ES*, whose preference for thematic treatment opened the way to the viewpoints which could have contributed to the growth of rationality in western civilization. Seen in this light, *ES* belongs to a stage of the investigation that, on the one hand, pursues the economic and social consequences of the Protestant ethic on modernization, the *PE* conceiving only of the 'spirit' behind this process, and, on the other hand, searches further back in history for the roots of Protestantism and inner-worldly asceticism. The fruits of this inquiry were the chapters on domination and bureaucracy on one side, and those on city and law on the other.[37]

What had not yet been attained was a unified conceptualization of the irresistible rise of rationalization and disenchantment. But taken together with his studies on the sociology of religion,[38] Weber was able to formulate an approach to the development of rationality through a comparative study of world religions. The search for the historical antecedents of European modernization was replaced by the more comprehensive question: how could one religion foster a matter-of-fact orientation to, and a practical concern with, the world, and why was this not the case with other religions? Occidental development would be situated within a chapter on Christianity and would be explained by reference to a comparison to the development of other civilizations.

The planned volume on Christianity that was to provide a definitive answer to the triumph of rationality in the west was never written. Little notice has been taken of this circumstance, and still less has been inferred from it. This reveals a more general weakness of commentary: it has been ready to assume that Weber's published works can be taken to be the realization of his plans – or, at most, regretting that the works were not finished. Yet, whatever the reasons for this, seldom have plans and actual publications been so discrepant.

While interpretation has to proceed from what is published, it is difficult to accept an interpretation as correct that excludes the author's original intentions and later plans. It was an accident that *ES* was (apparently) his last work,[39] since it was not envisaged as the conclusive principal work. Furthermore it has been overlooked that *WEWR* takes its present form only because Weber had to publish it prematurely and had even to forgo the chapters on Islam and Christianity.

Since the course of occidental rationality had not received a conclusive formulation and, indeed, had nowhere been the subject of a major coherent exposition, how could Weber have risked outlining the historico-religious process of disenchantment whose termination was inner-worldly asceticism, when only the Judaic component of Christianity had been considered? The *WEWR* collection poses the following puzzle: between Judaism and Calvinism unfolds the process of disenchantment – how could Weber have discovered this process, when he had not yet undertaken the study of Christianity? The answer is simple enough if one bears in mind the origins and formation of Weber's *oeuvre*. Only through a comparison of the conclusions, which Weber had drawn from his investigations of the development of rationality, could the general insight suggest itself that permitted Weber to pronounce from the known evidence of European development: namely, that modernization was a continuation of a process of disenchantment. And this conclusion from comparisons could occur nowhere else but in the 'Introduction' and 'Intermediate Reflections'.

Seen in this light the dominant position of *GARS* becomes much clearer; in place of its piecemeal and opaque character, the structure and import of the work emerges. When Weber began to publish the torso of *WEWR* in the *Archiv* in 1915, he formulated a hurried conclusion, namely, the 'Introduction' and 'Intermediate Reflections'. This exercise unexpectedly crystallized for him the data on the general issue of how rationality develops between ideas and interests. And he reached the conclusion (still to be expounded) that religious rationalization bore responsibility for the long term process of rationalization, with the proviso that the actual direction taken by religious rationalization depends on societal factors. This general insight now enabled him to discern a process of historico-religious disenchantment in occidental development whose elucidation he had until that moment expected only in the study (never written) on Christianity.[40]

So *WEWR* in its incomplete form leads to an unanticipated and valid continuation and conclusion of the question first posed by the *PE*. The *PE* and *WEWR*, inadequate as they are in their form, form a unity that, in spite of deficiencies and lack of cohesion, provides an understanding of the separate path taken by occidental development by virtue of the insights gained through a comparison of the processes of religious rationalization.

In order to publish this newly attained position, he combined the *PE* and *WEWR* to form *GARS*. Both parts were enlarged – again in a hurry – so that the collection, with the new additions and changes, would reflect his most recent conceptualization. The whole collection, published in 1920, was further unified by the addition of the well known 'Author's Introduction' (*Vorbemerkung*) with its famous but puzzling opening sentence: 'Anyone who is heir to the traditions of modern European civilization will approach problems of universal history with a set of questions which will appear to him as both inevitable and legitimate. These questions will turn on the combination of circumstances that has led to the appearance in the Occident, and here alone, of cultural phenomena which, as we like to believe, lie in the path of development that is of universal significance and validity.' This sentence, written on the basis of the 'Introduction' and 'Intermediate Reflections', documents a level of thinking that had not previously been attained in the substantive chapters of *ES* and *WEWR*. And it makes clear that *GARS* is not a collection of scattered, if related essays, but was supposed to be the cohesive report, though imperfect and incomplete, on the findings obtained from the preceding major studies on universal history. *GARS* is the work on which Weber laboured most persistently, in which he felt free to define his own problems and issues, and in which he finally attained a certain degree of resolution to his studies.

One important point remains to be discussed. Weber had twice intended to embark on a unified account of European development: first in the brief programme outlined at the end of the *PE*, second, in the chapter on Christianity, as part of *WEWR*, in which the interplay of religion and society on the course of western rationality would have been as thoroughly investigated as in those chapters on China and India.[41] It comes as no surprise that Weber, having reached in *WEWR* a general understanding of the process of disenchantment, spoke in the 'Author's Introduction' 'of the still to be completed analysis of occidental development'.[42] This testament, written shortly before his death and when the main sections of Part II of *ES* had been ready for the printers for seven years, should have made it perfectly clear that *ES*, while undoubtedly containing valuable contributions to the problem of occidental development, had neither confronted the problem nor had it been intended to do so. *ES* is not the principal work that honours the programme, albeit in a fragmentary way, that was so diffidently set out at the end of the *PE*, but instead it is in the *WEWR* collection that Weber deepened and broadened his conceptualization of a universal history.[43]

Universal history and rationality

Leaving aside the hard-to-interpret statements of Weber's late work, *GARS* represents his final cognitive stance (*Erkenntnisstand*) toward a theme that occupied him throughout his life. This final position is not to be found in the substantive chapters but in those sections ('Introduction', 'Intermediate Reflections', and 'Author's Introduction') which have been pushed aside as either introductory comments or philosophical addenda, or else, given the absence of a critical edition, could not be identified as the work of the final hand. These sections are the *summa* of Weber's inquiry into the processes of rationality and, as far as is feasible, are subsequently imposed on *GARS* in order to provide an articulation of the whole.

GARS contains two sorts of material, the empirical studies and the theoretical inferences. The relation of the two presents interpretation with three unusual problems that, as far as I know, have not previously been approached. First, interpretation has to compare the three studies of *WEWR* so that the similarities in the development of economic ethics can be sociologically identified. Second, it must show whether the conclusions to these studies (having regard also for the *PE* and *ES*) correspond to the inferences that Weber drew from them. And the final problem is to reconstruct the conclusions that Weber had submitted in such a fragmented and enigmatic form in the 'Introduction', 'Intermediate Reflections', and 'Author's Introduction'.

This involves the reader in an almost insoluble problem. Weber never bothered himself with the first two problems. For reasons internal to his programme and other external factors, he leaves it up to the reader to test the results against the researches. The theoretical passages should be read sentence by sentence, asking what proposition is based on which passage in the *PE*, or *ES*, or the chapters on India, China, and Israel.[44] However, they can only be read in this way after a systematic comparison of the studies has been performed. Interpretation has to make up for this deficiency; it has, therefore, to reconstruct from the mass of research work the train of reasoning and generalizations which led to the 'Introduction', 'Intermediate Reflections', and 'Author's Introduction'.[45]

Given the major problems that interpretation is faced with, Weber's conclusions can only be reconstructed here in so far as they shed light on his universal-history stance. This in itself is difficult owing to Weber's disregard for the form in which he set down his conclusions. Only a painstaking reading can retrieve the logic and system of his ideas.

For this purpose it is helpful to rehearse the rough outline of the comparative researches of *WEWR*. Weber undertook to show by an investigation of the history of China, India, and Israel, how, and through what forces, there emerged in the world religions a dominant economic ethic. In particular, he was interested in how human rationality appears in the course of history, and the role played by religious ethics in this process.

Weber starts from a position that postulates the basic similarity of primitive religions and solidaristic clans which then break up and open the door to social conflict and cultic pluralism. The issue then becomes: which forces, singly or combined, are involved in the emergence of a dominant religious image of the world (*Weltbild*) and, in particular, how have they contributed to the establishment of a characteristic religious economic ethic; in addition, whether and how the economic ethic has shaped the relation of man to reality? In examining the issue the data always falls into two parts: how the 'world image' is formed, and how it is established against social and religious rivals.

On the basis of these researches – the conclusions from the sociology of religion in the *PE* and *ES*, and the inferences drawn in the 'Introduction', 'Intermediate Reflections', and 'Author's Introduction' that together constitute a life-time's concern – Weber reaches his final cognitive position, namely, a universal-historical conceptualization of the processes of rationalization. The most obvious sign that Weber has reached a new stage in his thinking, in what are otherwise encoded texts, is a clear change in position. Everyone knows that ideal types were a methodological tool to aid sociological analysis as, indeed, they know that Weber never grew tired of stressing that they were conceptual constructs and should not be taken for real. It comes as a shock, therefore, to read in the 'Intermediate Reflections' that in one instance Weber didn't wish to exclude 'real' types.[46]

From this methodological shock there emanates a whole series of sociological shocks as soon as one has comprehended the situation. The exception, the quasi-real types, are religious world images. The growth of these world views produces predominantly rational compulsions that make the genesis of religion a contribution to the progress of rationalism, and the stages of this development become a sociology of rationalism that Weber outlines ideal-typically. The proof of the quasi-real validity of these types is to be found in the empirical sections of *WEWR*.[47]

Weber, who throughout his life had upheld the uniqueness of history against the laws of progress, is now encountered in his work on religion in the opposing camp of evolutionism. Even more surprising is his conception of this evolutionism. The nineteenth century had split into two schools over the question of the origins and growth of religion. One held that religion was a massive fall from grace in terms of man's cognitive view of the world. Man turns away from reality and invents a world behind a world (*hinterweltlich*) of powers and beings, and only science and its explorations can ensure that man is called to the sphere of rationality. For millennia man has gambled away his right to rationality with religion and metaphysics, the original and irrational sins. Against this extreme position were the gradualists who saw in religion, understood in subjective terms (though objectively deficient), a forerunner to knowledge and rationality. Religion and metaphysics were the first fumbling attempts of rational knowledge whose progress depended on the elimination of the metaphysical and transcendental elements, and whose rationality was to be measured by its increasing capacity to account for the facticity of the exterior world. Both schools assessed rationality according to its cognitive grasp of the world, and so, ultimately, according to a model of science.

For Weber it was entirely different; religion advanced according to its own specific problematic. As we shall see, this is at root what Weber termed the problem of theodicy, and has nothing to do with the cognitive investigation of reality. The rational compulsion, to which religions have to accede, derives from the need to possess a rational answer to the problem of theodicy. The stages of religious advance are the more and more articulated conceptions of this problem and its solution. The rational development of religion occurs neither in, nor for, the outer reality of the world. On the contrary, for Weber the rational unfolding of the problem of theodicy operates in opposition to the world.[48] He states that a rational development of religious images of the world proceeds apace with the rational logic specific to religion and is not concerned with the question of the cognitive interpretation of reality.

That religion advances according to its own laws is further emphasized by the assumption that the rules governing the practical conduct of life (*Lebensführung*), and consequently man's understanding of reality, remain within the sphere of religious ethics. Weber thus radically departs from a position that his age (and ours) despite all its other differences, held for a certitude: that man exemplified and acquired his rationality in the service of his reasoned interests directly in and through the world, and which derived from a cognitive as well as a practical mastery of reality (*Bewältigung der Tatsachen*). For Weber on the other hand, religious rationalization with its own logic demanded priority. As we usually see it, man's rationality developed to its final form, occidental rationality, on its own strength. For Weber though, occidental rationalism resulted conditionally from a specific course of religious rationalization, rather than directly from man's rationality.

If one is to understand this novel thesis in an organized way, one has to return to Weber's concept of rationality. Already in the

PE, he had said that one can rationalize life from more than one ultimate standpoint. Fifteen years later he appended to this the sharp reminder: 'This simple statement, which is so often forgotten, should stand at the beginning of every study that is concerned with rationalism.'[49] 'Rationalism' is a historical concept and, conceptually speaking, it cannot be reified.[50] One can rationalize the most varied spheres of life – law, economy, education, but one can also rationalize contemplation, or asceticism and the mode of conduct in general, and, furthermore, from a diversity of viewpoints. What is always valid is that: 'what is rational from one point of view may well be irrational from another'.[51]

From the axiom of freedom from value judgement (*Werturteilsfreiheit*), that in today's reawakened discussion is disposed of as solely a methodological postulate, Weber draws sociological conclusions. The impossibility of rationally substantiating values played a fundamental role in Weber's sociology. The rationality of ends, the reasons why goals are desired, is not itself susceptible to rational proof; the most diverse and contradictory modes of behaviour may be rational in terms of means-end relations. What actually is rational, and in what regard, depends ultimately on irrational grounds.[52] One has in addition to know the meaning which men hold in order to be able to judge whether their behaviour is rational.

In a similar fashion the content of religious images of the world proceeds from irrational grounds. 'Whereof' and 'whereto' one will be saved depends on historical and social factors. Weber contrasts the formation of what constitutes the ultimate possession of grace and ways to salvation in the wake of the interests of leading social groups, so that what is valid for a warrior stratum will be quite different for a peasant or bourgeois population. The ways in which man ultimately relates to the world become ingrained and reveal themselves as enduring cultural legacies; although modified by generational and social structural change, they are hardly disturbed.

What characterizes the distinctiveness of Weber's approach is that world images, the product of irrational circumstances, succumb to a double pressure of rationality. First, the image of the world has to satisfy the structure of theodicy; that is, those obscure aspects of existence that are perceived as unfathomable have, at their own level, to be explained theoretically and, at a practical level, overcome. Second, in meeting this demand, they have to contribute to a more unified and comprehensive explanation of the world from the standpoint of a rational theodicy. Under such pressure, as we shall see more precisely, the specific ends and ways to salvation that at first were merely experienced are being progressively conceptualized into explicit and dominant perspectives of reality, in order to provide a systematic theodicy of the world as a whole and, at the same time, a complete rationalization of practical conduct.

As part of this inquiry, Weber had shortly before in the 'Introduction' formulated the memorable sentence: 'Not ideas, but material and ideal interests, directly govern men's conduct. Yet very frequently the world-images that have been created by "ideas" have, like switchmen, determined the tracks along which action has been pushed by the dynamic of interests.'[53] The meaning of this formula, central to *GARS*, is unambiguous, and it is unambiguously supported, as well as demanded, by the 'Introduction', 'Intermediate Reflections', and 'Author's Introduction'. Notwithstanding the fact that human action is motivated directly by interests, there occur periods of history whose direction in the long run is determined by ideas so that, in a way, men work themselves to death in the pursuit of their interests, and in the long run the water of history is conducted by the mill of ideas and men's actions remain under the influence of ideas.

Interpretation has carefully avoided touching on this, let us call it for the moment, ruse of ideas in Weber's works, partly because contemporary sociology in its conceptualization is so ill-accustomed to the notion of ideas, and partly because it is very difficult to make sense of the formula without first deciphering *WEWR*. The formula has sometimes been taken as an argument for the ineffectiveness of ideas! In most cases, however, it is simply shrugged off – ideas exist as just another factor. Bendix too can make little of this 'cryptic remark'.[54] The less familiar we are with Weber's terminology, the less sociologists, even with the best of intentions, are prepared for this 'remark'. Sprondel completely misrepresents its meaning, and with it the problem of *GARS*, when he takes it to mean that ideas are identical with ideal interests.[55]

Weber's usage is that of the preceding century. Ideas are those suprapersonal, transmitted viewpoints that articulate the fundamental aspects of man's relationship to the world. In a broader sense they are 'images of the world', more precisely they owe their existence to the need for, and the striving after, a coherent account of the world and, as such, they are created predominantly by religious groups, prophets, and intellectuals. In a world he had not yet mastered, man faced forces which appeared mysterious to him. When these forces were no longer regarded as immanent within things themselves but, instead, as an essence that stood behind and beyond, then, for Weber, a new idea had entered the world; and when this essence was made into a personal being (*personale Wesenheit*) this represented another new idea. The monotheistic concept of a supramundane God, for Weber, was another idea that first had to be conceived and, once accepted, had far-reaching consequences. Fully formed, a new idea proposed that there was a punishing and rewarding deity, particularly so, when taken with the further supposition that the destiny of men in this world and beyond was directed essentially according to the observance of ethical commandments. A further new idea is represented by ethical prophecy (*Sendungsprophetie*), as in Judaism, because man then had to consider himself acting in the world as the instrument of God. A further extension of this – again a new idea – is the Protestant belief in predestination.

In treating ideas as historical and social facts Weber is completely conventional.[56] Entirely unconventional is his 'cryptic' theory (not 'remark') of the role of ideas as switchmen. Imbued with historical knowledge, scholars in the nineteenth century were all ready to acknowledge that ideas, once they acquired dominance, could easily determine a period of history. For Weber, however, not the power of ideas through their persistence but the dynamic of their own logic makes them the switchmen in history. Certain ideas under the compulsion of an inner logic (*Eigenlogik*) develop their rational consequences and thereby effect universal-historical processes; this is the import of *WEWR*.

Passing beyond the empirical corroboration of these conclusions, there are two theoretical branches, an anthropological analysis and a multilinear typology, of the development of religion. It has been frequently noted and lamented that Weber lacked an anthropology,[57] and indeed under this name one hardly existed in his time. Actually though, Weber had developed an anthropological theory of his own and set it out in the 'Introduction'.[58] Here, and not in the more meagre 'Basic Concepts', is where Weber conceives of action and man's relationship to the world.

He starts out from the acceptance of an original pragmatist orientation of action that is geared to success in its encounter with the surrounding world. Although it may also make use of magical intervention, which, in terms of our knowledge, is not properly rational, action is subjectively rational in its concern with the immediate effects it has upon objects (*Dinge*) which are perceived solely in terms of their facticity. This 'original (*urwüchsige*) freedom from constraint in the relation to the world' bears the seeds of its own supersession, for human action is not sufficiently successful. In the encounter with the world there occur surplus experiences that demand elucidation. These experiences originate from the experience of suffering that derives directly from deprivation or social injustice. The original solution to this was the search for charisma – it is here, and not in the political sociology, that the concept originates – that is, a magic-based superiority over the insecurities of a world full of suffering. The personal experience of the everyday world in both the natural and social order is by itself insufficient, and so, from the beginning, man searches for experiences that transcend the everyday, and through which he acquires a magical power over the world, so becoming a bearer of charisma.

Weber developed what is overall a modern anthropology in the 'Introduction' under the unfamiliar title of theodicy of fortune (*Glück*) and suffering (*Leid*). Fortune and suffering, these are the abstract categories for those personal experiences that extend man's action beyond his normal encounter with a purely factual and material world (*Dinge in ihrer schieren Tatsachlichkeit*). The experience of fortune and suffering shatter the purely purposive-rational categories of a pragmatic orientation to things; the elucidation and solution to these experiences can neither be explained nor overcome by technical or artificial means. At this point, Weber breaks with that conception, proper to the nineteenth century, according to which the uncertainty of an action's outcome could be reduced by an increase in knowledge. For Weber, the purposive rational orientation encloses a perpetual need, a search for charisma that lies beyond the everyday; charisma promises an immediate deliverance from the uncertainty of action, and the desire that action should result in success goes hand in hand with the reality of the uncertainty of action.

Weber proceeds from a constant and universal anthropological problematic: the experience of the world – possibly in its most simple form, that of acute suffering – is perceived as something senseless. Therein lies another anthropological constant, the search after charisma, that is, experiences that go beyond the everyday; these can take the most varied forms, for example, magical power over things, protection from a dolorous world through techniques (ecstasy, drugs). It also results, as in the particular theodicies of world religions, in the explanation of those aspects of existence devoid of meaning as transitory, superficial, encumbered (*verschuldet*) yet surmountable.[59]

From these universals there develops a dynamic, for every solution remains partial and unsatisfactory; every charismatic explanation reaches out beyond itself so long as a unified and comprehensive elucidation of the lack of meaning in the world has not been attained, as is sought by articulated theodicies. When, for example, primitive man imagined he had power over certain things through analogous magic (*Analogiezauber*), then this charismatic praxis (it, in its turn, requiring further explanation) is close to assuming that a controllable force inhabits those things. When this force is presumed to inhabit numerous similar objects, an area of control is formed over this sort of object, and when extended over an area of life, this probably led to a personalizing of the deities. In such a process the charismatic praxis would develop from a magical incantation and ritualistic control to a religion of sacrifice – of wills and gifts. This could give way to the view that the experience of suffering was not simply tolerated or ordained by the Gods (and so unalterable by prior sacrifice) but was rather the result, the punishment, for individual transgression of the basic commandments of a personal deity. This would mark the beginnings of an ethical religion, and could lead from pantheism to monotheism and to a type of ethical religion of redemption that discloses the prospect of permanently overcoming the experiences of suffering and the absence of meaning.

I have sketched, rather crudely, the main strand of early religious development, in order to indicate that the rationality of the dynamic is based on a necessity to unify that ties the systematization of facts (or their elucidation) into the systematization of action. Every charismatic practice (recourse to analogous magic) demands an account (of the controllable forces inhabiting things), and every elucidation (of the personal powers behind things) opens up new possibilities for 'charismatic' praxis (sacrifice). Weber holds that the original and, in a certain sense, natural relation of man to the world is, subjectively, purposive-rational; because of this man conceives of reality as a multiplicity of disconnected facts and isolated situations. The effect of this for the individual was that, reality being so splintered, action itself could be only fragmented and situational.[60] Religious development, therefore, is a rationalization, because it systematizes facts (and explanations) and unifies standpoints of action, but always under the spur of 'charismatic' needs, and so leads to further questions of theodicies. Under the pressure of this rationalization religions are forced to provide comprehensive images of the world and articulated theodicies, which present the most consistent forms of rationalizations of the world from the viewpoint of a comprehensive explanation of these specifically meaningless aspects of reality and according to the viewpoint of supramundane salvation.

The principal strand, outlined above, is only one branch in a multilinear 'genealogical tree' of religious rationalizations. As in a decision tree, this can run along several paths, some of which are 'blind,' others going further to higher levels which is why, in

universal-historical terms, they were both successful and conse-
quential. Whether a society remains stationary at one point, or
whether it is embarked upon a particular path depends on
circumstances. For every option taken, other future options are
excluded. The 'genealogical tree' reproduces the specific logic of
religious rationalization and the directional role (*Weichenstellung*)
of ideas. The genealogical tree performs two functions: it presents
the important facts of the developmental history, and provides an
ideal-typical explanatory schema of religious rationalization. While
allowing for deviant and intermediary forms, Weber claims that
from a universal perspective explanatory hypotheses and history
coincide. There is a historical probability that some of the
developments specified in the genealogical tree will in fact follow
the direction outlined.

With the arrival of ethical religions of salvation and monotheism
religious rationalization reaches an important threshold, because
here the problem of theodicy is encountered in a comprehensive
and articulated manner. This is particularly clear in the case of
monotheism. So long as man recognizes several powers, he must
serve each differently; because the world is split into spheres over
which a different God holds sway, man has, so to speak, to serve
both Apollo and Aphrodite. The idea of one supramundane God
of creation, or the notion of a deity immanent within the universe,
crystallizes man's heterogeneous and heteronomous reality into an
order that discloses the work of a single hand or will. This has
decisive consequences, because now the unitary explanation of the
world becomes a continuous problem of intellectual theodicy, in
the same way as the ethical unification of action becomes a
practical problem.

While Weber had originally thought that the concept of a
supramundane God of creation finally set the direction for a
religious ethic of asceticism, he later changed his mind.[61]
Nevertheless, he adhered to the view that the conceptualization of
an ethical religion of salvation increased the tempo of rationalization, bringing out its inner logic. It is here that those determining
ideas are imprinted which consequently hold sway over interests.
The aims of salvation and the ways towards it, although at first
established in a fortuitous and incomplete manner, perforce
become a permanent and explicit intellectual problem, demanding
consistency in its formulation; given the nature of the problem
and requirements, viewed sociologically this becomes specifically
the work for intellectuals. Early on in this process there occurs an
important bifurcation: the one branch leading to a view of the
world in which man is an instrument of God and free from
attempts to attain salvation through the intervention of magic, and

the other leading to the merging of man and deity by means of
mystical contemplation in which man becomes the receptacle of
the deity. The first way becomes embedded in Judaism, the
second in India, and both produce ultimately rationally consistent
solutions to theodicy: belief in predestination, and the Indian
religion of the intellectuals, the Karma. A third rational solution
is, in historical terms, discarded by Weber as developmentally
uninteresting, and the remaining world religions, although they
have a decisive impact on the relationship to the world and
economic ethics, present composite forms of rationally incomplete
solutions.

One cannot understand this (unavoidably) cursory reading of
Weber if only variations in the cognitive view of the world and
ethical precepts are perceived. Overall we may infer that *GARS* is
concerned with how man produces his cultural reality. Primitive
man missed the route to rationalization not, according to Weber,
because he was 'alogical' or 'irrational'; so long as he took things
to be identical with their simple facticity, his purposive rational
behaviour could only terminate in magic. When man created for
himself a hinterworld behind the facticity of things, he produced
not only a supposition of reality, from which practical maxims
derive, but he also created through cultural transformation
additional dimensions of inner and outer reality. In the same way
the ethical unification of action is not simply the logical
consequence of the conceptualization of the unitary order of
things, and so simply a principle. As the counterpart to his
conception of the world, man creates his cultural reality, and in
the conceptualization of the world as an order he gains that inner
and outer realm of experience, from which the ethical unification
of conduct can be carried through at the practical level. The
reality of men is, as Weber knew, their own cultural web, and
anyone who holds this to be of no consequence will scarcely
understand his sociology.

With the disclosure of religious rationalization Weber brings
back reason into history. He restores the unity of human history
by readmitting to authentic history all those forms, periods, or
cultures which scientism and modernism, in their evolutionary
bent, had regarded if not as insane then as senseless aberrations
from the due course of development. Weber saw reason at work
everywhere, though it did not automatically result in what is now
understood as rationality and progress.

As Weber notes, man acts directly according to his interests.
With certain reservations he presents reason as a means, according
to which, subjectively, primitive man was also purposive-rational.
Weber's entire work evinces the view that no comprehensive and

continuous rationalization of reality can proceed from interests. From his sentence on the role of ideas one can read, indeed must read, that interests are blind. Interests are directed only for limited periods on specific aspects of reality. They contribute to rationalization only in as far as their goals are attained, and are short-lived forces whose attainment inhibits further rationalization. The world, for Weber, is made of partial rationalizations which are called into being according to the interests of the moment – economic, technical, military, and administrative. Just as pre-modern adventurer and booty capitalism had little chance of leading to a rational economy, so other rationalizations of aspects of reality remained stuck fast for, quite simply, interests stood in their own way. The modern economy originated from the pressure of discipline and not from the gratification of interests. The switchpoint of ideas is, therefore, only the reverse side of the blindness of interests.

This takes us to the kernel of *GARS* and Weber's concept of the rationalization process. A comprehensive rationalization of reality, as has occurred in European modern times, could only originate out of the disciplining of interests in the sense of a rational and methodical conduct of life. While all religions in their way have sought to provide for a methodical conduct of life, such rationalizations were bounded by inner-worldly interests or had been directed upon supramundane salvation. Only inner-worldly asceticism created a rationally ordered mode of conduct which had to prove itself in a world free from the influence of magic. Everything that had previously been subject to the partial rationalization of interests could now unfold, and partial and divergent interests could be combined into a comprehensive and continuous rationalization of the world.

In this respect, Protestantism reveals itself as the heir to the Judaic religion which, despite all the inroads of magic, had retained a rational ethic free from the influence of magic. The idea of a world susceptible to the influence of rational action maintained its efficacy with Christianity – consolidated by the institution of the Church and underpinned by the legacy of the classical world; for instance, it changed monasticism into an order of work or favoured those partial rationalizations to which interests had already given the lead. Only Judaism had set religious rationalization on the path towards the disenchantment of the world, along which Christianity continued. While a rationally consistent solution to the problem of theodicy remained unfulfilled, the possibility always existed that magic could gain a foothold.[62] It was the Protestant ethic which sealed the fate of magic, and the belief in predestination accomplished a rational solution to the problem of theodicy.[63]

Thus the inner logic of religious rationalization had contributed to the unfolding of the idea which had remained latent in the Judaic ethic and which came to realization in inner-worldly asceticism. Weber herewith joined up the beginning and the end of the process religious disenchantment in the comparative study of religious rationalization:

> The rationale, in the sense of the logical and teleological 'consistency', of an intellectual-theoretical or practical-ethical attitude has, and always has had, power over man, however limited and unstable this power is, and always has been, in the face of other forces of historical life. Religious interpretations of the world, and ethics of religion created by intellectuals and meant to be rational, have been strongly exposed to the imperative of consistency.[64]

Knowing this, Weber could speak of the historico-religious process of disenchantment without undertaking the exposition of occidental history and in which other contributing factors could be left unspecified.[65] The conclusion to this process was inner-worldly asceticism. It had finally demagicalized reality and laid the way open for theoretical and practical rationalizations for which it had furnished the 'spirit'. From this point onwards, rationalization takes the form of modernization, born by worldly forces that no longer had to reckon with magical powers.

Thus the Protestant ethic shows itself to be part of a universal-historical process, and universal history is the key concept with which Weber in the 'Author's Introduction' sets out *GARS*. Sociologists are forced to confront universal-historical questions because all societies had to face the same fundamental problems to which they have found different solutions, and historically unique among those are the ones that have actually overcome, established, and thereby have produced, from the point of universal-history, significant cultural phenomena. Their explanation is possible not by recourse to general laws but only by reference to historical constellation. The subjects under study in *WEWR* are the major world religions seen from the viewpoint of universal history. Behind the ebb and flow of history, Weber reveals in bold outline how ideas perform the role of switchmen. This was no mere vignette within the traditional history of ideas, in which the power of ideas is sociologically defined and explained, but rather it was the discovery of the significance (*Bedeutung*) of ideas for universal-historical processes. The 'Author's Introduction' could have ended with the words of Goethe, that he who does not take into cognizance three thousand years of history, does not understand the world.

Max Weber's work

Taking into account what has been said about the position of his works and the development of his thinking, a summary would be superficial and a detailed exposition impossible. Nevertheless important new contours have emerged calling for an appraisal of the *oeuvre*.

Along with other commentators it may be taken for granted that Weber's writings, often including his occasional pieces, were the unravelling of a fundamental problem that almost totally dominated him. His undoubted and marked interest in occidental rationalization was, however, only the condensation and starting point of a theme that preoccupied him throughout his life. In fact only a small part of his *oeuvre* was directed to specifically occidental development, while the entirety of his work, including the methodology, owes its existence to the question: what is rationality?[66]

His interest in European development too is only comprehensible in the light of this question. Assuredly his concern with the causal explanation of the process, a concern that led from the *PE* to *ES* and then to *WEWR*, was not a private preoccupation; instead the impulse behind this concern was the question as to the destiny of capitalism, or in more general terms, rationalization on a comprehensive scale as the predominant form of life. Now one can adopt this view of Weber's without having to engage in causal explanation, even less so, universal-historical explanation, as sociology has sufficiently demonstrated. For Weber, however, a twofold demand is contained in the *factum brutum*: why had man at only one point in his history come to what he hence took for his rationality? This was both a question about the rationality of human action and the unity of human history. Secondly, what meaning should be attached to the fact that this rationality is now globally the predominant form of life? This contains the joint question whether and how man was able to live with his new rationality, and how he was able to come to terms with this situation. All this is not a matter of outlining historical causes and effects, but concerns the intellectual relatedness (*Anverwandlung*) to a new reality of colossal import; or, to salvage a neglected central concept from his methodology, the concern with the 'cultural meaning' (*Kulturbedeutung*) of the rational order. What I have termed 'relatedness' may not seem to be a very compelling existential proposition. But Weber was of the opinion, as may be confirmed by the methodology, that social science was only meaningful if it did not remain committed to the explanation of factual sequences (through subsumption of events under laws), but exposed the cultural significance of phenomena, since only in this way did phenomena disclose their meaning to man, allowing him to adopt a meaningful attitude. This is only possible if one gauges the individual and social possibilities that historically have been open to man, which then leads to the central question: what is rational, and to the further questions, what norms can man adhere to, and where do they lead him? Weber's insatiable hunger for reality, born of a desire to assay its comprehensibility, led him to probe into the most distant reaches of thought and reality, as evidenced by the mass of materials and broad themes.

Given the inclusive scope of his endeavours, interpretation has hardly bothered with the development of his thought, nor with the exact chronology of the texts which seemed to be but fragments of a life-time theme for whose unity one had to rely on *ES*. Now it is true that Weber had created in *ES* a conceptual *instrumentarium* and laid out a provisional plan of the separate fields of reality. To this extent it was not an accident that he took on the burden of this labour, and thus drove himself to a conceptual acuteness that for him was a necessity. Whoever in this sense labels *ES* a major work, may do so. However, much as Weber's being is breathed into every sentence of the work, little can be seen of the deeper development of his sociology. In terms of developmental history *ES* stands between the *PE* and *WEWR* and, as such, represents a period when he was still groping his way to an understanding of European rationality.

The work stands as a systematization in contrast to the problem-oriented research of the *PE* and *WEWR*, and therefore, ultimately, as an ideal-typical compendium. Weber could not have envisaged this as his life-time's work, because he did not share today's belief that sociology could, or even should, as far as possible be a complete system of concepts and finalized theory. In terms of biography *ES*, both its parts, was written in two separate attempts that put together took three years, whereas the main issues of the *PE* and *WEWR* extended over the whole period of his maturity, forming a continuous concern with the question of rationality.

Whoever wishes to penetrate to the vital centre of Weber's thinking and sociology must lay hold of *GARS* and even more *WEWR*, that is, they must turn to those sections, sketched in this article, that form the framework of *GARS*. From this stance alone can the open-endedness of Weber's writings be brought to a more than formal unity and the previously indiscernible later work of the mature Weber be brought to light.

In the course of *WEWR* Weber acquired a universal-historical perspective which, apart from bringing the earlier versions under revision, opened up new problems and a late phase in his sociology; and against this perspective I would want to assess all the texts which proceeded, or should have proceeded, from the themes and perspectives attained in *WEWR*.[67] Unfortunately, for various reasons, these texts are not many. Of these only sections from them can serve as clues as to how Weber would have transposed his universal-historical perspective to the characteristic situation of modern times. This had been the purpose and aim of his researches, and had been carried out to a degree in the *PE*.[68]

I shall attempt to show in an example why it is worth the trouble of deciphering these late texts, working from the assumption that the key to them is to be found in *WEWR*. Everyone, whether professor or student, knows the academic lecture 'Science as a vocation'. In the stunted interpretation of Weber this has been understood as a political expression of the axiom of freedom from value judgement, as a call to the unlimited discipline of detail and application.[69]

However the passages, in which Weber articulates his later sociology, remain out of view, as if they were some indecipherable hieroglyphic. Who has noted that Weber in this work paints a completely different picture of the cultural significance of science to the one he had outlined in the 1904 essay on 'Objectivity'? Who has been able to make anything of the final passages on fraternity, mysticism and new prophets? And what should one make of the sentence that begins, 'The many old Gods, demagicalized and taking the shape of impersonal forces, rise from their graves, strive to gain power over our lives, and once again begin an eternal struggle with one another.' The rump of sociologists will, I fear, read this sentence as 'infill', and those who find it opaque are unlikely to quote it as a scientific observation.

However the sentence, read in the context of *WEWR*, explains quite precisely that we are taking leave from a distinct period of a few thousand years of human history. The cage of capitalism is the expression that Weber used at the end of the *PE*; the structure continues but the spirit by which it was attained has vanished. *WEWR* appraised him that we stand at the end of a process of some thousands of years of disenchantment. The ethical unification of the mode of conduct, which for millennia man had previously achieved by means of theodicy, above all through an image of a supramundane God of creation, was dissolved. Weber held this to be a fundamental fact of modern reality and for man, culture and society. Through scientific knowledge and the purposive-rational domination of the world reality became demagicalized, and thereby, religion was pushed into the byways of the irrational. The theodicy problem, which when conceptualized in the form of a creation of the world or a salvation religion had posed a rational question, could no longer practice that profound effect upon man that it had enjoyed, despite conspicuous compromises over the preceding thousand years, namely, the ethical unification of action. With it there also disappeared those suppositions, formed in the epoch and under the influence of world religions, that so characterized the features of man and society.

Today's normal sociology, it appears, is quite capable of accounting for this historical fact. It places it under the rubric 'changes of value' and introduces it as a new variable into the vacant position labelled 'values'. Weber was familiar with the theory of value pluralism and was well aware that it was anchored within social differentiation. But he only understood this occurrence from a perspective of universal history, and only then was he able to assess its meaning and significance (*Bedeutung*). Man creates his reality not merely and primarily through social structures, he creates his own inner and outer realms of meaning, he produces the inner dimensions of his self and the outer field of cultural meaning (*äusseren Sinnfelder seiner Kultur*) through the counterpart (*Gegenbild*) of his rationalized image of the world. In a sentence, the reality in which man lives, at any rate the reality which he is himself, is a cultural web that he weaves from a conceptualization of the world.[70]

And if the old Gods rise from their graves and take up their struggle anew, the world is again fragmented into the spheres of competence of the different powers. But while the ancient Greeks in their original orientation to the world were able to sacrifice first to Apollo and then to Aphrodite, the tragedy of such polytheism being action that led to the jeopardizing of the value claims of the competence of a God – first revealed by Aeschylus, Euripides, and Sophocles – (and consequentially leading to the metaphysical transcendental searches for a solution of Greek philosophy), all that modern man is able to do is to call up the several Gods by their abstract names: communism, emancipation, equality, freedom, socialism; these are now the powers, which within the heart of the individual, come into unresolvable conflict in the social and political arena, decided only by fanaticism, political belief movements and *Kathederprophecie*, or else accepted due to forms of caution – of apathy or adaptation. Here we reach the point at which Weber's sociology breaks off. The questions still confronting us are what image of the world today produces itself in the interplay of ideas and interests of intelligence and power, and through what sociological interplay? What is the characteristic individuality of our modern civilization?

These are only brief indications to show that one may with great precision come to grips with the many hieroglyphic sketches and comments of Weber's late work, if one approaches them with the key to *WEWR*. Important material that until now had been neglected as too sketchy or as personal comment can be placed within the contours of his later sociology. The deciphering, in general, the final presentation of Weber's development, and so also the final interpretation of his sociology, will remain a difficult task so long as today's editions cover up rather than reveal these sections of the work.

There remains the question of what contemporary sociology might accomplish from the universal-historical perspective of the mature Weber in which ideas play a determining role. I limit myself to a couple of observations.

The question is not whether sociology should become a universal history, but whether it is capable of handling its issues if it forgoes the universal-historical perspective. The question is not whether we comprehend the present by means of the instruments of social research, but whether we should forgo the data of history and the questions that can be drawn from history in addressing the present. The question is not whether we should make sociology into a history of ideas, but whether we can proceed from the premiss that ideas *vis-à-vis* interests are ideologies, in any event, epiphenomena of what alone are the real structures. The question is not whether we ignore the problems of the present, but how we are able to recognize them.

Notes

* This translation is a slightly condensed version of the article which originally appeared as 'Das Werk Max Webers', in *Kölner Zeitschrift für Soziologie und Sozialpsychologie*, 27, 1975, pp. 663–702.
1. This appears to be the view of Reinhard Bendix, when he notes, 'as a comprehensive whole his work remains relatively unknown', *Max Weber, An Intellectual Portrait*, New York, 1960, p. 17.
2. Similarly R. Bendix says that Weber's work has served as 'points of departure for the most varied interpretations', 'Max Weber's Sociology Today', *International Social Science Journal* 17, 1965, p. 9.
3. My own work on Weber written in the 1950s and 1960s contains not only this error but other shortcomings of interpretation which I have tried to avoid in this article.

4.   J. Winckelmann, 'Max Webers Opus Posthumum', *Zeitschrift für die gesamte Staatswissenschaft* 105, 1949, p. 369.

5.   Ibid., p. 387.

6.   I naturally do not doubt the contribution that the editors Roth and Winckelmann have made to the arrangement, the architectonic structure and the systematization of *Economy and Society*. *ES* can only be understood if one continually bears in mind that sociology cannot be and ought not to be enclosed within a system of concepts. From this conception *ES* as a *summa* of sociology does not contain a systematic substantive argument and in default of this unity permits no intelligible whole. And certainly one should not do this, as though *ES* allowed the interpretation of a thematic unity concerning, for instance, the question of occidental rationality were it not for the unfortunate lack of fit of some few parts. The issue is not one of the number of gaps, nor enlargements, however welcome; neither could alter the character of *ES*. This gives rise to the doubt whether one ought to explain *ES* exclusively as the principal work of an author who on his side regarded the sociological *instrumentation* as a means to the end of knowledge of historical reality and, above all, historical courses (*Abläufe*).

7.   For the proof of this see Winckelmann, op. cit., p. 368.

8.   Karl Jaspers, *Max Weber, Politiker, Forscher, Philosoph*, Bremen, 1946, p. 41.

9.   See René Konig and Johannes Winckelmann, *Max Weber zum Gedächtnis*, Kölner Zeitschrift für Soziologie und Sozialpsychologie, Sonderheft 7, 1963, where Troeltsch himself observed, 'What is the scientific achievement in the face of the totality of this commanding personality?', p. 43.

10.   W. M. Sprondel, 'Sozialer Wandel, Ideen und Interessen: Systematisierungen zu Max Webers Protestantischer Ethik', in Seyfarth and Sprondel, *Seminar: Religion und gesellschaftliche Entwicklung*, Frankfurt, 1973, p. 215.

11.   *PE*, Unwin University Book, p. 105.

12.   Ibid., p. 27. (Translator's note: Parsons's translation should include the word 'enlarged'. So, 'In the *enlarged* studies collected here we shall be concerned with these forces', but see his preface p. ix.)

13.   (Tenbruck is referring to the German editions.) On this see his article, 'Wie gut kennen wir Max Weber? Über Maßstäbe der Weber-Forschung im Spiegel der Maßstäbe der Weber Ausgaben', *Zeitschrift für die gesamte Staatswissenschaft* 131, 1975.

14.   The far reaching consequences of failing to note and distinguish the composition dates of the essays and their additions have been taken up by Benjamin Nelson, 'Max Weber's Author's Introduction', *Sociological Inquiry* 44, 1974, and F. Tenbruck, 'Max Weber and the Sociology of Science: A Case reopened', *Zeitschrift für Soziologie* 3, 1974.

15.   'Ancient Judaism', New York, 1952, p. 5.

16.   *The Sociology of Religion*, Methuen, London, 1965, p. 179.

17.   Ibid., p. 269.

18.   The term is indexed only once, *ES*, New York, 1968, p. 333.

19.   *PE*, pp. 77–8 and 26 ff., *From Max Weber* (ed.), Gerth and Mills, pp. 293 and 280 ff.

20.   It has not been sufficiently appreciated that while the 'Objectivity' essay was concerned with general methodological questions, it was also written essentially as a methodological justification for the *PE*.

21.   The research programme outlined at the end of the *PE* doesn't detract from this argument; Weber scarcely mentions the history anterior to Protestantism, as will be shown below.

22.   'Ancient Judaism', p. 4.

23.   Bendix, op. cit., p. 13.

24.   G. Abramowski, *Das Geschichtsbild Max Webers*, Stuttgart, 1966.
25.   I am following Winckelmann's dating here, in the foreword to *Wirtschaft und Gesellschaft*, instead of G. Roth's, who in the English edition dates it 1910 to 1914. What is needed is a biography which dates precisely Weber's activities and studies, using and considering all the sources, and producing virtually a diary-based account of his life. The often disconnected and chronologically vague biography of Marianne Weber is as deficient in this respect as the damp squib offered by Eduard Baumgarten, *Max Weber, Person und Werk*. Certainly the exact dating of his studies and lectures could be depended upon to provide a better understanding of the genesis of the problems and goals of Weber's works.
26.   Cf. R. Bendix, *Max Weber, An Intellectual Portrait*, pp. 284 ff., and also p. 285, where he says, 'His essay on Judaism is only the starting point of an explanation that occupied him for the rest of his life.'
27.   Bendix, op. cit., p. 285.
28.   Ibid., and more sharply expressed, 'these continuations are addressed in large part to the question how the basic assumptions of that rationalism had become the dominant value orientation of the Western world'; this is in agreement with the quote cited n. 26.
29.   Marianne Weber states (*Max Weber, Ein Lebensbild*, 1952, pp. 387 ff) that the preparatory work for the substantive chapters of *WEWR* was done at the same time as *ES*, about 1911, and that both works in part were 'created out of the same source'; this accords with the many overlaps. However it was in 1915 that Weber first added the result of his comparisons from the substantive studies, the result being the 'Introduction' and 'Intermediate Reflections' of *WEWR*, leaving then probably only the chapter on ancient Judaism in note form – cf. the introductory note to *WEWR* and the remark by Marianne Weber (op. cit., p. 382) that the main parts of *WEWR* were ready in 1913. Since Bendix depends almost exclusively on the substantive chapters of *WEWR*, it is understandable that he maintains the chronological reversal. Weber only makes the decisive summation of the substantive chapters of *WEWR* for the first time, as is still to be shown, in the 'Introduction' and 'Intermediate Reflections'. There is also indeed substantial overlap with the sociology of religion from *Economy and Society*, and many details are identical in both presentations. *ES*, however, lacks the systematic bringing together of the individual perceptions as a sociology of religious rationalization, which attains a universal historical perspective in the 'Introduction' and 'Intermediate Reflections'. This falls in line with Weber's testimony in n. 1 of *GARS*, Bd. I, p. 237 that the essays of *WEWR* were designed 'to interpret and enlarge the sociology of religion section (of *ES*) and also on many points to be interpreted through it'. That the sociology of religion studies of *ES* were prepared at the same time and essentially from the same sources as *WEWR*, is clear since preliminary perceptions from the comparative studies of *WEWR* appear in *ES*; and it is the case that Weber set this down very early on, also though to be worked on at a later date. Nevertheless it is perfectly clear that Weber drew up for the first time the result of comparative studies in the 'Introduction' and 'Intermediate Reflections'.
30.   Bendix, op. cit., p. 103.
31.   Ephraim Fischoff had commented in 1944 that the *PE* was read without any regard to Weber's later writings, especially *WEWR*.
32.   See *GARS*, Bd. I, p. 237, n. 1 and p. 382 of Marianne Weber's *Lebensbild*.
33.   See n. 29.
34.   On the dating of 'Intermediate Reflections' see Marianne Weber, op. cit., p. 367. That it was a hurriedly inserted section conceived after the 'Introduction' was already in print is clear from the contents. Max Weber's comment (*GARS*, Bd. I, p. 237, n. 1) that 'the first parts remained unchanged from when they

were written down and read out to friends' can only have applied to the
substantive chapters.
35. *PE*, p. 284, n. 119.
36. Marianne Weber speaks (op. cit., p. 381) of the enlargement which
Weber's studies underwent as a result of the work for *WEWR*. Although she
avoids mentioning that the explanation 'of the uniqueness of the whole of western
civilization' can only be answered by turning to the more general question of the
long run destiny of rationality between ideas and interests, her statements are
very informative in one respect. According to her, Weber, when he alighted upon
the theme of *WEWR*, was continuously preoccupied with the question that he
later articulated in the 'Author's Introduction' to *GARS*: why is it only in the
West that there are rational forms of science, art, the city, bureaucracy and the
state? This makes it clear at a stroke that *ES* could not have been intended to
provide the answer. It is apparent that ranging over capitalism and modern
Fachmenschentum, Weber had uncovered other rational components of European
civilization, so in science, art, etc. He could use this in one way to explain the
accumulation of rationality leading to modernization. But there then still
remained the question, one that continually preoccupied him according to
Marianne: how is it that the Occident has experienced the development of these
aspects of rationality? Simply because *ES* had discovered the large number of
rational features, the work pressed on to further question which it could not
solve. It could scarcely provide the answer to this further question, since it was
the site on which it was first posed.
37. See note 36 above.
38. Weber's studies in the sociology of religion were significantly advanced by
the influence of the 'Eranos-Circle', which in its turn was probably influenced by
Weber who after a short period was setting the tone. See Marianne Weber, op.
cit., p. 392, and the situational presentation of Paul Honigsheim, *Erinnerungen an
Max Weber*, Sonderheft 7, Kölner Zeitschrift für Soziologie; also M. L. Gothein,
Eberhard Gothein, 1931, p. 149 and p. 213.
39. While it is well known that *ES* still was not ready for the printers at the
time of Weber's death, little notice had been taken of the fact that he planned
more works of a different sort, in particular, a sociology of culture. The place of
ES as the definitive, though unfortunately incomplete, life's work would perhaps
be relativized if notice had been taken of Marianne's information, op. cit.,
p. 745, 'Weber sunk himself completely into his task, and once said that the
scientific problems he saw before him would last for a 100 years.'
40. I do not share Bendix's opinion (op. cit., p. 289) that after the publication
of *WEWR* Weber stuck to his plan for chapters on Islam and Christianity. The
abandonment of this design is clearly spelt out in the introductory note to
WEWR, and I know of no counter evidence. Nor do I share Bendix's view that
Weber in *WEWR* was concerned only with early Christianity. If one takes the
chapters on China and India as the base line, then one would expect that the
chapter on Christianity would concern the further destiny of rationality up to
Protestantism between, on the one side, the different churches and directions
and, on the other, the societal interests. As will soon be shown, after he had
copied down the prosecution of *WEWR* he adhered to the plan to depict the
development of the Occident. This is to be counted as part of the grand design of
the late phase, and it could scarcely be followed by a volume on Christianity.
This is to be classed with the many displacements that the great life-time's theme
of rationality underwent.
41. The last written work, which concerns ancient Judaism, differs from those
on India and China in that social relations are concerned only in broad outline.
Whether this is in accord with the nature of the work, or whether it was because

of the hurried publication of an unfinished manuscript I cannot judge.

42. *GARS*, Bd. I, p. 12. (Translator's note: Parsons's translation misses the sense of this point.)

43. On the complex relation of *WEWR* and *ES*, I have discussed this in notes above. Weber was committed to the large conception of *ES* which excluded and forced him to sacrifice plans that for him were more important, viz. *WEWR*. For evidence for this see G. Roth's 'Introduction' to *ES*, p. lvii.

44. On the relation of *WEWR* to the chapter on the sociology of religion in *ES*, see n. 29. The many overlaps allow one to realize that it was only in *WEWR* that the universal-historical concept and the 'sociology of rationalism' clearly emerged.

45. Abramowski's book (see n. 24 above) provides a serviceable comparative analysis outlining the typical variations of the city, domination, etc., between the Occident and the Orient, which are certainly there to be emphasized. The shortcoming of this undertaking, as I see it, is the comparison of social and historical processes and the contribution of the dominating ideas of the different world religions. This, though, is the consequence of the understanding of *WEWR* and so *GARS* as an empiricist work. I might take the opportunity here of announcing that Steve Kalberg has worked on a dissertation at Tübingen for the University of New York (Stony Brook) and is nearing completion.

46. Cf. the first pages of 'Intermediate Reflections'.

47. A worthwhile contribution to the 'affinity', as he terms it, of religion and rationality is Günther Dux, 'Religion, Geschichte und sozialer Wandel in Max Webers Religionssoziologie', in Seyfarth and Sprondel, op. cit.

48. The religious rejection of the world is indeed the independent theme of one paragraph of the sociology of religion chapter in *ES* and, further extended and deepened, in the 'Intermediate Reflections'. The latter therefore serves for the transition to the later work, as it is depicted in 'Science as a Vocation'. Central to this is the new though rather dismal estimate of the cultural significance of science, which would probably have played an important role in the planned sociology of culture. I refer here to the proximity of Weber's ideas to Simmel's account of the 'tragedy of culture'. Consideration of the stages and directions of religious rejections of the world – the sub-title of 'Intermediate Reflections' – is no cultural and philosophical aperçu but a central strand of Weber's theory.

49. *PE*, pp. 77–8.

50. Ibid. and *passim*.

51. Ibid., p. 26, and *passim*.

52. Gerth and Mills, *From Max Weber*, London, pp. 281–2 and *passim*. The concept of 'irrational elements in the rationalization of reality' is crucial for the train of thinking.

53. Ibid., p. 280.

54. Bendix, op. cit., p. 68.

55. In the above work.

56. Weber therefore takes the findings of the historical cultural-sciences, but not their theories.

57. See G. Dux, in Seyfarth and Sprondel, op. cit., p. 221.

58. Weber meant psychical anthropology wherever he used the word 'anthropology'. Moreover Weber's usage is very similar to the theory of human action developed by Simmel, especially in the *Philosophy of Money*.

59. Cf. the relevant sections in my work on the role of everyday experience on action, in F. H. Tenbruck, *Geschichtserfahrung und Religion in der heutigen Gesellschaft*, Freiburg, 1971, pp. 18–41 and particularly pp. 38 ff.

60. Cf. particularly Gerth and Mills, op. cit., pp. 327 ff., and other passages on systematization, sublimation, and the methodical conduct of life.

61. The insertion of 'Intermediate Reflections' gave Weber an occasion to make
a late correction to the 'Introduction', though this is neither very clear nor
clearly made, see Gerth and Mills, op. cit., pp. 327–8.
62. *Ancient Judaism*, p. 214.
63. *Sociology of Religion*, p. 269.
64. Gerth and Mills, op. cit., pp. 323 ff.
65. *Sociology of Religion*, p. 269, 'The impediments of capitalism must be
sought primarily in the domain of religion . . .' This comes very close to the
conclusion of *WEWR*.
66. The *Wissenschaftslehre* is more than simply a methodological work and is
fundamentally tied into the other work. Particularly the Logos essay of 1913, but
also 'Science as a Vocation' articulate the link between sociology and
methodology, and for which the central concept of *Kulturbedeutung* is important.
I hope on some occasion to expound the *Wissenschaftslehre* and to revise the
doubts raised in my 1959 article (*Kölner Zeitschrift für Soziologie*) as to whether
the works and the methods of Weber were in agreement.
67. Several of the plans, mentioned earlier, indicate the intention to write a sociology of culture. Some of the letters dating from the final period of Weber's life,
handed down to us in Marianne's *Lebensbild*, make it clear that Weber believed
himself to be entering into a new creative period and occupied with great plans.
68. Above all in the iron cage of capitalism from which the spirit has flown.
69. Cf. F. H. Tenbruck, 'Science as a Vocation, Revisited', in *Festschrift für
Arnold Gehlen, Standorte im Zeitstrom*, Frankfurt, 1974.
70. Weber also lacked the conceptual instruments and disciplines of today's
science, above all that of anthropology and action theory. Perhaps we should not
regret this since the position of the sciences of man gives one cause to fear the
phenomena, the reality, with which it is particularly concerned will disappear
behind a technical terminology.

Gesammelte Aufsätse zur Religionssoziologie
(The English translations are listed in brackets)
'Vorbemerkung', 1920.
'Die protestantische Ethik und der "Geist" des Kapitalismus', 1905.
(These two texts appear as the 'Author's Introduction', and *The Protestant Ethic
and the Spirit of Capitalism*, trans. T. Parsons.)
'Die protestantischen Sekten und der Geist des Kapitalismus', 1920.
Earlier, but shorter versions, appeared in 1906.
('The Protestant Sects and the Spirit of Capitalism' in Gerth and Mills, *From
Max Weber*.)
Die Wirtschaftsethik der Weltreligionen. This is a collection of essays and
studies that were originally published in serial form in the *Archiv für
Sozialwissenschaft und Sozialpolitik*. They comprise:
'Einleitung', 1915.
('Social Psychology of World Religions', in Herth and Mills, op. cit.)
'Konfuzianismus und Taoism', 1915.
(*The Religion of China*, trans. H. Gerth.)
'Zwischenbetrachtung: Theorie der Stufen und Richtungen religiöser Welt-
ablehnung', 1915.
('Religious Rejections of the World and their Directions' in Gerth and Mills, op.
cit.)
'Hinduismus und Buddhismus', 1916–1917.
(*The Religion of India*, trans. H. Gerth and D. Martindale.)
'Das antike Judentum', 1917–1919.
(*Ancient Judaism*, trans. H. Gerth and D. Martindale.)

CHAPTER 4

Prussian agriculture – German politics: Max Weber 1892–7

Keith Tribe

> Historical research is thus not charged with establishing the
> meaning of the past as it was (Ranke) nor with revealing that
> which with historical necessity lies before us (Marx) but rather:
> to make intelligible how *we are today* what we have become, and
> to this history of *our present* (*Gegenwartsgeschichte*) (itself only an
> 'excerpt from the course of the fate of mankind') 'capitalism'
> especially belongs.
>
> (Löwith 1932: 64)

Max Weber's political life can be divided into three periods,
superficially distinguished first by his long period of illness from
1897 to 1903, and second by the outbreak of the First World War
in 1914. But while the resulting periodization (1892–7, 1903–14,
1914–20) is quite accurate, there is more at stake here than a life
whose turning points are provided by personal and national crises
which simply redirect and develop a fundamental set of 'beliefs'.

That there is a fundamental set of beliefs is not here disputed,
but it is evident that the continuities of such themes as
'disenchantment', a 'politics free of illusions' and 'nationalism' in
the person of Weber obscure the shifting significance of such ideas
in the restructuring of politics in Wilhelmine Germany. For
Weber lived through a period in which quite radical alterations in
the political domain took place, and an effective appreciation of
'Weber's politics' must needs take account of this. The writings of
Weber are quite plainly chronologically differentiated by the
domain of engagement and the *form of intervention*. This only
becomes quite obvious if the writings are systematically read
through in the order in which they actually appeared or, as near as
possible to judge, were written. Reading the writings for 'themes'
combined with a conventional view of Wilhelmine politics as the
prelude to the First World War and Nazism – from Bismarck to
Hitler – either places Weber as a *promoter* of this historical fate
(e.g. Lukács, Marcuse) or views him in his vain struggles against
the tide of history (Wehler). Both these options *judge* Weber in
terms of a conception of subject and object which is dubious: the

unity of the authorial subject confronts the objectivity of a course of historical inevitability. 'Weber' becomes then either the sign for a predestined history and his writings are ransacked accordingly;[1] or alternatively he becomes 'all psyche' and the history of Germany is read in terms of his personality and circumstances.[2]

This essay has the limited objective of demonstrating the political consequences of Weber's involvement with the problems in Prussian agriculture during the period 1892–7. The principal objective is not, however, to write an account of Weber's politics, but rather to show that his extensive engagement with the rural labour question, internal colonization, and the Junker estates was stimulated by, and more importantly is demonstrative of, a basic political orientation.[3] This will be shown by a detailed exposition of his 'agrarian writings'. Engagement with the 'agrarian problem' (in fact a range of issues which were not uniformly present in the various regions) during the 1890s brought with it automatically an engagement with the central field of German politics. This relation of economy and politics in Weber's writings has therefore nothing to do with that established by Marx, where a knowledge of politics was necessarily preceded by and was epistemologically subordinate to a knowledge of economics.[4] During the 1890s agrarian Germany became the switchboard through which a reconstitution of the political domain was effected. Investigating Weber's place in this process on the basis of his writings will therefore reveal something of his conception of the *contingent* relation of politics and history.

What are the characteristics of the 'three phases' proposed above? The first period, which will be examined here, is one of 'public' politics played out in the new institutions of post-Bismarckian politics: the *Verein für Sozialpolitik*,[5] the *Evangelisch-soziale Kongress*, the *Alldeutscher Verband* – institutions which held conferences, addressed themselves to a 'public opinion' and circulated literature and newspapers. The Inaugural Address at Freiburg in 1895, which Mommsen has called 'the most significant document for the political being Max Weber until the war years' (1974: 38) is in many respects a summary of the work of the previous three years, while this phase of work is brought to a close by the critique of Oldenburg's address to the 1897 meeting of the *Kongress* on 'Deutschland als Industriestaat', a critique which clearly presents two alternative paths for national policy only one of which will assure Germany's role as a world power. The most significant writings in this period take the form of survey reports, newspaper articles, and contributions to conference proceedings.

When in the early years of the twentieth century Weber began to recover from the worst effects of his illness this engagement was not renewed, for German politics had by this time moved on, the agenda had been changed. If we glance at Weber's bibliography for this second period it is evident that his focus has become more strictly academic: opposing certain aspects of University appointment policy, taking up the editorship of a social science journal, assisting in the foundation of a Sociological Association. Here the domain of engagement and the forms of intervention are 'academic'.

This alters, however, with the outbreak of war: the bibliography alternates between writings on religion and reflections on the consequences of the war for German politics. The former naturally continues earlier work; the significance of the latter is that Weber conducts a growing political involvement through the medium of newspaper articles, culminating in the (failed) attempt formally to enter the new party-political structure of post-war Germany.

It is quite possible to detect the development of a set of political principles running through these phases and blurring their differentiation. But to approach Weber's politics in this way obscures the manner in which he was able to adopt the posture of 'opinion-leadership' in quite different circumstances and for divergent sets of 'opinions'. Weber stood at the 'leading edge' of German politics and culture and *this* is why he is important for us today. Any amount of exposition of his 'sociology' or his 'politics' must necessarily be of limited value if the nature of their *articulation* in contemporary society and politics is not properly understood.

Here the perspective will be firmly limited to Weber's 'rural sociology', as it is generally known. Or rather, not generally known, since no appraisal of any depth has been made of Weber's agrarian writings, whether on Prussia or Antiquity.[6] Curiously, the most serious analysis of the East Elbian writings published to date is to be found in Mitzman's 'psychohistory' of Weber, where unfortunately the socio-economic problems of Junkerdom are dealt with as an allegory for the socio-economic tensions of the Weber household (1970); not the most fruitful of approaches to Weber's politics. As with other bodies of Weber's writings – on the stock exchange, on the psychophysics of work, on Russia, to name only a few at random – discussion has passed them by as perhaps too specialized or dated to warrant anything more than the most superficial investigation. And so the accepted interpretations are passed down through the commentaries without pause for the thought: why did Weber, who was, it can be agreed, an astute thinker, spend so much time and effort on these 'specialized' studies? Which are in fact more than occasional studies, they are substantial bodies of work – comprising for our attention here a *Verein* report of over 800 pages and more than 100,000 words of newspaper articles, conference proceedings, and journal contributions. For many academics this might today be a respectable life's work, both in terms of volume and quality. But before we turn directly to these writings, it is as well to outline some leading politico-economic features of Germany in the 1890s as a prelude to situating the writings.

The modern liberal conception of Germany's political and economic development since the foundation of the Reich in 1871, a conception that was virtually unchallenged until recently, is dominated by the problem: how was the Third Reich possible? This problem has been current since the late 1930s and Gerschenkron's *Bread and Democracy in Germany* articulates the version of this history relevant here quite concisely. Writing in the 'Preface' to the first edition of the book, published in 1943, he states:

> The primary purpose of this study is to show, first, how, before 1914, the machinery of Junker protectionism in agriculture, coupled with the Junker philosophy – the true forerunner of the Nazi ideology of our days – delayed the development of democratic institutions in Germany; and second, how the Junkers contrived to escape almost unscathed the German Revolution of 1918 and how this fact contributed to the constitutional weakness and subsequent disintegration of the Weimar Republic.
>
> (1966, p. xiii)

Three main elements are of importance here: the economic basis of the Junkers, their hegemonic role in German culture, and the consequent 'uneven' development of the German nation, a progressive industrial power with an authoritarian and non-democratic political structure. The last element had been outlined by Veblen in 1915, and presupposes a model of western economic development in which industrial advance is conditional upon and accompanied by political reform and 'democratization'; as in Britain, the first and paradigmatic model. Germany, so runs the argument, was a late but rapid industrializer, and furthermore only formally became a national power in 1871. Its modernization was thenceforward out of phase; and this combination of industrial *economic* power with agrarian *political* hegemony brought with it a series of fatal consequences.

Socially, as Eckart Kehr argued in 1932, the bourgeoisie

became 'feudalized' – a term drawn from Weber's writings during
the war and not, it must be noted, used in his actual analyses of
Junkerdom during the 1890s. Instead of assuming the role of a
historically progressive force, the bourgeoisie allowed themselves
to become suborned by Junker culture; specifically, adopting
Junker militarism in the form of the reserve office corps (Kehr
1965: 99).

Economically, the great coalition of rye and iron laid the basis
for the development of an advanced industrial power whose
external economic policies were, however, dominated by the needs
of agrarian protectionism. Consequently Germany's international
economic posture was limited and distorted by a powerful lobby
whose estates had to be protected against the falling prices in the
world grain market (cf. Rosenberg 1976).

Politically, the watchword of German politics became, in Kehr's
phrase which turned the conventional Bismarckian view inside
out, governed by the 'primacy of internal politics'. The development of government policy was directed to suppressing internal
forces felt to be hostile to Junker supremacy. While the SPD was
legalized in 1890, this marked the beginning of the formation of a
number of reactionary pressure groups – such as the *Bund der
Landwirte* and the *Ostmarkenverein* – which carried the Junker
politics to the people. The development of imperial ambitions was
also a response to internal political conditions and was seen as a
means of shoring up the political hegemony of the Junkers.

This general perspective on modern German history is one
therefore which seeks answers to questions such as: was Germany
to blame for the First World War? (the famous Fischer
controversy of the early 1960s); and how was Nazism possible?
Such a perspective seeks causal factors; as we have seen in the case
of Gerschenkron above, the Junkers get the blame, along with the
socio-economic structure of Prussian agriculture.

Now it cannot be denied that 'Junkerdom' and its surrogates
played a major role in Wilhelmine Germany, but the way in which
this is inserted into a teleological interpretation of German history
obstructs our understanding of the social and political forces of the
1890s. Treating the *Kaiserreich* as a 'pre-capitalist state dominated
by the landed aristocracy' has, as Geoff Eley argues, propagated a
view whereby the problems of German society are identified as
'survivals' from a feudal or pre-industrial past (Eley 1978: 738–9).
Mommsen in his detailed study of Weber's politics (1974: Ch. 5)
tends to such an interpretation, consequently placing Weber as the
theoretical originator of the so-called 'Kehrite' view of modern
Germany.[7] But this 'view' is fundamentally 'un-Weberian': in the
first place Weber would have no truck with a historical teleology

which suppressed the contingency of historical development; second, and more importantly, as we shall see Weber regarded the most economically progressive Eastern estates, farmed intensively on capitalist lines, as the most *politically* dangerous for the nation. It was not the backwardness of the Junker estate owners that concerned him so much as the consequences of their progressivism for the social organization of the East.

These comments on the conventional historiography of Wilhelmine Germany cannot be here elaborated in detail, for this would divert us from the principal object of investigation, namely the nature and significance of Weber's agrarian writings. There is, however, by now an extensive literature on the 'Kehrite' interpretation, together with monographs from the two main English critics, Geoff Eley and David Blackbourn.[8] The former examines the significance of a number of Rightist popular organizations, and thus emphasizes the heterogeneity of Wilhelmine politics; the latter investigates the fortunes of the *Zentrum* in South Germany, the Catholic Centre Party that was the principal competitor with the SPD for working-class votes. The SPD has finally been granted an English-language treatment which properly deals with it as the first mass socialist organization whose problem was to convert its support into political force (Guttsman 1980). Handicapped by the electoral system of the *Reich*, apart from local persecution, the SPD in general failed to win the mass rural electoral support necessary in the 1890s to effect this conversion (see Hussain and Tribe 1983: Ch. 3). It is true that the SPD were much feared as a political force by their contemporary enemies; it is also true that much of Wilhelmine historiography has centred on the 'ambiguities' of Social-Democracy as a potential alternative model for pre-war politics. But in the 1890s the SPD failed miserably to win the various sections of the rural vote and they are therefore, within this period, politically insignificant on a national plane.

Quite why this was so will be outlined shortly, but this 'insignificance' must be understood as one which derives from the political options of the time. Without any doubt, Social Democracy was a mass organization the like of which had never been seen before; it embodied progressive ideals and was possessed of a vision of the future which retains its fascination. But these virtues and strengths endowed it with an indefinite potentiality rather than a political weight in the national arena. Having in many ways invented a new vocabulary of politics it found itself on legalization in 1890 rapidly confronted with rival organizations which imitated its organization and activities. As Geoff Eley puts it,

The new technology of mass communications dramatised the
fact that Wilhelmine politics were fast becoming the scene of a
battle for *consent*, to implant the popular legitimacy of
bourgeois values in their specific *German* form. The efforts of
new mass organisations like the Navy League to wage a battle
of *words* and *ideas* meant partly that the right had cynically
'modernised' its politics. But in practice it also meant that
concessions were being made to new popular forces and that the
SPD was being fought increasingly on its own ground.

(1980: 213)

In the early 1890s, the material basis of this struggle was rural
Germany – not the major towns and cities, already shared between
the *Zentrum* and the SPD. At the end of the decade this
bifurcation of town and country would become expressed in the
prospects of the Agrarian and the Industrial States – alternative
futures for the German nation in which Weber decisively opted for
the latter as the only path which could make possible a greater
Germany. But Weber came to such a conclusion from intensive
study of agrarian policy and development, not from some vision of
an inevitable industrialization of civilization.[9] The problems of
agrarian Germany provided the material basis of the decisive
struggle between competing political forces; the SPD failed to
establish a firm foothold in the countryside and hence were unable
to participate in this struggle effectively.

Quite why did the Germany countryside become so strategic in
the political domain? As Eley outlines, 'post-Bismarckian politics'
was not simply formed by the retirement of Bismarck and the
legalization of the SPD. It was instead constituted by the collapse
of the power bloc which had been the basis of Bismarck's
representational authority, based on the National Liberals.[10] The
demise of the National Liberals in states and *Reich* was the result
of the failure of their mode of political organization – the
Honoratiorenpolitik, which based party organization on 'prominent
figures' and then electorally placed such notables before the public
and waited for the votes to be registered. The SPD played a major
role in changing this, forging the modern structure of party
organization and treating the electorate as the target of political
campaigning. Since the constituency boundaries of Germany took
no account of the massive shift of population from countryside to
town, however, and since the numerous but under-represented
urban working-class was already divided between *Zentrum* and
SPD, it was in the rural areas that this new electoral politics
developed and destroyed almost at once National Liberal

predominance. This coincided in the early 1890s with the appearance of an agrarian radicalism stimulated by problems of the small farmer, indebtedness, the 'ruralization' of the rural economy with the disappearance of crafts and trades, and finally a foot and mouth epidemic in 1891–2 followed by drought in 1893 (Eley 1980: 21).

The SPD had already set the pattern of articulating the material demands of its supporters, but a consistent national rural politics of this nature was not possible because of the differentiation of the 'peasantry'. Instead the Conservatives reacted by composing a demagogic programme and forming the agrarian pressure group the *Bund der Landwirte*, while the anti-plutocratic populism of the peasantry in Central and Southern Germany was expressed by anti-semitic parties. The *Bund der Landwirte* is in turn usually regarded as a mechanism for the maintenance of Junker hegemony, forming an apparently uniform 'agrarian interest' whose objective was to recruit peasant support for the interests of Eastern large landowners. It is true that in terms of membership the East predominated, both numerically and in the leadership structure.[11] But more significant is the way that the *Bund* succeeded in inserting itself between the National Liberals and their traditional constituency, 'breaking the mould' of Central and Southern politics (Eley 1980: 28). The resulting political formation was certainly conservative, but this does not of itself indicate a *subordination* to Junker interests (cf. Hussain and Tribe 1983: 34–5).

This new form of electoral politics was not, however, typical of the East, where an independent peasantry hardly existed and large estates dominated the social and political landscape. Here there was an *absence* of political life in the new sense; but, on the other hand, the presence of socio-political problems crucial to national politics. While there was then a definite division between the agrarian politics of the East and that of the South and West, these were articulated in national politics in terms of the East. When, for example, the *Verein* compiled its questionnaire on rural labour in 1891, a great number of the items related exclusively to the East, as complaints from the South and West made clear (cf. Frankenstein 1893: 14). The East, as Weber was to stress, had delivered to Prussia and thereby to the German nation the political leadership and the military material which had made possible the creation of the *Reich*. Towards the end of the nineteenth century the economic basis of Junker power, the large estate, was threatened by international competition in grains, while the rural labourers were migrating to the 'freedom' of the cities and the New World. Seeking to maintain their position, the estate owners replaced German labour with Polish migrants; this was leading, argued many, to a gradual Polonization which laid the Eastern border open to Russia. In 1885 Bismarck had expelled 30,000–40,000 Poles of non-Prussian citizenship[12] and closed the frontier, limiting entry to a three-mile-wide border zone. But he came under increasing pressure from Eastern landowners to reverse this, and in 1890 this was done for the period 1 April–15 November. The landowners petitioned for a period 1 March–1 December, which they gained in 1898, reduced further in 1900 to 1 February–20 December (Nichtweiß 1959: 33–43).[13]

National government policy was not therefore a simple reflection of Junker interests; indeed pressure groups were formed precisely *because* of this disjunction, while the famous Kanitz motion, aimed at nationalizing the grain market for the benefit of estate owners, consistently failed to win the necessary political support to make it more than a programmatic demand.[14] The *Ostmarkenverein*, founded in the autumn of 1894 as the *Verein zur Förderung des Deutschtums in den Ostmarken*,[15] was certainly originally dominated by large Eastern landowners, but two of the founders were at the same time prominent entrepreneurs: von Hansemann was the son of the Director of the Discontogesellschaft, and Tiedemann was heavily involved in the export trade. Its principal strategic significance as a pressure group by the later part of the decade was not that its upper reaches were dominated by Junkers, but that 42 per cent of its membership were officials and teachers (Galos *et al*. 1966: 77). The 'struggle for the soil' in which the *Verein* participated together with official efforts at Germanization (the so-called 'inner colonization') resulted chiefly in driving up land prices, the Germans selling up and moving out, the Poles selling up and repurchasing elsewhere. In the period 1897–1904 in Posen and West Prussia the Poles had succeeded in buying 40,000 more hectares from the Germans than the Germans from the Poles; in 1900 in fact the Colonization Commission bought only 60 per cent of its land from Poles, 40 per cent was bought from Germans (Tims 1941: 153).[16]

The programme of Inner Colonization is certainly an important element in the national domain during the 1890s, but it is important to note that this importance is discursive and bears no direct relation to the actual results of the policy. The same goes for perhaps the most often cited aspect of agrarian politics, the issue of protection. Here, it might seem, Eastern landed interests were able to legislate in their own favour and dupe Western and Southern peasants into supporting such protective tariffs. This is argued by Gerschenkron and no rational economic ground for peasant support of protection in grains is identified by him (1966:

75–6). Instead it is suggested that protection had the general effect of preserving backward agricultural principles on large and small enterprises alike, introducing serious distortions into the German agricultural structure. Instead of adapting to changing world conditions as had in their different ways Britain and Denmark, protection preserved outmoded systems of production to the eventual social and economic cost of Germany as a whole.

The central problem of the world market in grains during the later nineteenth century – at least the problem from the point of view of high-cost Western European producers – was the rapid fall in prices consequent on the opening of the North American prairies. The cultivated area in the United States rose from 19.37 million acres in 1869–71 to 36.08 million acres exactly ten years later; the freight rate for a ton of wheat from Chicago to New York fell from 51.12 marks in 1873 to 26.64 in 1879; and the shipping rate from New York to Liverpool fell in the same period from 32.97 marks to 19.27 marks (Hardach 1967: 74–5). Not only did this herald the invasion of the German market by foreign grains; export markets previously enjoyed were eroded as well. Over half of Britain's imported grain had in the period 1834–40 originated in Germany; by 1871–80 the proportion was 7.45 per cent, although this figure represented more than twice the volume of grain since British imports were increasing (Hardach 1967: 73).

Britain 'adapted' to this by more or less abandoning serious production of bread grains, but the picture is not quite so straightforward as might appear from the above. Differences in the quality of different strains of wheat for instance complicated the 'reception' of North American wheat which on its own was not that suitable as bread flour. Second, the relation of grains for human and animal consumption must be taken into account, particularly in the case of Eastern Germany with its poorer soils and cultivation of rye. Third, this flooding of the world market by the United States was a very transitory event; by the end of the century its growing urban population took up an increasing share of the grain produced not by a rise in productivity but by extending the cultivated area and having a transport network capable of rapidly distributing its product. Argentina, India, and Australia became significant world suppliers of grain then in the place of the United States.[17]

Agrarian protectionism dates supposedly from 1879, with the introduction of duties on the import of wheat, rye, and legumes of 1 mark per 100 kg, and 50 pfennigs per 100 kg of barley and maize (Conrad 1891: 481). These rates were trebled in 1885 and then raised to 5 and 2.25 marks respectively (2 marks for maize) in 1887. Imports did not, however, fall and perhaps the most unambiguous result was a rise in government revenue. Hardach can find no clear lobby for the introduction of tariffs, and at the time the only region in which protectionism was at all prevalent among agriculturalists was in Western and Central Germany where producers were oriented to nearby industrial regions. North East Germany was at this time export oriented and hence was opposed to tariffs in principle.[18]

Concentration on the fate of grain producers means concentration on those who market the bulk of their produce, that is large farmers. At this time meat and animal products were primarily marketed by smaller enterprises, loosely the peasant enterprises. Gerschenkron suggests that the broad effects of the tariffs were to make bread dear for the urban consumer and fodder dear for the peasant producers of Central and Southern Germany. Hunt has, however, demonstrated that a series of Health Regulations operated in favour of such producers more effectively than the grain tariffs ever did in favour of the large estate owners of the East (1974: 314f.). Furthermore, in so far as the peasant producer was committed to a mixed pattern of production (as Moeller shows this was what was conceived as 'rational farming' in all textbooks of the period) peasant producers would ideally consume their own grains and if there was a surplus to sell then they too would benefit from any protection afforded to home-grown crops.[19]

The above discussion seeks merely to outline some of the problems in directly concluding from the existence of a set of import tariffs that protectionism as a policy existed, was effective, and served the interest of one particular class, the estate owners of the East. The attention gained by the grain tariffs has furthermore obscured another development in German agriculture in the later part of the century, a development which had direct impact on the issues which Weber was to confront: the extension of root crops, especially potatoes and sugar beet. During the period 1878–1900 the proportion of arable land devoted to roots rose from 13.7 per cent to 17.7 per cent, which while less than half that of grain crops far outstripped them in terms of energy produced.[20] Central Germany became a major producer of sugar beet and the rise in significance of such crops is clearly shown by the statistics on artificial fertilizers. In 1878 50,000 tonnes of nitrates were imported from Chile; by 1900 this had risen to 484,000 tonnes (Perkins 1981: 84). The expansion of root crops depended on massive inputs of artificial fertilizer and the application of pesticides, combined with the use of mechanical ploughing and drilling. The agricultural consequence of the new course was the extension of cultivable land through the elimination of fallow, the intensification of livestock holding on the basis of the fodder provided by the by-products of processed sugar beet – and a massive increase in the demand for seasonal labour.

Perkins has estimated that in the 1890s in Mecklenburg on holdings devoted to cereals, legumes, and pasture 77.9 labour days per hectare were required; 110 on farms with 20 per cent of the area given over to roots other than sugar beet; and 173 on holdings with more than 20 per cent of the area given over to sugar beet (1981: 99).[21] Not only did intensive root cultivation require approximately twice the number of workers as the more conventional mixed farming; the requirement was concentrated in a need for seasonal, in this case particularly female workers. With the development of Saxony as a rootcrop region from the 1860s migration to the region became such a regular feature that it gained a name – *Sachsengängerei*, literally 'going Saxony'. Many of these migrant workers came from the eastern provinces, and we can conclude this preliminary survey of political and economic structural transformation by considering the structure of landholding in the East, for this takes us to the heart of the 'labour problem'.

Broadly speaking, the characteristic feature of Germany east of the river Elbe was the domination of the rural landscape by large estates and the relative absence of a village pattern of settlement. Hence the estates not only occupied a significant proportion of the land, they also structured the geographical pattern of settlement and hence the social and political landscape. By comparison, in Westphalia there was also a settlement pattern marked by an absence of villages, but here this was because the countryside was dominated by independent peasant farmsteads, reflected in the predominance of holdings between 2 and 10 hectares (Dillwitz 1973: 57). The socio-political structure that this gave rise to was one quite distinct to that of the East and which came to form a model for reform proposals in the East.[22] The physical dominance of the estates in the East was underwritten by the landowner having local police and administrative powers, apart from being sole major local employer.

There were variations of course, but these were variations within the general format of a combination of large holdings with dwarf holdings. In Mecklenburg-Strelitz, for example, 83.8 per cent of all holdings were less than 2 ha. while in Mecklenburg as a whole 60 per cent of the land was occupied by holdings of 100 ha. and above. Those residing on the small holdings could not hope to live off them and represent in fact a settled force of wage labourers. The greatest concentration of large holdings was in the late nineteenth century in Pomerania, *Regierungsbezirk* Stralsund, where enterprises over 100 ha. occupied 75 per cent of the cultivated area; this compares with 55 per cent in Posen and 35 per cent (the lowest) in Silesia (Dillwitz 1973: 56). For all these areas, however, the bulk of the remaining land is taken up by enterprises from 20–100 ha. and those under 2 ha. This represents in economic terms large enterprises, on the one hand, and a settled permanent labour force, on the other. But, as we shall see, the picture is more complicated than this; the East was in more capital-intensive areas, chiefly the more southerly regions, undergoing a process of change in crops which was changing the structure of the labour requirement towards seasonal workers;[23] the whole area had since the 1860s been characterized by heavy permanent emigration, which during the 1880s had in places exceeded the birth-rate,[24] and lastly, many of the *Sachsengänger* originated not from Poland, but from the eastern provinces of Prussia. Rather than work for their local landlord, they migrated to the West annually and thus created a local labour shortage that was made up by Polish migrants.

We shall see that this is the problem that Weber takes up: a problem of 'rural labour' which does, however, have the profoundest implications for the political future of Germany. It is not possible to more than sketch such problems in the foregoing, but the main purpose has been to present an image of the Prussian countryside, and its place in German society, independent of Weber's account of it.[25] It must be emphasized, however, that more recent research has not seriously questioned his account of the technical aspects of the organization of agricultural enterprises, of the distribution of landholding and its effects, and of the various forms of labour. Modern research has supplemented Weber's findings, it has not superseded them; nevertheless, for our purposes here it is necessary to establish this 'truth value' prior to and independently of an analysis of such writings. For at stake here is not the 'accuracy' of the agrarian writings, but their structure and hence how it is possible for Weber through them to pick up the main threads of the changing political order in Germany. That he happened to be quite correct in his perception of the agrarian order is important in this respect to the extent that it prevented political opponents dismissing his political and theoretical conclusions with empirical rebuttal. The 'truth value' of his writings performs a rhetorical function: it blocks evasion of his political intentions. In this as we shall see Weber was supremely successful; nobody during the 1890s managed successfully to identify error or deficiency in his 'empirical' work. But if we treat Weber's writings on agrarian issues simply as 'specialist' work this rhetorical function disappears, the relation of empirical analysis to political intention becomes contingent. Examining the *structure* of his analysis will show how his political argument is formed; and from the foregoing it will be clear that by virtue of the condition of contemporary politics, he was thereby projected into a leading position in the field of national politics.

In September 1890 the organizing committee of the *Verein für Sozialpolitik* met and decided, on the suggestion of Max Sering, to plan an investigation of the rural labour question in the *Reich*. This was not the first time that it had addressed itself to rural questions: in 1883 the results of an investigation of the condition of the middle peasantry had been published in three volumes,[26] while in 1887 a survey of rural usury had appeared.[27] Neither of these surveys was, however, conducted in a particularly systematic fashion, nor were the reports particularly accessible for comparative purposes. The study of the rural labour question was conceived and planned in a more thorough fashion, and it was intended to present the results for discussion at the 1892 meeting of the *Verein*. Significantly, it was at the same time planned to hold this meeting in the city of Posen, in the heart of the Eastern borderlands; usually meetings were held, for the sake of convenience, in one of the central cities where academics could combine attendance with other business. As it turned out, the meeting planned for September 1892 was postponed, in part because of a cholera epidemic, but also in part because of a danger of a poor attendance. The meeting was instead held in March 1893 in Berlin.[28]

By early 1891 Thiel, Conrad, and Sering[29] had agreed on the general objective of the survey and the method of investigation, and Sering was charged with constructing a questionnaire. It was intended to send this questionnaire around to landowners, for them to complete and then return to the *Verein*. This was as we shall see to cause some criticism, for not only were the landowners to be asked about the conditions confronting rural labourers, it was felt that objectivity was best served by requesting information not on the landowners' *own* enterprises, but rather on 'local conditions'. The combination of these two features conspired to rob the responses of precision, but the sheer volume of the response did provide some counterweight by permitting a degree of cross-checking.

By July 1891 addresses of around 4,000 landowners had been obtained from their national association, and in December 3,180 questionnaires were sent out; followed by a second, more impressionistic questionnaire to 562 addresses in February 1892.[30] A total of 49 were undelivered, and 168 returned unanswered, but the overall response was far beyond the expectations of the organisers: 2,277 to the first, and 291 to the second, question-naire.[31] The original idea of assembling the results as a summary of the various reports had to be abandoned, and the work farmed out to individuals who could write up the responses in time for the (planned) September meeting. Max Weber was given the task of covering the material on the rural labour problem East of the Elbe, recognized as the most important section of the survey.

How this came about must for the time being remain a matter for speculation, but the most likely general reason is that Weber had, six months previously in October 1891, published his *Habilitationsschrift* on Roman agrarian history. But why should the author of a treatise on the agrarian law of ancient Rome, who apart from his doctoral dissertation on medieval trading companies had only published a couple of reviews in his supervisor's journal *Zeitschrift für das Gesammte Handelsrecht*, be selected to write up the most important section of a *Verein* survey on the condition of rural labourers in modern Germany?

Part of the answer is given by the dedication of the *Römische Agrargeschichte*: to August Meitzen, who at the time was a member of the Prussian Statistical Bureau and part-time professor at the University of Berlin, where he had taught Weber. In 1865 Meitzen had been commissioned by the Prussian Ministers of Agriculture and Finance to compose a comprehensive survey of landed property in Prussia together with an evaluation of the existing system of agricultural taxation. Accordingly Meitzen published in four volumes between 1868 and 1871 *The Land and Agricultural Relations in the Prussian State*, which became the standard work of reference for years to come. Further, Meitzen had been the author of the article on agrarian policy in Schönberg's *Handbuch der politischen Ökonomie*, and here we can find a definition of the nature of agrarian policy which could be regarded as programmatic for Weber in his agrarian studies:

> Scientific agrarian policy must then be represented primarily in terms of agrarian history. It must take as its object the elucidation of the acts of agrarian policy in modern civilised states out of the entire course of development of their agrarian structure. Specifically, it must show how relations could arise which were more or less incompatible with the natural requirements of the agricultural enterprise, and how the consequent evil is completely or partially confronted, with whatever fortunate or unfortunate results.
>
> (1882: 671)

These recommendations were to shape the way in which Weber

wrote up the *Verein* report and also in part form the link between his studies of ancient agrarian organization and modern policy. Not that the one can be reduced to the other, but rather that both historical investigation and the analysis of contemporary agrarian structure are marked by common procedural methods.[32]

The method of investigation in the *Römische Agrargeschichte* is explicitly attributed to Mommsen, and it could perhaps be argued that it was precisely in the study of ancient society, characterised by (even then) a sophisticated philological method, that *theoretical* questions could be introduced without being cast out of the guild. Approaching the problem of the Roman Wars of Conquest, Weber asks: who conducted these wars? That is, not the question, were did the resources come from, but rather

> what social strata and economic interest groups constituted
> politically the motive force, and hence also: to what tendencies
> can the apparent displacement of the centre of gravity of
> Roman politics mentioned above be attributed, is it for example
> the *conscious* product of the endeavours of particular interest
> groups?
>
> (Weber 1891: 6)

The actual project of the study, to investigate the relation between the organization of Roman agriculture and the changes in Roman political structure need not detain us here apart from noting that this formulation of the problem translates without a great stretch of the imagination into the study of Prussian agriculture in the 1890s. In fact when discussing the labour requirements of the large estates in the Imperial era the problem of matching seasonal needs to the existing free and slave labour forces explicitly invokes the case of East Prussia (Weber 1891: 237). What is important, however, about such historical cross-reference (it arises in reverse later when Weber compares the migrant workers in their barracks to the slaves of ancient Rome) is not that one is a metaphor for the other, but that it emphasizes Weber's interest in *differential forms of economic organization*. Similarly, at times the *Agrargeschichte* contains references to 'capitalism' and 'capitalist tendencies of development'; Sombart drew attention to this in a review, and while emphasizing that it was impermissible to associate 'capitalism' simply with widespread commodity production in isolation from the social classes supporting this, he suggested that Weber's usage was casual and did not involve an evolutionary perspective (1893: 353). It might be suggested that Weber's 'casual usage' reflected more thought that Sombart gave him credit for, signifying an interest in the problem of the characteristics of capitalist as opposed to non-capitalist modes of organization.

Weber quite clearly states at several points in his book that he is not seeking to write *an* agrarian history, but rather to uncover the *tendencies of development* at work in the agrarian order of ancient Rome, imbricated in and traversed by others. Such tendencies were in no sense law-like, such as those which suffuse Marx's *Capital*; they were the result of quite specific circumstances and forces, they were in some respects empirical, possessing their own logic. The tendencies which he focuses upon primarily, and through which the analysis is concentrated, are those involving various labour forms, particularly the *colonus* and the slave. Since these were not governed by natural laws of development but rather by specific circumstances, the purpose of the investigation was to assess the forms and evaluate the conditions which governed their alteration. Some of these conditions would be determined by laws, some by particular enterprise structures, some by specific agricultural products, some by sets of social relations. Depending on the actual combination of these determinations, deliberate intervention on the part of administration or landlord was possible and its effects might be calculated. Which brings us back to the interrelation of agrarian history and agrarian policy, and the rural labour problems of Prussia East of the Elbe.

By March 1892 Weber had reviewed the reports assigned to him by the *Verein*, and the extent to which he had already arrived at a comprehensive appraisal of the problems can be seen in his first printed statement on the issue, which appeared 1 April 1892:

> The classical soil of the 'rural labour question' is the German
> East. Here can be seen uniform changes under way on an
> extensive scale, posing to landed property as well as to the state
> to an incomparably greater degree than elsewhere grave
> problems of fateful import. The root of all difficulties lies in the
> way in which the need for agricultural labour, especially on the
> part of the large estates which here predominate, is distributed
> through the year.
>
> (1892a (4): 3)

This declaration opened the first of three articles printed in the newspaper of the *Evangelisch-soziale Kongress* which not only offer a summary of the rural relations in Eastern Germany, they present an argument for a *further* survey to be undertaken by the rural clergy. What is of particular interest to us here is the manner in which the need for this second survey is presented.

Beginning with the seasonality of demand for agricultural labour and the intensification in fluctuation of demand with a transition to root crops, in particular sugar beet, Weber makes an initial distinction between permanent and seasonal workers. The first part of the article is to deal with the former, who appear as either servants or *Instleute*, labourers who are settled on small plots of land. The latter are of greatest significance for Weber, and he concentrates exclusively upon them.

The *Instmann* is provided with a house and a small plot of land on the estate, is assigned a share of the threshed crop, and receives for the rest of the year a small day-wage or a fixed sum of money. The household can keep a cow and pasture it on estate land receiving fodder in the winter months; other animals may be kept and fed off the estate. Firewood and cartage is also provided. In return the *Instmann* is contractually bound to work on the estate and provide one, perhaps two, additional hands. The latter are the so-called *Scharwerker*, who are boarded at the expense of the *Instmann* in the event of the *Instmann* having no children of an age able to perform a full day's work.[33] The outcome of this, argues Weber, is that the household budget is made up of receipts from the estate in kind (housing, firewood, raw materials for clothing, bread, and fodder grain) and the products of the household's own labour, in the form of vegetables, milk, eggs, and meat. Cash received for the labour of the *Instmann* and the *Scharwerker* is divided half between other household requirements which have to be purchased, and payment of the *Scharwerker*. The possibility exists in good years of selling some of the product of the garden land and also potatoes and grain supplied by the landowner; pigs, fattened on roots supplied by the estate, can also be sold.

The result of this situation is for Weber the following:

> In this relationship the rural labourer has a decided interest in favourable prices for grain and animals, since he is himself a petty entrepreneur; there is in general between him and the lord of the estate a community of interest which daily confronts him; the composition of his own budget depends on the fortunes of the estate; sun and wind, rain, frost and hail, epidemic and low prices from economic crises and foreign competition decide his economic situation in the same way as that of the estate owner.
>
> (1892a (4): 3)

The *Instmann* is thus not only physically bound to the estate, his economic interests are bound up with it in a quite specific fashion, for it affects the manner in which he regards the economy. His community of interest with the estate owner arises from the fact that they both confront 'market forces' as entrepreneurs without

there existing any degree of competition between them – they
supply different markets. This subjective position is for the
Instmann, Weber suggests, underwritten by the life-cycle of the
household: beginning as a servant in the household of the estate
owner, his future wife is employed as a maid. Together they save
for a cow and related needs, and on marriage they are given an
Inststelle. The first fifteen years are hard, but as the children of the
marriage grow up they are able to assume more of the work of the
household and occasionally work elsewhere for wages, so that with
time the financial situation improves. The nature of this life-cycle
ties the individual to the estate as surely as does the community of
economic interest existing between *Instmann* and estate owner.

This is, however, states Weber, an ideal picture (*Idealbild*)
which is increasingly in decline. The important question concerns
the rate and form in which it is declining: which elements are
changing fastest and what are their consequences? What is the
outcome of the grain or potato income falling short, so that either
animals cannot be fed or there is not enough for sale? Posed in this
way, the household budget of the *Instmann* is both indicative of
the tendencies of development and plays an important role in the
evaluation of his economic circumstances. Available statistics,
related to general trends, cannot supply information on this
crucial *subjective* element of the rural economy; despite this,
Weber notes that it is 'most pressing to establish as far as possible
total overviews of the constitution of the labourer's budget' (1892a
(4): 4). The *Verein* survey, limited as it was financially and
through its administration to landowners, was unable to investigate this aspect of the problem. The rural clergy of Protestant
Germany, however, enjoying the trust of their congregation,
would have access to reliable information in a way impossible for
other investigators. The important matter was not the actual state
of affairs, but the tendencies of development; and these were
ascertainable in their *subjective* consequences only through an
assessment of the household budget.

Two primary changes are identified by Weber which alter the
structure of this budget: first, the intensification of grain
cultivation had led to the introduction of steam threshing, upon
which the share of the threshed crop falling to the labourers had
been reduced to the point where even in good years they had to
purchase grain; and second, the landowner sought to maximize
the use of his cultivated land and sought therefore to transform
the land assigned to the *Instleute* into a *Deputat* of potatoes and
grain, transferring the animals of the household to the estate's own
stalls. Through these two factors the community of interest
between *Instmann* and estate owner is destroyed. The first factor

undermines the interest of the *Instmann* in the level of the estate harvest, while the second robs him of an interest in prevailing prices of grain *qua* producer – indeed here his interest becomes the opposite of that of the estate owner to the extent that he is forced to purchase grain. The permanent estate worker becomes a mere day labourer, who might experience this transformation as an increase in freedom, but for whom the future looked uncertain.

The 'free labourer', the subject of the second article, clearly lacks the community interest with the estate owner enjoyed by the *Instleute*. Instead the propertyless worker was inclined to see his interest as one in common with similar workers. What was not, however, clear and which could be ascertained by the clergy was the way in which these free, seasonal workers viewed the situation of the contractually bound workers – were they perceived as better off? Did they feel a community of interest with them as an emergent proletariat? Did such views mark the beginning of a fusion of a general class consciousness uniting rural and urban proletariat, or did they herald a desire for economic independence of a peasant kind? Here again, it was the incomings and outgoings of the individual households which provided the indicators of this, combined with the attitudes to work. It was suggested by some that the problems of rural labourers of this kind could in part be solved by settling them on small plots of land; but Weber suggested that where this had happened the labourers preferred to starve than work for the local estate owners. Here emerged what was referred to by Weber as a land-owning proletariat.

Payment by the piece, introduced by 'progressive' estate owners, worsened the general situation, since this encouraged the workers to make comparisons – Weber poses the question here of the effect of such forms of payment on the calculability of the household budget:

> But as always it is not the fact of the wage level itself which is of greatest interest, but rather the question: whether the system of payment in question makes possible suitable and ordered household management (*Wirtschaftsführung*), whether it in fact occurs, whether the people are happy with this, or if not why – in their *subjective* view – this is the case.
>
> (1892a (5): 5)

It is the subjective views of the free labourers which govern their decisions concerning when and where they will work. Kaerger in his study of *Sachsengänger* had already shown the virtue of direct approach to the workers[34] and indicated that *psychological* dispositions were decisive in migration and a preference for long

winter 'vacations' in their home areas. The *Verein* survey was here
structurally unable to deliver any detailed information. Those
areas experiencing the greatest out-migration were not those of
labour surplus or any other factor visible to the landowner – these
areas also experienced the greatest immigration from Poles and
Russians. The reasons for this exodus remained to the estate
owners matters of supposition and conjecture, and yet this was a
vital feature of *their* labour problem.

The third and final article was devoted to an examination of the
various measures proposed for this solution of this problem. Prime
among these was the idea of renting land to a labourer, together
with house, garden land, pasture or fodder, use of an estate
plough team, and milling of grain at an agreed rate. In exchange
the labourer was obliged to work for day rates on the estate, or as
in Northwest Germany, only at harvest time, or a variety of other
possible combinations of rent and duties. This might seem to be a
similar situation to that of the *Instmann*, but in fact the position
was quite different:

> The tenant of a parcel of land is *separated from the household of
> the estate*, his economy is not at every point interlaced with that
> of the estate owner, like that of the *Instmann*, or as in the case
> of the *Deputant* simply that of a boarded servant – for the most
> part *both Instmann* and *Deputant* are in the East subordinated to
> the *Gesinde-Ordnung*, in the case of the *Deputant* this is always
> the case – and payment is constituted in terms of a *money
> economy*: the tenant feels himself a 'free' day labourer but
> simultaneously a smallholder.
>
> (1892a (6): 1)

Two questions are associated with this: how does the labourer
view this possibility, and how far is the estate owner prepared to
rent out marginal land? The former question is a psychological
one which only an investigation on the part of the clergy can
clarify; as far as the latter question goes, it is clear that some
owners were already renting out marginal land, correctly perceiv-
ing this as a means of tying their supply of labour to the land and
consequently to them.

Weber emphasizes that if the East is not to be depopulated
small peasant property must be encouraged, although in some
areas it was only possible to farm on the basis of larger holdings.
Where conditions permitted, however, the advantages of peasant
enterprise were decisive: the self-exploitation of labour made such
enterprises relatively less dependent on free wage labour; and
following from this, the enterprise was insulated from price

movements in that it tended to consume its own produce rather than sell it and then in turn purchase its necessaries. Free trade and socialist perspectives on the peasantry suffered from an erroneous assumption that conditions in industrial and agricultural enterprises were comparable. On the contrary, maintained Weber, peasant relations are not simply the product of social relations, but have their own psychological effectivity.

There were then various possibilities for a reorganization of settlement and labour supply in the East, but the prospects were not that bright for any single policy. For example, the transformation of the rural labourer into a settled smallholder presupposed abilities of household management, in particular on the part of the wife, that were not common among such social groups. However such possibilities might appear, one thing was clear: the *Inst*-relation was in decline and there was no restoring it. How the various alternatives would develop depended to a great extent on the individuals who would appraise them and opt for one or the other:

> Again and again we arrive at the conclusion that the problem that we are dealing with, insofar indeed as it relates to external, material relations, is of a *subjective* nature and lies in the breast of the people concerned. The *perception* of those concerned – often in objectively similar circumstances quite various and all equally unjustified – of their situation is more important to us than this situation itself; for the further course of development it is also the more important factor.
>
> (1892a (6): 4)

It could of course be argued that Weber emphasized this subjective moment principally to persuade the *Kongress* to put its facilities at the service of a survey which would supplement Weber's section of the *Verein* survey, and nothing more. But as the earlier argument has sought to demonstrate, there was general agreement that the 'Eastern Question' was the major one in German agriculture, and all the more so in the Protestant, mainly northern, regions of Germany open to the *Kongress*. Above all, the emphasis on the subjective perception of economic change as a decisive factor in the prospects of such change was to find expression in later work, in particular the studies on the industrial worker. As we shall see, although the *Kongress* survey was carried out, Weber experienced something of a loss of interest in it, and this psychological appraisal of the rural labour question remained for the most part a programme.

During 1892 in any case his attention was fully occupied in writing up his report for the *Verein*, which on publication later that year was recognized to be a major piece of work eclipsing other contributions.[35] It was therefore Weber who addressed the meeting held to discuss the survey, but before examining his contribution there are several features of his book that deserve attention.

Distinguished from the other reports not only by its length but by the inclusion of a general essay on conditions, remarks on method, and a concluding chapter on 'Prospect', the actual procedure differed from the usual tracing of detected variations to differentiated local conditions. Major local variations existed in the East, argued Weber, that could not be explained by reference to prevailing circumstances; for neighbouring enterprises, presumably enjoying similar conditions, often demonstrated wide variations in their organization. He suggested that instead:

> The differences present are in the main expressions of diverse
> economic stages of development. The disappearance of the
> three-field system and the fallow, as well as the summer pasture
> for cattle, the reduction in the relative importance of grain
> production in favour of the cultivation of commercial crops,
> and in particular the penetration of sugar beet – have led to
> alterations in the organisation of labour in comparison with
> which local factors are completely overshadowed.
>
> (1892b: 4)

To assess the *direction* of this process of development two earlier studies were pressed into service: von Lengerke's report on a survey conducted through agricultural associations in 1848;[36] and von der Goltz's report on a survey of 1873.[37] As with the *Verein* survey, these expressed the viewpoint of the employer, but rather than considering this as introducing bias Weber emphasized that it simply led to 'blind spots' on issues not known to the landowners. The level of wages and income, which the employer might be able to estimate, was not of major significance; the question was rather whether it made ordered economic conduct possible.

Preceding the detailed presentation of the data organized on a region-by-region basis, Weber included an essay on the general structure of labour relations which elaborated the outline already presented and again drew attention to the question of the community of interest between employer and employee. It was, however, in his 'Ausblick' that he for the first time outlined the general economic issues arising from the changes under way in labour relations. Broadly speaking, a more patriarchal, traditional type of estate was being displaced by a more capitalistic, intensive form. The patriarchal estate tended to conserve conditions for the labourers, they were more settled, and since they were not so intensively farmed and therefore so heavily committed to migrant seasonal labour, conditions were in fact better here than on the capitalist estates. But as we have seen, the *Inst*-relation was in decline, it had 'no future' (Weber 1892b: 781). Continuation of payment in kind was chiefly a consequence of a shortage of cash, and wherever capital intensive farming developed there was a strong tendency to shift all remuneration on to a cash basis.

Those who bought up ailing estates naturally tended to try and run them on 'rational' lines, and in doing so they contributed intentionally or unintentionally to the proletarianization of the labourers. In the long run this was reducing the economic and physical situation of the inhabitants of the East, together with its 'nationality and defensive power' (1892b: 795). This was no longer simply a question of rural decline, it was rather an issue which directly concerned the state. It was up to the state to alter this situation through the reorganization of labour relations; and however this was done, the result had to be a more differentiated rural social landscape where the labourer was provided with a course of upward mobility (through the acquisition of land) which did not necessitate emigration. If economic 'progress' were left to itself the East would be depopulated and Polonized by the advanced capitalist estates. Weber concluded as follows:

> The future of the German East will depend on whether the conclusions resulting from this are decisively drawn. It is not the vocation of the dynasty of Prussian kings to rule over a homeless rural proletariat and slavic nomads alongside Polish dwarf peasants and depopulated latifundia, as with the present course of affairs in the East will eventuate; but instead over German peasants alongside a stratum of large landowners whose workers bear the consciousness that they can in their homeland find their future in an ascent to independent existence. Whether this objective can be achieved is not clear. But whoever has a low estimation of the capability of the state to guide the forces effective in social life will admit that its power in the agrarian sector is extremely great. How it should be used will be discussed at the approaching assembly of the *Verein*.
>
> (1892b: 804)

Before this meeting took place, however, Weber published another summary of the *Verein* survey which introduces some

points worth considering in passing. Again in a more popular
format Weber summarized the purpose of the project and
defended it from criticism, and then proceeded to explicitly
construct a comparative analytical framework for rural labour
organization whose purpose seems mostly didactic. This took the
form of outlining two extreme cases, between which the agrarian
relations of civilized peoples were to be found.

The first case involved permanent unfree labourers – the slaves
of antiquity. These were held by their owner all year round, and
either had to be supplemented if at all possible for harvesting, or
alternatively the estate had to put up with being generally
overpopulated for the greater part of the year (1893a: 24). This
burden was what made a slave economy either in the long run
extremely inefficient or caused it to collapse.

The second case was one that had come to Weber's notice from
modern Argentina.[38] In the interior there existed colonial farms
which grew grain for export in a kind of 'slash and burn'
economy, although unlike that economic form it was purely
destructive of the soil. A farmer would sow an area of land and
maintain it, if at all, with the help of one permanent worker, who
acted as overseer. When the time for harvest came, semi-nomadic
workers from the deep interior were engaged, and these needed no
accommodation, lived in the most chaotic social order, and
required in effect only to be fed. Once the harvest was in they
were dismissed, the grain was threshed by machines brought
around by contractors, sacks were filled and left in the fields for
collection, and that was that. Threshing and ploughing was done
by contract, virtually no equipment on the farm was necessary,
and no buildings.

Both forms of organization are characterized by Weber as 'social
barbarism'; the one rests on the total slavery of the worker, the
other on their total 'freedom'. Each presents in monetary terms
competition for developed rational economies which they cannot
match. Each is, however, based on a structure which leads to its
own collapse: the slave economy cannot in the long run support
the number of workers that it requires, while the Argentinian case
lasts only as long as the fertility of the soil. The latter especially,
however, could last long enough to destroy more advanced
economic forms, if this were allowed.

Through this sequence of writing there gradually emerges an
argument concerning the future of the German nation, more
specifically the economic conditions which make possible the
existence of the nation as a power and the particular internal
configuration of classes which arise on this basis. It should be
clear, however, that this movement does not force either the

material with which Weber is working, nor the method which he employs. It is quite possible to examine these texts as so many contributions to a rural sociology; as pointed out above they are suited to this not least because of their accuracy. But to restrict the attention to this aspect of the writings is to ignore the energy which informs them, and which means that there is a movement towards the theses of the Inaugural Address, and not just the bald summary of rural conditions, as delivered by other *Verein* contributors. It was for this reason, one can suppose, that he was chosen to address the assembly on 20 March 1893.

After a preamble defending the *Verein* survey and asserting that the critics had given no clear indication of how the rural labourers could have been directly approached by the *Verein*, Weber turns first briefly to the conditions prevailing in parts of South and West Germany. Here, it seems, there is no 'rural labour problem' in so far as no separate group of workers exists – there exist only small peasants whose economies are interwoven with those of the larger peasants. The problem that arises in these regions is not one of the organization of labour within the enterprise, but rather that of the distribution of landed property, which is one that is at present not under discussion. But this deviation had been made to emphasize a point about the conception of work resulting in these areas, which is described as a 'psychological moment' (1893c: 64). Since there is no *social* division between the large and the small peasant here, each working alongside the other, the 'worker' regards himself as an equal party and there is no relation of subordination.

This contrasts strongly with the conception of work prevailing among labourers in the East, dominated as it is by the conception of work as a duty which rigidly pervades all life.

> This psychological moment which is often overlooked has enormous significance for the question: is such an arrangement of the organisation of labour, which would go together with the radical breaking up of all larger enterprises, politically desirable as an objective? – I believe not. It is no coincidence that the regions of Germany where this form prevails have not been blessed with the political organisation and the formation of the political spirit which have created the unity of the *Reich*.
>
> (1893c: 65)

Weber was to be mistakenly praised by Conservatives who read into such statements an open defence of Junkerdom, but such readings were sharply rejected at the time by Weber himself.[39] He drew a clear distinction between recognizing the national services of Junker and Eastern peasant, and justifying the contemporary

political role of the Junkers. As far as Weber was concerned, the
Junkers were to disappear just as surely as the *Instleute*: for both
there was no future: 'I did not wish to ascribe to the eastern
Junkers a *personal* merit, but only in the circumstances a relative
merit in the form of social organisation' (letter to Lujo Brentano,
20 February 1893; Weber 1936: 365). This social organization was
in decline, however,

> The patriarchal disposition of the lord over the fate of the
> labourer, as in the old *Inst*-organisation, just this will no longer
> be tolerated by the people. Psychological forces of
> overwhelming power lead to the movement into the towns just
> as much as to the disorganisation of this organisation of labour.
> (1893c: 70)

What concerned Weber was not that one order was passing
away, but that the new order which appeared to be taking its place
was much worse from the point of view of the nation. As far as the
labourers were concerned, he emphasized repeatedly the fact that
it was their perceptions of these changes which were of crucial
importance, a 'psychology of the labourer' had to be constructed.
Only then could effective policy be formed and implemented; one
of the primary targets of such policy being to reshape these
perceptions through definite changes in landholding and labour
relations. The Prussian labourers of the East migrated to the West
and returned every winter for a 'vacation' and gained thereby the
illusion of earning more than if they had stayed at home. This
created problems for the state in so far as they were replaced by
foreign migrant labourers. This process was most marked where
the great estates were: 'the agricultural large enterprise of the East
is the most dangerous enemy of our nationality, it is our *greatest
Poloniser*' (1893c: 72).

This address to the *Verein* marks Weber's first explicit
confrontation with the issue of Polish migration, which was for the
next two years to play such a role in his thoughts. As we have
seen, the issue had been touched on in previous pieces, but as
asides, as a consequence of his more central exposition of labour
relations. Speculation on how this developed would at this point
be idle, given the paucity of the material available; apart from the
use of the codeword *Ostmark* in his *Das Land* articles (1893a: 43)
there is little in his published writings to go on apart from a steady
increase in ferocity which culminates, as we shall see, not in the
Inaugural Address, but over a year previously at the 1894 meeting
of the *Evangelisch-soziale Kongress*.[40]

The demand which Weber advanced in the short run was

closure of the frontier in the face of a chorus of protest from the
Junkers. Drawing implicitly on the example of Argentinian
competition outlined in fn. 38, he argued that the Polish worker
would drag the German worker down to his cultural level if free
competition were permitted to exist between them – the Pole
would simply put up with conditions which the German labourer
would not. Two such different nationalities could not be
permitted to compete for employment in the same area; the border
would therefore have to be closed, else the Germans would give
way entirely to the Polish migrant workers. The Junkers, if they
protested against this, were availing themselves of the same kind
of arguments as the free traders – the privilege of following their
own economic interests independent of those of the state. The
Germans could not be regulated – tied to particular estates or
contracted for specific periods. Limiting the freedom of movement
of labourers who clearly wished to be mobile was no longer
possible. The future of the nation was at stake, and what was
required was responsible policy which would construct this future
for the nation.

But even in this rhetoric of national policies there is a clear line
connecting the statements that Weber makes and the analysis on
which it is based. Here he summarizes his position:

> I regard the 'rural labour question' here completely as one of
> *Staatsraison*. For me it is not a problem of rural labour,
> decidedly *not* the question: is the worker doing well or badly,
> how can he be helped? . . . even less is it a question of how
> labour is to be found for the eastern large landowners. The
> interest of the state and of a nation can differ from that of each
> *Stand* – not just from that of large landed property which is
> occasionally forgotten, but also from that of the proletariat,
> likewise often forgotten. The state interest in the rural labour
> question of the East is solely to be found in the question of the
> condition of the foundations of social organisation – can the
> state rely on it in the long run to solve the political tasks which
> exist in the East. In my opinion the answer is *no*.

(1893c: 74)

What the Junkers cannot do as a *Stand*, the state must effect
through specific measures of policy,[41] as for example the purchase
of estates by the Settlement Commission, preserving them as
German property or splitting them into smaller holdings.
Technical problems then emerged which the *Verein* was in a
position to evaluate, and the viability of systems of tenancy,
ownership, or leasing of different-size plots could be evaluated.

Weber tended to favour tenancies, and suggested that the domain administration should set a good example to the private landholding sector.

> Certainly, Gentlemen, we make high demands of the future, we
> believe that it will effect the transformation that we seek, we
> hope that in the evening of our days we will be granted that
> which we were denied in our youth: to be able to go forward
> with a steady gaze into the future of the nation and deal with
> the cultural tasks placed before us, secured by a firm
> foundation of the social organisation of the state and the people.
> We hope at that time to be able to say as we look back: at this
> point the Prussian state recognised in due time its social
> vocation; on its own initiative it put a spoke in the
> wheel of social development and met with success – and it for
> the first time ventured this intervention before it was too late!
> (Loud applause)
>
> (1893c: 86)

A little more than a year later Weber, together with Göhre, faced the annual conference of the *Evangelisch-soziale Kongress* and sought to give an account of the survey that had been carried out. Questionnaires had in December 1892 been sent to around 15,000 clergy and country doctors (of which perhaps 9,000 were actually rural clergy, since there was no certain way of distinguishing rural from urban parishes). By 1 May just under 1,000 had been returned, a response rate of approximately 10 per cent and far below that of the *Verein* survey. The results were also much more uneven than those for the previous investigation; there were objections at 'interference' and at the amount of work expected, but on the other hand some of the responses were extremely detailed and the work of a number of clerics working together. The distribution of responses was also uneven;[42] and altogether Weber and Göhre were rather bewildered by the results and unsure how to process them. At the meeting Weber expressed the hope that printing would begin 'in a few months' but as with many such expressions scattered through his work this remained a pious wish (Weber 1894d: 61). Not until 1899 was a partial publication of the results begun.[43]

The presentations of Göhre and Weber failed to summarize the results of the survey; instead they settled for the easier option of outlining recent work and interspersing their remarks with material drawn from the new survey. Weber, dealing with the East plus the province of Saxony-Anhalt noted that no discrepancies of any importance emerged with respect to the *Verein*

study; and where the information supplied by the clergy indicated
that the labourers resisted the restriction of payment in kind he
for example took leave to doubt its validity (1894d: 69).

Three main features distinguish this general outline of the
Eastern Question from earlier versions: some preliminary remarks
on the relation of economic to political and social conditions; an
evaluation of the political options implicit in peasant enterprise;
and a rising tone of aggressiveness and belligerence which can
here, unfortunately, only be 'translated'.

'Our modern scientific method had made us accustomed to view
technical-economic conditions and interests as a fundamental
point of departure from which the social stratification and political
formation of a people can be derived', states Weber (1894d: 66).
In the East, however, he suggests, other conditions prevail which
have a reciprocal effect, such that the economic factor does not
occupy a leading role. The form of population grouping, the
distribution of enterprises and landholding, the legal organization
of labour relations are all within the districts the principal
elements governing the situation of the labourer. These relations
govern the economic situation of the labourer; the wage is
determined by the living conditions, and not vice versa. Wage
levels are, however, no certain indicator of the general conditions
prevailing, for it is not through the wage that the worker is able to
determine the comfort or lack of it in his existence. In
Mecklenburg, where the wage levels are highest, there is the
greatest exodus of local workers and inflow of migrants; and in
general it is the most economically well-off worker who moves to
the towns and cities, not the poorest. The depopulation of the
East is not the result of economic forces so far as the availability of
work or the level of pay is concerned; it is primarily a
psychological question, the lack of prospects for local self-
improvement and the desire for an existence free of the
domination of the landowners.[44]

This becomes a national political question with the replacement
of these workers by seasonal Polish 'nomads' (here Weber makes
implicit reference to the Argentine 'savages') (1894d: 68), or as he
later says, 'Polish animals' (1894d: 81). As we have seen, German
labourers could not easily be prevented from responding to
conditions as they perceived them; hence these conditions had to
be changed through a policy of internal colonization. This would
be expensive, and Weber was not as optimistic as Göhre about the
potential success of such settlement; but this was the only way in
which the conditions of the worker could be improved, by
opening up the opportunity for local social mobility.

I do not believe that the colonisation of the German East –
initially at least – will lead to an improvement in agricultural
technique, for example because the technique of the peasant
was better than that of the large enterprise – the reverse is true
– but I rather regard it therefore as necessary and possible
because the prevailing international relations of competition
render the land of the German East valueless from the point of
view of production for the world market.

(1894d: 79)

The advantage of peasant cultivation was not that it was efficient,
but that it was insulated against fluctuations in the world market.
The purpose of placing peasant producers in the East was not to
strengthen the German economy (in fact a deterioration in the
agricultural production of the East could be anticipated) but
rather to secure the German nation:

We want to fetter them to the soil of their fatherland, not with
legal, but rather with psychological chains. We wish, we say it
quite openly – to make use of their hunger for land to bind
them to their homeland, and even if we have to hammer a
generation into the land to secure its future, so we should
assume this responsibility.

(1894d: 79)

As he went on to say, the object of social policy was not to make
people happy, but to secure the future of the nation.

This address to the assembled members of the *Evangelisch-
soziale Kongress* articulates clearly for the first time Weber's
'politics free of illusions'. The stake was the future of the nation,
as was to be outlined the following year in Freiburg. This future
was on the one hand knowable, in that a number of tendencies
could be detected which would give it shape (the relation of the
classes, the movements of the German population, the political
reorganization of Germany, to name a few); and on the other there
were in the hands of the state means which could *act on* the
progress of these disparate tendencies. Note that these factors are
not in principle reducible to a uniform process of development:
the 'uniformity' of Germany's future prospects was derived from
the manner in which these tendencies combined, and this was not
in principle governed either by the dominance of economic or of
political forces. The labourers of the East might be driven by
illusions; a responsible *Staatspolitik* could not, however, afford
this luxury. The 'facts' had to be confronted squarely; and the role
of social investigation was to provide the material of such 'facts'.

No social grouping appeared to Weber ready to assume the vital task of political leadership: the Junkers were in decline; the bourgeoisie was and remained unprepared for rule ('As a class-conscious bourgeois I can maintain such a view without suspicion of prejudice' (1894d: 77)); and the proletariat with its aspirations was under the leadership of petty-bourgeois elements:

> There is no greater danger confronting us in Germany today for our political life than that of falling under the domination of the petty bourgeoisie, of *Spiessbürgertum*. And the typical features of *Spiessbürgertum* – the absence of great instincts of national power, the limitation of political endeavour to material objectives or even to the interests of its own generation, the absence of a consciousness of the responsibility borne with respect to succeeding generations – that is what permanently separates us from the social-democratic movement – for it as well is to a great extent the product of German *Spiessbürgertum*. Interest in the power of the national state is for none so great as for the proletariat, if it thinks of more than the morrow.
>
> (1894d: 81)[45]

This was no mere rhetorical flourish. Weber treated social democracy as a potential participant in the shaping of Germany's future – this was inevitable and it was an illusion to oppose this. The bourgeoisie on the other hand were failing to assume the responsibilities that were placed immediately before them, and it is perhaps this that generates the relentless anger which suffuses Weber's prose.

Some flavour of this can be seen in Wagner's contributions to the discussion of Weber's presentation. Prominent in the *Kongress*, a popular speaker and leading economist, Wagner's attitude to the Eastern Question contrasts strongly with Weber's by virtue of its flaccidity. The Junkers, he suggested, were important, and should be preserved. Colonization appeared to be massively expensive – nevertheless, if things were permitted to continue, urban capital would as in England and elsewhere invade the East. For Wagner, this was the worst that could happen:

> Or do we wish that the matadors of the stock exchange enter in general possession of the large estates? No, as far as I am concerned rather Prussian Junkerdom with its faults, but also its virtuous side. (Applause)
>
> (1894d: 89)

His main policy suggestion, apart from proceeding with the process of colonization, was a raising of the grain tariff. Is it any wonder, he asked, that the large landowners used so much Polish labour, when the wage levels were so high?

Confronted with such asinine thinking it is no wonder that Weber got annoyed. Wagner apparently failed to grasp the most fundamental point of Weber's analysis, that the 'labour problem' was a *psychological* one, as he put it. The contrast with Wagner, and other contributors to *Verein* and *Kongress* discussions, serves to highlight the rigour with which he developed his political perspective out of a thorough analysis of the labour problem. Wagner's criticisms and comments need only be referred to statements actually made shortly before. Likewise when Kaerger criticised Weber's analysis of the *Inst*-household, accusing him of assuming that grain supplied in kind was consumed entirely by the household and not partially sold, it was only necessary to point to the relevant passages and tables in the *Verein* report to rebut such claims (Kaerger 1893: 20ff.). No matter how crude and reactionary Weber's attitude to the Poles in Germany might seem, from the point of view of the 'German national interest' he was quite right – after all, the greater part of 'Germany east of the Elbe' is now part of the state of Poland, if not (as is the case of East Prussia), part of the Soviet Union. The 'threat from the East' no longer takes the shape of Polish migrant workers, but that of a vision of a permanent visitation of Warsaw Pact tanks.

But to return to Weber's writings. By now the main principles of Weber's agrarian studies are in place, and there remain three further pieces which are developed on their basis.

The first of these is the article 'Developmental Tendencies in the Situation of East Elbian Rural Labourers', which appeared twice in 1894, the second version being somewhat revised.[46] Mitzman in his psycho-history of Weber does in fact give a detailed account of this article, the most detailed account in English; he lays particular emphasis on the nature of the revisions made by Weber between the supposed date of the original drafting (autumn 1893) and that of the revision (spring 1894) (1970: 120). The variations that he detects are employed as evidence for his thesis concerning the relation of Weber's domestic and personal circumstances to his analysis of the Junkers. Independently of the plausibility of such a procedure, or even its accuracy given the 'Weberian' cast of Weber's thought, Mitzman is led to over-emphasize the consequences of the revisions for the argument. Furthermore, by neglecting to examine some of the more obscure sources outlined above, Mitzman is led to identify as novelty that which had already been said. The 'modification' or 'development' of Weber's position that he perceives is thus spurious (cf. Mitzman, 1970: 134).

What then is the difference between the two versions? Is there perhaps some significant variation? For the most part the newer version improves by clarifying passages, omitting complex expressions, and adding supplementary sections. The long footnote stretching between pp. 33–6 of the first version for instance, which replies to the criticism of Kaerger noted above (fn. 44), was deleted entirely. A new introduction is added, and apart from clarification this emphasizes the comparative historical perspective of the study associated with the identification of 'developmental tendencies'. But this was fundamental to the *Verein* book of 1892 and had been indicated in its introduction. Mitzman implies for example again that the analysis of Junkerdom in the opening pages has emphasis added (DT, this volume: 159) but this is identical in the two versions.

In sum, there is quite a great deal of minor stylistic alteration in the second version; it is important to note that Weber made the effort to clarify his prose, however unsuccessfully. *Left out* are primarily criticisms of Kaerger and Quarck, with their associated lengthy footnotes; *added in* are sections which summarize the argument, and also the final remarks on internal colonization, which are interesting but not that different to earlier statements. There is, however, one alteration that has more than editorial significance: in telescoping a bridging section (DT, this volume: 117) the 'Lebenshaltung der Arbeiter' becomes the 'Nationalität der Arbeiter' (1894f: 463; 1979: 195). This is nothing new, Weber had made clear already that the question of 'standard of living' was one of 'nationality' – but the way in which the one is substituted in a summary for the other points towards the Inaugural Address, where the question of nationality was to be made one of the major themes.

The second of the texts developed on the basis of the agrarian writings is in fact the Inaugural Address, delivered in Freiburg in May 1895. As with the 'Developmental Tendencies' essay, however, this is available in English and does not add new material to that already presented. Both require detailed analysis but that is not the objective of this article, which restricts itself to a detailed exposition of the agrarian writings. This task is now almost complete, apart from one final and little-known contribution of Weber: his reply to Oldenberg's address to the 1897 meeting of the *Evangelisch-soziale Kongress*, 'Deutschland als Industriestaat'. This inflects the arguments already advanced into a new form, that of alternative forms of economic development – the industrial versus the agrarian state.

Oldenberg began from the dubious supposition that if the trend apparent in occupational statistics continued unchecked, then within 70–80 years Germany would be a purely industrial country.

An economy was, however, an organism, requiring both industrial and agrarian production, in which moreover the latter was of greater importance. An industrial population, suggested Oldenberg in Physiocratic tones, was fed from the surplus produced in agriculture. Too great an expansion of industrial production for export was risky, it brought with it a dependence on foreign markets dangerous for the nation, for with the collapse of such markets the basis of national production was destroyed. Independence was conceived chiefly as *supporting the nation by its own produce*, although later Oldenberg maintained that this argument was not an agrarian one in the sense of promoting agrarian interests (1897: 43). The point of departure was the national interest and conclusions were developed on this basis.

It could be said that if a general tendency is to be ascribed to Oldenberg, it was not agrarianism but anti-capitalism. He saw the forces of capital as undermining the national interest: investing in more profitable industry than agriculture, attracting a rural workforce to the cities, and making the national population increasingly dependent on the production of goods for *others* (i.e. foreigners: German workers were oppressed not by producing goods, but by producing goods for foreigners (1897: 11)). The promotion of an export-oriented industry identified irrevocably the interests of capital with those of the nation, which was in fact being undermined by capitalist interests.

Oldenberg's arguments are quite clear and not at all vague and muddled like those of Wagner (1901). Proceeding from a conception of autarchy, conceived as subsistence production, he viewed capitalism as a robber baron abroad in the world, plundering the colonies for profit and raw materials and in turn undermining the developed nations by making them dependent on the supply of raw materials. But this self-expansion could not go on for ever, and when the foreign markets were closed to the developed countries, or when harvests failed, they would suddenly discover the precarious nature of the economies they had built up.

Weber was not impressed by these arguments, and he emphasized that there was no *positive* side to the argument developed; no positive 'model future' (*Zukunftsideal*) could be developed out of it.[47] The crucial question was for Weber: can capitalist development be prevented? The answer: *not, it cannot be prevented*, for us it is unavoidable and it is only possible to economically influence the course which it takes' (IS, this volume: 214. The prospect held up by Oldenberg of an independent Germany, argued Weber, was one in which the cream of the working class and technicians were banished as surplus to national requirements, leaving behind a small urban sector and a depopulated agriculture farmed on rational lines. The East-West division of Germany into agricultural and industrial regions would lead to a depopulated East employing foreign workers. Self-sufficiency in foodstuffs required intensive, rational agriculture in large units. This highlights the political nature of his previous argument in favour of peasant cultivation of large tracts of the East. The demands of economic rationalism ran counter to this, for peasants would consume too high a proportion of the crops that they produced with greater relative effort than the larger units. Oldenberg, in presenting arguments for national security based on economic self-sufficiency, overlooked the political conditions for establishing such an autarchic state. In Germany in the late nineteenth century one could either import foreign labour to produce foodstuffs or import foreign foodstuffs in exchange for industrial products. While there was no real prospect of self-sufficiency for Germany (that is, without ridding the country of a majority of the population) a rigorous model of such a state would require inputs of seasonal agricultural labour on a massive scale, since (as in the slave model outlined years earlier) these 'mouths' could not be supported for the whole year within the territory. The absurdity was thereby produced of a rational economic model of self-sufficiency in food which was heavily dependent on foreign migrant labour.

Neither Oldenberg nor Wagner could grasp the simplicity of this argument in discussion; Oldenberg, for example, did not understand why Weber laid such emphasis on a depopulated countryside. This had only occurred, as in England, with a decline in agriculture, not with its expansion. Wagner in his contribution did little more than reiterate points already made by Oldenberg. It is apparent that the strength of Weber's argument here is one that derives from his analysis of the tendencies of development in the East combined with his future-oriented, 'illusion-free' politics. As he stated in his closing remarks:

There are pessimists and optimists in regard to the future of German development. Now I do not belong among the optimists. The enormous risk with which the unavoidable economic expansion of Germany abroad presents us is recognised by me as well. But I regard this risk as unavoidable and thus say: 'so must you be, you cannot escape it'.

(IS, this volume: 220)

As Weber was later to write:

The social science that *we* wish to pursue is a *science of reality*.

We want to understand the *specificity* of the reality of life which
surrounds us, in which we are placed – the relation and the
cultural *meaning* of its individual appearances in their
contemporary organisation, on the one hand; on the other, the
bases of their historical form-ation as this and no other.

(1968: 170–1)

'Methodology and Politics in Max Weber'? Or even *Science and
Politics* . . . – but that book has already been written. It was
remarked above that Weber was a Weberian – he took his own
'methodology' seriously. And this is apparent from the two
quotations juxtaposed above. Or is it? Is it in Weber a question of
a methodology, on the one hand, and a political orientation, on
the other?

One of the objectives of this essay has been to implicitly argue
against such a view. It has been shown how a particular mode of
analysis develops into a particular political position – the latter
'political' in terms of Wilhelmine politics, but also in its 'future-
orientation', its 'reality', its 'freedom from illusions' a basic
conviction. The fact that empirical analysis is formed by a political
orientation does not alter the effectiveness or scientificity of this
analysis: Max Weber's agrarian writings are *value-free* in a strictly
Weberian sense. Not in the modern (American) sense of being
neutral,[48] but in the sense that their scientificity is open to
argument and evaluation:

The notion that there exist independent economic or 'socio-
political' ideals is revealed as an optical illusion as soon as one
seeks to establish these 'peculiar' canons of evaluation by using
the literature produced by our science . . . . Value judgements
are made everywhere in a nonchalant and spontaneous manner,
and if we abandon the evaluation of economic phenomena we in
fact abandon the very accomplishment which is being
demanded of us. . . . In truth, the ideals we introduced into the
substance of our science are not peculiar to it, nor have we
worked them out independently: they are *old-established human
ideals of a general type*. Only he who proceeds exclusively from
the pure Platonic interest of the technologist, or, inversely, the
actual interests of a particular class, whether a ruling or a
subject class, can expect to derive his own standard of
judgement from the material itself.

(IA, this volume: 200)

These passages are to be found in that 'political' tract, the
Inaugural Address.

This essay has not attempted to assess the more institutional aspects of Weber's political engagement in the 1890s: his role in the *Verein*, his relation to Naumann, his reasons for joining and then leaving the *Alldeutscher Verband*. For although a thorough digestion of the agrarian writings is a presupposition for this, the intention was to show how such an engagement was for Weber *possible*. As Löwith acutely observed, Weber was interested in *Gegenwartsgeschichte*, a 'history of the present'. The most basic definition of his politics could be: from the history of the present to the politics of the future. The history was, as we have seen above, neither evolutionary nor propelled by some basic motive force, the 'natural laws' of the economy which determined in advance the options which the future held. To see what the future held, the present had to be confronted in its reality, its reality as a configuration of forces, moments, and 'developmental tendencies'. Here lie Weber's 'methodological writings'.

Notes

I would like to acknowledge the financial support of the Alexander Humboldt Stiftung and the hospitality of the Max Planck Institut für Geschichte which made the research on which this article is based possible.

1. The clearest case of this is Lukács' *The Destruction of Reason*; but the same would apply to any treatment of Weber as prophet of bureaucracy, of the problems of socialism, as demagogue, and so forth.
2. Which is what Mitzman does, as will be demonstrated below.
3. 'Political' in its widest sense, as opposed to a 'party' or 'academic' concern.
4. That is, as established by the theoretical framework of *Capital* which identified the 'laws of motion of capitalist social formations'. These laws were economic laws which provided the motive force for historical development and were expressed as tendencies. Political forces were conditioned by and subordinated to these economic forces. Weber rejected any such law-like teleology, and in this rejection lies one of the most significant differences between Marx and Weber, registering at the same time Weber's decisive *advance* on Marx.
5. Formed much earlier of course in 1872. Initially conceived as a pressure group directly influencing legislation, this role was formally abandoned in 1881 in favour of one which focused on the education of officials and ministers (Lindenlaub 1967: 27–8).

As we shall see in the case of the survey of rural labour, the government possessed no regular investigative apparatus, and in some cases, as this, sponsored *Verein* work (ibid: 34–5). Schmoller pithily summarized the work of the *Verein* in opening the 1893 General Assembly – to rise above class interest, for in a free constitutional state legitimation could not rest on a single class interest, but on the consent of public opinion, science, and the press.

In this mass-psychological process organs such as the *Verein*, with its publications and discussions, have a justifiable, important and influential place. We enlighten, we remove misunderstandings, we reveal interests, but always however in the context of the whole; we seek the course along which social progress is possible. Gentlemen! We are at the service of science, of truth.

(*Verein* 1893, Bd. 58, pp. 2–3)

6. Honigsheim's article of 1946 is no more than a précis of the articles on 'Developmental Tendencies' and on the *Fideikomiß*, together with a review of his treatment of the Polish Question and that of rural Russia. Honigsheim succeeds in completely garbling the Polish material since he combines a summary of the *Verein* and *Kongress* material from 1892–4 with the citation of 'political views' from the writings of 1915 and 1916 without noting that in the meantime Weber's position had changed. The 'historical' treatment of the agrarian writings is also very poor (1949).

The more recent article by Munters (1972) broadly repeats the content of Honigsheim and briefly outlines the historical studies; this is again of little use. Another treatment of this area, to be found in Lazarsfeld and Oberschall (1965) relies for the *Kongress* work solely on Weber's article in *Christliche Welt* (1893b); lamely excusing themselves on the grounds that 'other material' (such as for example the proceedings of the 1894 meeting of the *Kongress*) was not available in the United States (p. 186).

Heuss's article finally, dealing with the studies on antiquity, is quite routine, and quite incorrectly suggests that the *Habilitationsschrift* was poorly received, since Weber was 'hard to understand'. This is clearly a problem which afflicts modern academics rather than Weber's contemporaries; as Käsler (1979: 197–8) indicates, it was this work which brought Weber to the attention of the academic world, and the basis on which, it might be presumed, he was assigned the task of compiling the East Elbian study for the *Verein*.

7. Complicated by the fact that Mommsen coined this term in criticizing the historiography of Wehler and others (1973: 8). Wehler edited a collection of Kehr's writings in the mid-1960s, and in some ways this marks the beginning of a distinctive revision of German historical writing which became established as a 'school'. In fact Weber began to use this characterization first in 1897, *after* he had completed his East Elbian studies.

8. Eley (1980) and Blackbourn (1980). See also their (1980); and the level of hostility such arguments have provoked can be judged by Winkler (1982). The central text of this 'Kehrite' version of German history is Wehler's textbook (1973), criticized devastatingly in Nipperdey (1976). The 'failure' of German development, according to Wehler, is that of an inability to 'synchronize' economic and political force. Nipperdey shows how Wehler's approach forecloses problems and imposes a uniform 'failed development' on what are in fact heterogeneous forces and agencies.

9. There is this idea at work of course, but as will be indicated his argument attacks the vacuity of the notion of an 'agrarian state'. It was rather the agrarians who possessed a vision of immutable industrialization.

10. Weber's father was a prominent National Liberal politician – here Mitzman's analysis might have some purchase, since Weber's political thought in this period is clearly marked by a rejection of National Liberalism.

11. In 1896 89,000 members came from west of the Elbe, and 99,000 from the east (which was at the same time less densely settled) (Puhle 1975: p. 38). He goes on:

The developing campaign in the West and South of the *Reich* which gained pace from 1895 had the sole effect of shifting the body of membership to the West, and had no impact on the East Elbian involvement of the *Bund* since its inception: thus the membership of 1903 was indeed composed of 139,000 western and 111,000 eastern members, but at the same time the numerical relation of the local groups, the lowest organisational level of the *Bund*, displayed a reversed relation: of 31,999 groups 14,153 were from the areas to the west, and 17,836 from those to the east, of the Elbe (p. 39). Cf. Blackbourn (1980: 12–13).

12. In 1890 10 per cent of Prussian inhabitants, i.e. 2.98 million spoke Polish or a related dialect as their first language (Tims 1941: 11). Of 1,751,163 inhabitants of the province Posen, 697,286 in 1890 gave German as their native tongue (ibid.: 44).

13. One solution canvassed at this time was the import of Chinese coolies to work on the eastern estates (Nichtweiß 1959: 38–9).

14. This is often obscured by those who focus on the class interests of the Junkers. A classical statement of this is to be found in Rosenberg: 'In socio-historical perspective state agrarian policy proved itself, in essence as well as in its practical effects, as a merely superficially concealed body of class legislation' (1978: 113). This essay expresses concisely the kind of approach which, it is suggested here, obscures the *heterogeneity* of political forces during this period. The Kanitz motion (named after the deputy who moved it) proposed the monopolization and restriction of the grain trade in such a way as to ensure a high and steady price for grains produced in Germany. Schmoller rejected this in part because he saw it leading to a socialist state (1895: 612).

15. The 'Ostmarken' was a collective name for the eastern borderlands which was *coined* by the *Verein*. Such 'traditional neologisms' are important for understanding Junker 'conservatism' which was not by any means 'traditionalistic' in orientation, as Schmoller had noted with respect to the Kanitz motion.

16. Delbrück in a biting attack on eastern settlement policy calculated that at the rate at which colonization was proceeding, after 100 years 100,000 Germans would be settled among 1.5 million Poles, at enormous cost to the German taxpayer (1894: 7).

17. Germany became a net importer of rye in 1852, barley in 1866, oats temporarily in 1872, and legumes in 1873. By the later 1870s 11–13 per cent of the domestic market for rye was imported, 60 per cent from Russia and 10 per cent from Austro-Hungary. Only from 1876 was there a net import of wheat, composing in 1876–8 6–9 per cent of the domestic market. Only 15 per cent of this came from the United States; 50 per cent came from Russia and 30 per cent from Austro-Hungary. During the 1870s there was a series of poor harvests in Europe, only in the 1880s did normal supply conditions prevail (Hardach 1967: 80–6).

It is also important to take account of the consuming and producing regions of Germany. The East, in which we are primarily interested, was productive of a net surplus, apart from Silesia. Adding surplus and deficit areas together shows that the shortfall could not be covered by domestic production in gross, independent of any internal problems of transportation. It was for example far simpler to export the net surplus from the Bremen and Oldenburg region direct to Britain rather than to Baden where there was a shortfall. The cost of shipping grain from the East to Mannheim was twice that from Rotterdam to Mannheim (Lexis 1889: 211). See also Tirrell (1951: 20–1).

18. Protective tariffs might exist on the statute book, whether they have any effect and thus whether it is relevant to talk of protection is a different matter. Barley and oats, for instance, were not protected since the tariff rate was superfluous; and these grains made up 44.4 per cent of the product of the cultivated area devoted to grains (Reuter 1977: 206). No protection was afforded to home wheat production in the first five years. Rye was the only grain which gained from the beginning definite protection, but as we saw above the rye

market was not at this time seriously penetrated and the problem was not that of 'American grain', but its falling popularity as a bread grain. Reuter's detailed analysis concludes with Hardach that the tariffs were more important as sources of government revenue than as 'protection' to a sector of the economy.

19.   This view is disputed by Webb (1982: 324) but he does not examine in any detail the market situation of differing scales and forms of enterprise in the various regions. Any exhaustive treatment of the impact of protection would need to do this.

20.   'In the harvest of 1900 under two per cent of the arable area that was devoted to sugar beet yielded 1,364,000 tonnes of beet compared with a total of 2,295,000 of cereals from over fifty per cent of the arable land. In the same year the potato harvest amounted to over 30 million tonnes. In terms of calories sugar beet in the period 1909–13 yielded an estimated 23.8 billion per hectare and potatoes 9.6 billion, whereas rye and wheat yielded 5.1 and 6.5 billion respectively' (Perkins 1981: 80–1). The root cultivated area in the *Reich* increased as follows:

1878	176,000 ha.
1893	395,000 ha.
1907	513,822 ha.
1913	533,000 ha.

Changes in taxation in 1888 ended the advantages of root cultivation in Saxony and shifted the centre of production to the East, this being decisive by 1891. In Posen the area tripled 1893–1913, while in the same period the area in Rgb. Merseburg (Prussian Saxony) only rose by 2 per cent (Nichtweiß 1959: 31).

21.   Nichtweiß (1959: 32) also produces the following labour calculations: on a 60 ha. farm, the labour requirement was:

		Male days	Female days
I	three field system	573	139
II	Norfolk rotation	567	1048
III	Rotation with heavy influence of roots	774	2405

22.   Particularly the 'Heuerling' relation, see Kaerger (1892).

23.   Winson in his discussion of estate farming (1982: 395) suggests that Weber was not clear on the origin of the changes in the labour supply. As we shall see, this is not so; the whole thrust of Weber's argument turned on this problem, which he approached by considering the organisation of enterprises and their consequent *requirement* for labour. It was for Weber self-evident that root crops played a major part in this, and he referred repeatedly to Kaerger's book on *Sachsengängerei* in part because this was a leading example of recent rural labour research (1890).

24.   In 1890 75 per cent of the East Prussian surplus of births over deaths migrated (Sering 1893: 7).

25.   The account presented aims to indicate in outline the reasons for agriculture occupying a strategic place in German politics prior to Weber's engagement with it. It should not be taken to be an adequate outline of German agriculture in this period, partly because of its focus on the East, partly because several important issues are simply left to one side – e.g. indebtedness, and changes in productivity.

26.   *Bäuerliche Zustände in Deutschland, Schriften des Vereins für Socialpolitik,* Bde. 22–4.

27.   *Der Wucher auf dem Lande, Schriften,* Bd. 35.

28.   Schmoller, opening speech 20 March 1893 (*Verein*, Bd. 58, p. 1).

29.   Thiel was a member of the *Verein* and Privy Councillor in the Prussian Ministry of Agriculture; Conrad was one of the most prominent academics in Germany and Professor of Economics at Halle; while Sering was Professor at the Berlin Agricultural College.

30.   Both questionnaires are printed at the beginning of *Schriften* Bd. 53, 1892, xiv–xxiv.

31.   This information is to be found in Thiel, 'Einleitung', *Schriften* Bd. 53, 1892, vii–xi.

32.   As Weber emphatically states in his popular lecture delivered in Freiburg in 1896:

> For our social problems today we have little or nothing to learn from the history of antiquity. A contemporary proletarian and an ancient slave would comprehend each other as little as a European and a Chinaman. Our problems are quite different. The play of events that we observe possesses only *historical* interest, although indeed being one of the curiosities of history: the internal dissolution of ancient culture (1924: 291).

One could read ambiguity, in the light of his later religious studies, into this casual remark concerning European and Chinese culture. But these ancient studies have nothing to do with an evolutionary conception of history. Even the allusions in this lecture to the forces of disintegration at work within Germany remain at the level of allusions (cf. pp. 289, 297–8).

33.   Weber does not here state that the contract is in effect one between a landlord and a *household* (1892b: 11). Without a family the *Instmann* cannot fulfil the terms of the contract, for his subsistence is assured by the labours of family members on garden plot and in tending the animals.

34.   Kaerger had personally sought out workers during August–October 1889 in the root-growing areas, and then later in the year in their home regions (Neumark, Lower Pomerania, West Prussia, Posen, Silesia) (1890).

35.   The next most satisfactory was Kaerger's on NW Germany (1892); Frankenstein's contribution was lengthy but diffuse (1892); while the remainder were neither detailed nor very useful (Losch 1892; Großmann 1892; Auhagen 1892).

36.   This survey was aimed at assessing the *condition* of the rural labourer in terms of income needed, proportion receiving such an income, how their position could be improved (von Lengerke 1849: 2).

37.   The problem posed by this study, conducted in 1873, was how a share in the generally rising national wealth was to be assured to the labouring classes. Von der Goltz himself was responsible for the eastern Prussian provinces (von der Goltz 1875).

38.   A whole article was later devoted to this (Weber 1894a) where it was used to demonstrate the argument that the economic 'Darwinism' of the free traders would result in a general worsening of conditions, not their improvement. 'In order to be able to compete with economies like that outlined, we must not improve the character of our social structure and cultural level, but rather *reduce* it' (Weber 1894a: 57). He added: 'It is advantageous to a nation if it eats cheap bread, but not if this is done at the cost of future generations' (ibid: 59).

39.   The *Kreuzzeitung* 2 February 1893 had praised Weber's analysis of the East Elbian situation as exposed in the *Verein* book; then on 20 May after the meeting of the *Kongress* he and Göhre were attacked as being 'bookish' and accused of presenting data in such a way that they were free to draw any conclusion they wished. This volte-face was treated by Weber as symptomatic of the weakness of the Junkers: 'The visible decline of the self-consciousness of a *Stand* that permits itself *this* kind of Press representation is a symptom of its weakness, which speaks

clearer for any prognosis of the future than we ourselves can' (1894c: 673).
40. As some kind of comparative control, consider this rather later view of the Polish question in relation to Posen and East Prussia:

> The Pole, who has shown himself in history incapable of forming and maintaining a state, is dazzled by the mad idea presented to him by his leaders that this German *Kernland* should belong to a Polish *Reich*. They preach to those, who would only have allowed the land to become waste and barren, that they have a vocation to own and work this soil. Fanaticised by this ideology, the Poles went over to the offensive against *Deutschtum* in the eastern provinces (Höhn and Seydel 1941: 64).

41. This emphasis in no way differentiated Weber from his colleagues. Von der Goltz had in his own words 'broken a seventeen year silence' in 1893 to write a general review of the rural labour problem which, as Weber pointed out, shifted the emphasis from the role of the agrarian entrepreneur to that of the state (von der Goltz 1893; Weber 1893c: 289).
42. E.g. East Prussia 32; West Prussia 14; Posen 17; Pomerania 50; Silesia 58; Brandenburg 95; Mecklenburg 24; as against for example Saxony/Anhalt 141; Brunswick 72 (Weber 1893b: col. 540).
43. After Göhre left the organizing committee it seems Weber was left virtually on his own to work up the results and find a publisher. Some of his students eventually took over the task, but there was a great delay: 'So it arises that the following works, prepared at a time when there was a flood of interest in socio-political themes among our clergy . . . now appear at a point in time at which this has completely ebbed away' (1899: 11).
44. In the light of previous statements perhaps Weber's position should be summarized: broadly, E. Germany fell into two intermixed regions, the older, patriarchal estates (chiefly in the north) and the newer, capitalist estates of the south. The northern area mentioned here experienced the greatest out-migration, but since the more traditional relations prevailed here there were at the same time available permanent workers. The trend was, however, that intensive farming, with its high demand for seasonal labour, would prevail as the 'rational' form, and thus the future of estate farming promised an ever more heavy reliance on seasonal migrant workers.

Kaerger advanced the strongest criticism made of Weber when he suggested that the deleterious impact of intensive cultivation on the nutrition of the worker was unsubstantiated (1893: 33). Weber replied by denying having made a direct link in this way; he reiterated that the result of intensification was to proletarianize the worker and monetarize the forms of payment. This can lead to improvement in the condition of the labourer with respect to the smallholder; but according to Weber's observations this was only temporary (1894b: 33, n. 1).
45. In discussion Weber enlarged on this theme; forced to reconsider, he would say that it was a petty-bourgeois view to place 'throne and altar' on the shoulders of a sinking class. 'I have myself said that we do not at the moment have a proletariat that thinks on a large scale; but he who doubts that we could gain it in the form of a class-conscious, far-sighted labour aristocracy doubts the political future of the fatherland' (Weber 1894c: 93).
46. (Weber 1894b; Weber 1894f.) The second version has been translated and is included in this collection, as is the Inaugural Address. For this reason the discussion will not devote a great deal of attention to these texts.
47. See the translation below (p. 210ff.) of Weber's reply to Oldenberg.
48. Cf. p. 169 in Hennis (1983). The misconceived interpretation of 'value-free science' as 'neutral' science is one of the greatest disservices done to Weber by his American disciples. The essay on objectivity seeks repeatedly to make the relation clear: 'we are of the opinion that it can never be the task of an

experiential science to produce binding norms and ideals which can be the basis of practical recipes' (Weber 1968: 149). These ideals and norms existed, but they should not be permitted to determine the results derived from scientific work in the way that the natural laws of capitalism 'turned out' to lead unavoidably to the wished for social order of the future.

References

Auhagen, O. (1892) *Die ländliche Arbeiterverhältnisse in der Rheinprovinz und im oldenburgischen Fürstentum Bielefeld*, *Schriften des Vereins für Socialpolitik* Bd. 54, Leipzig: Duncker und Humbolt, pp. 651–765.

Blackbourn, D. (1980) *Class, Religion and Local Politics in Wilhelmine Germany*, New Haven: Yale University Press.

Blackbourn, D. and **Eley, G.** (1980) *Mythen deutscher Geschichtsschreibung*, Frankfurt a.M.: Ullstein Verlag.

Conrad, J. (1891) 'Die Wirkung der Getreidezölle in Deutschland während des letzten Dezenniums', *Jahrbücher für Nationalökonomie und Statistik* Dritte Folge Bd. 1, pp. 481–517.

Delbrück, H. (1894) *Die Polenfrage*, Berlin: Hermann Walther.

Dillwitz, S. (1973) 'Die Struktur der Bauernschaft von 1871 bis 1914. Dargestellt auf der Grundlage der deutschen Reichsstatistik', *Jahrbuch für Geschichte* 9, pp. 47–127.

Eley, G. (1978) 'Capitalism and the Wilhelmine State: Industrial Growth and Political Backwardness in Recent German Historiography, 1890–1918', *Historical Journal* 21, pp. 737–50.

Eley, G. (1980) *Reshaping the German Right*, New Haven: Yale University Press.

Frankenstein, K. (1892) *Die ländliche Arbeiterverhältnisse in Hohenzollern . . .*, *Schriften des Vereins für Socialpolitik* Bd. 54, Leipzig: Duncker and Humbolt, pp. 1–400.

Frankenstein, K. (1893) *Die Arbeiterfrage in der deutschen Landwirthschaft*, Berlin: Robert Oppenheim (Gustav Schmidt).

Galos, A. et al. (1966) *Die Hakatisten*, Berlin: VEB Deutscher Verlag der Wissenschaften.

Gerschenkron, A. (1966) *Bread and Democracy in Germany*, Berkeley: University of California (1st edn published 1943).

Göhre, P. (1894) 'Die deutschen Landarbeiter (Referat)', *Bericht über die Verhandlungen des 5. Evangelisch-sozialen Kongresses*, Frankfurt a.M., 16–17 May 1894, pp. 43–61.

von der Goltz, T. (1875) *Die Lage der ländlichen Arbeiter im Deutschen Reich*, Berlin: Wiegandt, Hempel und Parey.

von der Goltz, T. (1893) *Die ländliche Arbeiterklasse und der preußischen Staat*, Jena: Gustav Fischer.

Großmann, F. (1892) *Die ländliche Arbeiter in der Provinz Schleswig-Holstein . . . Schriften des Vereins für Socialpolitik* Bd. 54, Leipzig: Duncker und Humbolt, pp. 401–649.

Guttsman, W. (1980) *The German Social Democratic Party 1875–1933*, London: Allen & Unwin.

Hardach, K. W. (1967) *Die Bedeutung wirtschaftlicher Faktoren bei der Wiedereinführung der Eisen und Getreidezölle in Deutschland 1879*, Berlin: Duncker und Humbolt.

Hennis, W. (1983) 'Max Weber's "Central Problem" ', *Economy and Society* 12, pp. 135–80.

Heuss, A. (1965) 'Max Webers Bedeutung für die Geschichte des griechischrömischen Altertums', *Historische Zeitschrift* Bd. 201, pp. 529–56.

Höhn, R. and **Seydel, H.** (1941) 'Der Kampf um die Wiedergewinnung des deutschen Ostens. Erfahrungen der preußischen Ostsiedlung 1886 bis 1914', in *Festgabe für Heinrich Himmler*, Darmstadt: L. C. Wittich Verlag, pp. 61–174.

Honigsheim, P. (1946) 'Max Weber as Rural Sociologist', *Rural Sociology*, 11, pp. 207–18.

Honigsheim, P. (1949) 'Max Weber as Historian of Agriculture and Rural Life', *Agricultural History* 23, pp. 170–213.

Hunt, J. C. (1974) 'Peasants, Grain, Tariffs, and Meat Quotas: Imperial German Protectionism Reexamined', *Central European History* 7, pp. 311–31.

Hussain, A. and **Tribe, K.** (1983)

Marxism and the Agrarian Question, 2nd edn, London: Macmillan.

Kaerger, K. (1890) *Die Sachsengängerei*, Berlin: Paul Parey.

Kaerger, K. (1892) *Die Verhältnisse der Landarbeiter in Nordwestdeutschland*, *Schriften des Vereins für Socialpolitik* Bd. 53, Leipzig: Duncker und Humbolt, pp. 1–239.

Kaerger, K. (1893) *Die Arbeiterpacht*, Berlin: Verlag von Gergonne und Cie.

Käsler, D. (1979) *Einführung in das Studium Max Webers*, Munich: Beck.

Kehr, E. (1965) *Der Primat der Innenpolitik*, Berlin: de Gruyter.

Lazarsfeld, P. and **Oberschall, A. R.** (1965) 'Max Weber and Empirical Social Research', *American Sociological Review* 30, pp. 185–99.

von Lengerke, A. (ed.) (1849) *Die ländliche Arbeiterfrage*, Berlin: E. H. Schroeder.

Lexis, W. (1889) 'Die Wirkung der Getreidezölle', in *Festgabe für Georg Hanssen zum 31. Mai 1889*, Tübingen: Verlag der Laupp'schen Buchhandlung, pp. 197–236.

Lindenlaub, D. (1967) *Richtungskämpfe im Verein für Socialpolitik*, Beiheft 52/53 *Vierteljahrschrift für Sozial- und Wirtschaftsgeschichte*.

Losch, H. (1892) *Die ländliche Arbeiterverhältnisse in Wurttemberg, Baden und in den Reichslanden*, *Schriften des Vereins für Socialpolitik* Bd. 53, Leipzig: Duncker und Humbolt, pp. 241–455.

Löwith, K. (1932) 'Max Weber und Karl Marx', *Archiv für Sozialwissenschaft und Sozialpolitik* Bd. 67, pp. 53–99, 175–214.

Meitzen, A. (1868–71) *Der Boden und die landwirthschaftlichen Verhältnisse des Preussischen Staates*, 4 Bde., Berlin: Wiegandt und Hempel.

Meitzen, A. (1882) 'Landwirthschaft. II. Theil. Agrarpolitik im engeren Sinne', in G. Schönberg (ed.) *Handbuch der politischen Oekonomie Bd. I*, Tübingen: Verlag der H. Laupp'schen Buchhandlung, pp. 669–710.

Mitzman, A. (1970) *The Iron Cage*, New York: Knopf.

Moeller, R. G. (1981) 'Peasants and Tariffs in the *Kaiserreich*: How Backward were the *Bauern?*', *Agricultural History* 55, pp. 370–84.

Mommsen, W. (1973) 'Domestic Factors in German Foreign Policy before 1914' *Central European History* 6, pp. 3–43.

Mommsen, W. (1974) *Max Weber und die deutsche Politik* 2nd edn, Tübingen: Mohr (Paul Siebeck).

Munters, Q. J. (1972) 'Max Weber as Rural Sociologist', *Sociologia Ruralis* 12, pp. 129–46.

Nichtweiß, J. (1959) *Die ausländischen Saisonarbeiter in der Landwirtschaft der östlichen und mittlere Gebiete des deutschen Reiches*, Berlin: Rütten und Loening.

Nipperdey, T. (1976) 'Wehler's "Kaiserreich". Eine kritische Auseinandersetzung', in his *Gesellschaft, Kultur, Theorie*, Gottingen: Vandenhoeck und Ruprecht, pp. 360–89.

Oldenberg, K. (1897) *Deutschland als Industriestaat*, Göttingen: Vandenhoeck und Ruprecht.

Perkins, J. A. (1981) 'The Agricultural Revolution in Germany, 1850–1914', *Journal of European Economic History* 10, pp. 71–118.

Puhle, H.-J. (1975) *Agrarische Interessenpolitik und preußischer Konservatismus im wilhelminischen Reich 1893–1914*, Bonn-Bad Godesberg: Verlag Neue Gesellschaft.

Reuter, H.-G. (1977) 'Schutzzollpolitik und Zolltarife für Getreide 1880–1900', *Zeitschrift für Agrargeschichte und Agrarsoziologie* Bd. 25, pp. 199–213.

Rosenberg, H. (1976) *Große Depression und Bismarckzeit*, Frankfurt a.M.: Ullstein.

Rosenberg, H. (1978) 'Zur sozialen Funktion der Agrarpolitik im Zweiten Reich', in his *Machteliten und Wirtschaftskonjunkturen*, Göttingen: Vandenhoeck und Ruprecht, pp. 102–18.

Schmoller, G. (1895) 'Einige Worte zum Antrag Kanitz', *Jahrbuch für Gesetzbegung, Verwaltung und Volkswirthschaft* N.F., Bd. 19, pp. 611–29.

Sering, M. (1893) *Die Innere Kolonisation im östlichen Deutschland*, *Schriften des Vereins für Socialpolitik* Bd. 56, Leipzig: Duncker und Humbolt.

Sombart, W. (1893) Review of Max Weber, *Die römische Agrargeschichte*, *Zeitschrift für Sozial- und Wirthschaftsgeschichte* Bd. 1, pp. 349–56.

Tims, R. W. (1941) *Germanising Prussian Poland*, Dissertation, New York: Faculty of Political Science, Columbia University.

Tirrell, S. R. (1951) *German Agrarian Politics after Bismarck's Fall*, New York: Columbia University Press.

Veblen, T. (1915) *Imperial Germany and the Industrial Revolution*, New York: Macmillan.

Verein für Socialpolitik (1893)

Verhandlungen der am 20. und 21. Mai in Berlin abgehaltenen Gernalversammlung . . . Schriften des Vereins für Socialpolitik Bd. 59, Leipzig: Duncker und Humbolt.

Wagner, A. (1901) *Agrar- und Industriestaat*, Jena: Gustav Fischer.

Webb, S. B. (1982) 'Agricultural Protection in Wilhelminian Germany: Forging an Empire with Pork and Rye', *Journal of Economic History* 42, pp. 3, 9–26.

Weber, M. (1891) *Die römische Agrargeschichte in ihrer Bedeutung für das Staats- und Privatrecht*, Stuttgart: F. Enke.

Weber, M. (1892a) ' "Privatenqueten" über die Lage der Landarbeiter', *Mitteilungen des Evangelisch-sozialen Kongresses* Nr. 4, pp. 3–5; Nr. 5, pp. 3–6; Nr. 6, pp. 1–5.

Weber, M. (1892b) *Die Verhältnisse der Landarbeiter in ostelbischen Deutschland, Schriften des Vereins für Socialpolitik* Bd. 55, Leipzig: Duncker und Humbolt.

Weber, M. (1893a) 'Die Erhebung des Vereins für Socialpolitik über die Lage der Landarbeiter', 6 pts, *Das Land*, Jg. 1, pp. 8–9, 24–6, 43–5, 58–9, 129–30, 147–8.

Weber, M. (1893b) 'Die Erhebung des Evangelisch-sozialen Kongresses über die Verhältnisse der Landarbeiter Deutschlands', *Die Christliche Welt*, Jg. 7, Nr. 23 (1 June) cols 435–40.

Weber, M. (1893c) 'Die ländliche Arbeitsverfassung' in *Verein für Socialpolitik*, 1893, pp. 62–86.

Weber, M. (1893d) 'Contribution to Proceedings on "Die ländliche Arbeiterverhältnisse und die Enquete" ', in *Verein für Socialpolitik*, 1893, pp. 128–33.

Weber, M. (1893e) Review of von der Goltz (1893), *Jahrbücher für Nationalökonomie und Statistik*, 3, Folge Bd. 6, pp. 289–96.

Weber, M. (1894a) 'Argentinische Kolonistenwirthschaften' 2 pts *Deutsches Wochenblatt*, Jg. 7, Nr. 2 (11 January), pp. 20–2; Nr. 5 (1 February), pp. 57–9.

Weber, M. (1894b) 'Entwickelungstendenzen in der Lage der ostelbischen Landarbeiter', *Archiv für soziale Gesetzgebung und Statistik* Bd. 7, pp. 1–41.

Weber, M. (1894c) 'Zum Preßstreit über den Evangelisch-sozialen Kongreß', *Die Christliche Welt*, Jg. 8, Nr. 28 (12 July), cols 668–73.

Weber, M. (1894d) 'Die deutschen Landarbeiter (Korreferat)', *Bericht über die Verhandlungen des 5. Evangelisch-sozialen Kongresses*, Frankfurt a.M., 16–17 May 1894, pp. 61–82.

Weber, M. (1894e) Contribution to Discussion: 'Die deutschen Landarbeiter', *Bericht . . .* pp. 92–4.

Weber, M. (1894f) 'Entwickelungstendenzen in der Lage der ostelbischen Landarbeiter', *Preußische Jahrbücher* Bd. 77, pp. 437–73.

Weber, M. (1899) 'Vorbemerkung des Herausgebers' to S. Goldschmidt, *Die Landarbeiter in der Provinz Sachsen . . .*, Tübingen: H. Laupp, pp. 1–11.

Weber, M. (1924) 'Die soziale Gründe des Untergangs der antiken Kultur', in *Gesammelte Aufsätze zur Sozial- und Wirtschaftsgeschichte*, Tübingen: Mohr (Paul Siebeck), pp. 289–311.

Weber, M. (1936) *Jugendbriefe*, Tübingen: Mohr (Paul Siebeck).

Weber, M. (1968) 'Die "Objektivität" sozialwissenschaftlicher und sozialpolitischer Erkenntnis', in *Gesammelte Aufsätze zur Wissenschaftslehre*, Tübingen: Mohr (Paul Siebeck), pp. 146–214 (3rd edn).

Weber, M. (1979) 'Developmental Tendencies in the Situation of East Elbian Rural Labourers', below, pp. 158–87.

Weber, M. (1980) 'The National State and Economic Policy', below, pp. 188–209.

Wehler, H.-U. (1973) *Das deutsche Kaiserreich*, Göttingen: Vandenhoeck und Ruprecht.

Winkler, H. A. (1982) Review of G. Eley (1980), *Journal of Modern History* 54, pp. 170–6.

Winson, A. (1982) 'The "Prussian Road" of Agrarian Development: A Reconsideration', *Economy and Society* 11, pp. 381–408.

CHAPTER 5

From patriarchalism to capitalism: the theoretical context of Max Weber's agrarian studies (1892–3)

Martin Riesebrodt
Translated by Leena Tanner

Aim and method of the Analysis[1]

During recent years Max Weber's work has attracted renewed interest, which is likely to increase with the imminent publication of the *Gesamtausgabe*. It was above all Friedrich Tenbruck's fundamental rereading of Weber's late works[2] which provoked a debate which opened the way to new interpretations. Thus for example Wolfgang Schluchter has attempted to develop a theory of occidental development on the basis of Weber's work (1981). On the other hand, Talcott Parsons's systems theory is seen by Richard Münch to be the appropriate interpretive basis for Weber's concept of rationalization (Münch 1980). And Wilhelm Hennis shows us Max Weber as an economist (*Nationalökonom*) of the 'historical school' who, in the last analysis, bases his 'problematic' or 'theme' on a philosophical anthropology (1988). Aside from all differences, the common factor of these interpretations is the attempt to present Max Weber's works (seen as a whole or in parts) as a consistent theory or as variations on a constant theme. Consequently, all these interpretations are deficient inasmuch as they construct an idea of homogeneity and systematic uniformity which inheres in Weber's works (as a whole or in parts) and which one can seldom rediscover when reading Weber's texts. The reason for this is obviously the interpretive method shared by all the above-mentioned authors. They consider Weber's works from an 'ex post' perspective[3] which lends an absolute meaning to interpretations in fact only correct from one point of view.

In the context of the publication of the *Max-Weber-Gesamtausgabe* (1984) the opportunity arises once more of reviewing competing interpretations on the new basis of the historico-critical edition of his texts, whereby we might understand more precisely the work in its development and complexity. For this purpose, however, we also need a new methodological approach for textual interpretation. It is clearly not enough to present a purely immanent interpretation and systematization – as Münch and Schluchter in particular do – but there must be a change from the 'ex post'-perspective to an approach which considers genetic and contextual aspects. We do not sufficiently 'understand' the texts in their 'subjectively intended meaning' if we do not try to reconstruct them on the basis of their contemporary context and genetic development. Instead of internally systematizing the works or interpreting them as a development of one motif I suggest their reconstruction as part of a contemporary discourse. If sociology is not to betray its own claims, it should not interpret its 'classics' by means of a history of ideas, by individualization or by heroization.

Max Weber's early academic work, i.e. texts in which his academic socialization is likely to be most visible and reconstructible, is the most important source for a genetic and contextual reinterpretation. Up to now relatively little attention has been paid to Weber's early writings. This has very often been based on a biographic-psychological explanation of Weber's crisis without, however, any demonstration of this at the level of the contents, methodology, or categorization of the texts. Above all, Weber's extensive contribution to the *Verein für Socialpolitik*'s (Association for Social Policy) survey of rural labour, together with associated and subsequent articles have until now been improperly neglected. Thus, even in the relevantly titled essay by Paul Honigsheim (1946), the *Verein* survey does not appear in the bibliographical notes. Wolfgang Schluchter, Keith Tribe, Wilhelm Hennis, and Lawrence Scaff are among the authors who have dealt with Weber's early works in most detail.[4] Hennis and Scaff above all advanced beyond a primarily political interpretation of the texts in question, and they expressly point to their importance for Weber's scholarly work.

Reputable contemporaries have commented on the young Weber in a way that justifies our serious consideration of his academic early works. Marianne Weber writes: 'At the age of twenty-four he was a man whose basic structure was complete and self-contained, a man whom insights and experiences could enrich but no longer remold' (Marianne Weber 1975: 85). In the course of the customary disputation during the presentation of Weber's dissertation the septuagenarian Theodor Mommsen suggested that the younger generation often had new ideas that the older one could not immediately embrace, and that might be so in this instance. He went on: 'But when I have to go to my grave someday, there is no one to whom I would rather say, "Son, here is my spear; it is getting too heavy for my arm" than the highly esteemed Max Weber' (Marianne Weber 1975: 114). And Georg Friedrich Knapp, then the leading historian of Prussian agrarian development, stated in respect of Max Weber's contribution to the *Verein*'s survey of rural labour that he had 'provoked the feeling that our knowledge is insufficient, that we have to start learning from scratch' (Knapp 1893: 7).

Even if one should not overinterpret these characterizations, they must nevertheless be taken seriously in a research strategy. By doing this it certainly cannot be the aim to attribute to the texts on the rural labour question the same importance for sociology as for example the writings on sociology of religion or *Economy and Society*. The aim of the following is rather, through analysis of the concepts, theorems, and methodology of the early work to place it thematically, conceptually, and methodologically on a more secure footing than hitherto. Let us therefore take the statements of Mommsen and Knapp seriously and pursue the question: what brought about such a high opinion of Weber's academic achievements, and what might have been the basis of Weber's significance and originality in the context of competing approaches?

The difficulty of such an attempt consists above all in the fact that Weber did not usually disclose his sources and references, or he seems to proceed on the assumption that his contemporaries are familiar with them. Thus one has to be careful in establishing such references. It is not the use of the same concepts which is decisive but their specific contents. Likewise, when investigating Weber's early academic development, it is not sufficient to follow his formal career and to focus on his teachers in Göttingen, in Strasburg, and, in particular, in Berlin. On that assumption Weber's early work would essentially have been influenced by the concepts and theories of Levin Goldschmidt and August Meitzen, to whom he dedicated his dissertation and thesis respectively (Weber 1889, 1891). If one investigates the texts on the East Elbian rural labour question on that basis, it is clear that such a personal-biographical interpretation does not hold. It is far more likely that the young Weber tried to develop his own approach in debate with leading representatives of law and social sciences (*Staatswissenschaft*), of economics and historical science. An uncritical epigonism could not explain Theodor Mommsen's and Georg Friedrich Knapp's statements.

A textual interpretation on a genetic and contextual basis suggests that we consider afresh existing assumptions about continuities and breaks in Max Weber's work and thus do not proceed simply on old schemes of periodization. That is why the following analysis restricts itself to the study on rural labour and on its associated and successive articles written in the context of the *Verein*'s survey. In addition it refers to the *Roman Agrarian History*, that is to primarily academic texts published between 1891 and 1894, when Weber passed from the study of law to that of economics. On the basis of these texts Weber's central categories and theorems as well as his methodology are to be analysed and to be put into relation with those of contemporary authors. Weber's analyses of seigneurial rule (*Gutsherrschaft*), the capitalistic transformation of East Elbian agrarian relations, and the origins of this process form the centre of this analysis. The treatment of these themes should result in a profile of Max Weber's academic approach in the context of his time.

The East Elbian Rittergut as patriarchally-led association

Weber characterizes the estate enterprise as a patriarchal 'economic community' or 'house and economic community', and as 'monarchally centralized organism' on a natural economic basis.[5] With these characterizations he stresses all those elements which in his opinion disintegrated during the subsequent capitalistic transformation of agriculture. Weber underlines above all three structural features which distinguish traditional agrarian from capitalistic relations: the principally natural economic internal organization of the estate, the manner in which the labour relations are characterized by power relations, and the associational-communal elements within the estate enterprise. With his (implicit) ideal-typical construction of the estate economy, Weber primarily proceeds on relations prevailing before the Prussian agrarian reforms of the nineteenth century which abolished hereditary subjection. He suggests that initially the reforms scarcely altered these conditions. It is true that the new labour relations of the servants and the *Instleute* (comparable to smallholder) are based on contracts, but they still have seigneurial features. The labour relations within the traditional estate economy are based on the economic exploitation of seigneurial rights making possible a 'way of life appropriate to the *Stand*'. Accordingly economic processes are not oriented to gain but to the status-related need which holds true both for the lord and for his inferiors. Their income is also calculated on the basis of this criterion and not according to labour time, efficiency, general crop yield, etc. In addition, after the abolition of hereditary dependence, the basic character of East Elbian estates as seigneurial centres of dominance expresses itself in the rights of the lords over the people belonging to the estate. On entering the contract the *Instmann* places himself under the police power and patrimonial jurisdiction of the lord. This subjects him with respect to administrative law; up to 1848 he could physically be punished and forcibly returned to his work place by police authorities if he had left it prematurely. Furthermore, the *Instmann* is subject to the lord by private law, by his obligation to place himself and his family from dawn to dusk at his disposal. In the terminology of that time, Weber calls this direct, personal power relation 'patriarchal domination'. The function of this seigneurial organization of the estate consists in subsisting the *Stand* out of which the Prussian monarchs used to recruit leaders for political and military positions.

This seigneurial natural economic character is true up to a point; for, as we know, the East Elbian proprietors marketed their grain for centuries. The internal relations of an estate economy, on the other hand, are almost exclusively based on labour in exchange for land cultivation rights and payment in kind. The *Inst* relation still clearly shows these features. The *Instleute* are granted allotments of land and garden plots together with a cottage in which they live. They keep their own cattle, cows, pigs, chicken, geese, etc., and thus can provide themselves with milk, eggs, and meat. They grow flax which is later spun by the women and used for the production of their own cloth. In case of illness they are entitled to free medical care and treatment; they get fuel from the estate and for specific purposes they have rights of cartage. They come into contact with money only if they sell surpluses of grain, meat, etc. Thus Weber characterizes the estate economy as an organization defined internally above all by natural production, by division of labour, and largely by self-sufficiency.

In order to characterize the estate economy Weber cites a third element in addition to the aspects of natural production and power relations: he calls the *Instleute* 'comrades (*Genossen*) with minor rights', and talks of an 'estate organism' and 'economic community' (1984b: 889–90). So what are now, according to Weber, these cooperative and common elements in the relation between the *Instleute* and the lord? Weber underlines above all three factors: the economic position of the *Instmann* as a smallholder; the resulting parallelism between his basic material interests and the interests of his lord; and in particular, his legal position within the estate economy which implicitly interweaves his interests with those of the lord.

As mentioned above, the *Instmann* farms his own land by which, in addition to his obligation to work for his lord, he

secures his own and his family's living. He possesses his cattle, his
garden plots and gets a share of the yield from the estate's rotating
fields. From his lord he receives a cottage which he furnishes and
he owns the most important tools, for example a scythe and a flail.
In exchange for a fixed share he is granted threshing rights during
winter months. If he produces surplus this is sold on the market.
Therefore his basic economic interests, that is, to achieve a good
harvest and to obtain high prices for grain and other foodstuff, are
identical with the estate owner's interests. Furthermore, his
interest is that *his* lord achieves the best possible harvest, since he
gets a direct share of the estate's yields because of his threshing
rights. To this extent, and despite the seigneurial structure
(*Herrschaftsstruktur*), he is a 'comrade' within the estate economy
and consequently Weber generally characterizes the estate
economy as an institution in whose seigneurial relations cooperative elements have survived. Thus for all members of the estate
the subsistence of the respective *Stand* is guaranteed; though to a
different extent, all have their share in the estate's yields, *Gesinde*
and *Instleute* have fixed rights, for example to collect wood, access
to pasture, and to be looked after in case of illness and old age.

If one compares Weber's characterization of the estate economy
as a patriarchally organized cooperative (*Genossenschaft*) on a
natural economic basis with Knapp's[6] analyses, one can in general
detect a factual similarity in both theories. Thus Weber largely
bases his work on the East Elbian development on Knapp's results
and, for example, follows him in underlining the importance of
the Junker estates (*Rittergüter*) as power centres. Nevertheless,
Weber did not only employ Knapp's terminology for some of his
categories are not used by Knapp or by others. The features
stressed by Weber and the concepts used by him point to the fact
that he has been influenced in particular by the '*oikos*-theory' of
the economist Carl Rodbertus and the 'theory of association' of the
lawyer Otto Gierke, both of which he combines with Knapp's
material analyses.

Rodbertus's influence on Weber is proved by three explicit
references. Thus Weber stresses that essential points in his thesis
on *Roman Agrarian History* of 1891 'originally had been inspired
above all by Rodbertus' (1897: 18). In the preface to this text he
calls Rodbertus a 'major thinker' (1891). In a letter to Lujo
Brentano Weber supports Rodbertus's theses on Roman history,
despite their one-sidedness and calls them 'profoundly fruitful and
stimulating' (1936: 363). These three statements primarily substantiate only Rodbertus's influence on Weber with respect to his
studies on Roman agrarian history. It is possible, however, that
Rodbertus's tendency to draw analogies between Antiquity and

contemporary development motivated Weber also to think of parallels between late Roman and modern East Elbian agrarian development.[7] Weber only points explicitly to Rodbertus in one paragraph of the rural labour studies when he writes: 'The organization of the large estates, as it had come down to us after the reorganization, still bore the features of the isolated house economy (strictly speaking of the *"oiken-economy"* as Rodbertus calls it)' (DT, this volume: 160). Rodbertus characterized the *oikos* as a self-sufficient economic unit run on a natural economic basis under the rule of the pater familias (1865: 347). Obviously, above all with his typological description of the traditional estate economy, Weber oriented himself to Rodbertus's '*oikos* conception'. But beyond that Weber also draws a parallel between the political function of the ancient *oikos*, as described by Rodbertus, and the East Elbian *Rittergut*. Referring to the ancient *oikos* Rodbertus underlines the fact that it made it possible for the lord 'to dedicate himself totally and cost-free to the service of the state' (1865: 347). By comparison Weber writes of the *Rittergut*:

> Based upon Prussian traditions, they provided the material
> basis for a stratum of the population which was accustomed to
> possessing both political authority within the state, and the
> political and military forces of state power. . . . On this basis
> the domination of the politically important, yet socially and
> politically underdeveloped, eastern half of the state could be
> effected cheaply and without danger of corruption.
>
> (DT, this volume: 159)

Thus one can detect a clear parallel between Weber's typological descriptions of the traditional estate economy and Rodbertus's writings on the *oikos* of Antiquity with its political function, substantiated by Weber's explicit reference to Rodbertus.[7]

Weber's emphasis on cooperative elements in the traditional estate economy is likely to be due above all to his 'Germanistic' formation, a result of his studies of German law. Already in his thesis, *Medieval Trading Companies*, the concept of *Genossenschaft* plays an important part. This conception had been introduced by Georg Beseler and was developed into a central category of the historical science of law and economics, in particular by the work of Otto Gierke (1868–81). Gierke outlined his theory of *Genossenschaft* (association) in opposition to existing contract theories. Cooperative and contractually-based power associations are in principle antagonistic structures which, however, in the course of historical development have interpenetrated each other (Gierke: vol. I, 135 ff.). In this sense Weber describes the estate economy as a mixture of power elements and of communal cooperative elements in which the first dominate. Whereas Gierke, following the romantic tradition, sees in the cooperative a typical product of German 'popular spirit', Weber uses the conception with the aim of creating an 'ideal type', as called by him later, by which he underlines the elements of traditional estate economy forming a contrast to capitalistically transformed estate economy.

It cannot be demonstrated that Weber was directly influenced by Gierke, for the associational theory had been widely accepted. On the other hand we do know that Weber attended both Gierke's and Beseler's lectures in Berlin. Nevertheless, Weber explicitly rejected their Germanism and his appreciation of Gierke shows that he most likely agreed with Gustav Schmoller who considered 'many aspects which Gierke believed to be the result of German popular spirit more likely to be a typical form of given cultural stages'.[8]

Structural features of capitalistic development

In his analysis of the capitalist transformation of East Elbian agrarian relations Weber proceeds on the assumption that a basic change in the relation between domination and economy takes place during this process. The labour relations within the traditional estate economy were primarily based on a relation of power; the institutionalized aim is to reproduce this relation and to enable a standard of living defined as appropriate for the ruling *Stand*, to which end the exploitation of labour is also oriented. In the capitalist estate economy, on the other hand, labour relations are as a rule based on formal voluntary contracts which nevertheless imply a power relation; the aim of this institution is to maximize gain and the exploitation of labour is contractually oriented to this. Thus a relation primarily based on power is transformed into a legally established and primarily economic relation. The next question is: what are the intermediate stages in the transformation process from patriarchalism to capitalism in East Elbian agriculture, and what categories and concepts does Weber use for their description and analysis?

Again Weber follows the process by looking at the *Instleute*: their gradual transformation into smallholders (*Gärtner*) or *Deputanten* in the first instance, and then into wage labourers. According to Weber three interweaving factors above all determine this process of 'proletarianization', as he often explicitly calls it: the destruction of economic independence, the separation from the land, and the monetary transformation of relations. Initially land allotments, cattle rearing, pasture rights, and rights to collect wood are substituted by free grants of farm produce (*Deputate*). The economy of the *Instleute* is restricted more and more and eventually abolished; the *Instleute* become *Deputanten*. The natural economic element still dominates, but an important stage of social advance among the rural labourers has been abolished. The next step consists in the monetary transformation of labour relations. Contract labour is replaced by 'free' day labourers. Characteristic of such a transition are above all the '*Geldstübler*', i.e. land labourers who work for daily wages and live on the estate paying rents.

In this process Weber underlines above all the total reversal of the constellation of interests. If the *Instmann* was essentially producer and seller of foodstuff and also produced commodities for his own requirements, he now becomes during the process of proletarization more and more a buyer of foodstuff and other consumer goods. With that the community of interests between himself and his lord comes to an end, for henceforth he aims at low market prices and the harvest of his lord is only of marginal interest for him, as he no longer shares its yields. The communal elements of their relation have been destroyed. Also the lord himself undergoes a transformation and becomes a capitalistic entrepreneur. The community of interest is replaced by the 'struggle between landed capital and labour', the 'economic struggle of interests', and the 'wage struggle'.

If we now again compare Weber's analysis of the capitalist development of labour relations with Knapp's study we can establish an essential difference. While Weber considers the transformation from the estate economy into a capitalistic enterprise on the basis of the underlying organization of labour, Knapp sees the estate as a capitalistic organization right from the beginning. For Knapp the capitalistic enterprise 'is not at all linked with a definite organization of labour'.[9] Although Weber thought that agrarian capitalism had begun to develop in Prussia in the sixteenth century, the nineteenth century, itself a period of transformation, is the result of this long term process. If Knapp, with a view to Weber's studies for the *Verein* survey, comments that they 'have provoked the feeling that our knowledge is insufficient, that we have to start learning from scratch' (see above: 133) this could be a reference to this alteration in emphasis in the categorial description of the transformation process.

Weber's specific form of the concept of capitalism and the criteria stressed by him in that context seem to be strongly influenced by Marx. Now one could argue that several of the categories used can also be found in other socialist writers, as for

instance Lassalle or Rodbertus, and in social democratic popu-
larizations of Marx's writings. This is certainly true. We know,
however, that Weber read original texts of Marx as early as the
beginning of the 1890s, that is, most likely the first two volumes
of *Capital* and the *Communist Manifesto*.[10] Thus he was at least not
dependent on secondary socialist literature. On the other hand it is
striking that Weber often refers to specific concepts used by Marx.
He talks for example of the 'social ensemble' (DT, this volume:
160), of the 'socially necessary' expenditure of labour (DT, this
volume: 186), of 'wage struggle', of 'struggle between landed
capital and labour', of 'economic struggle of interests' and of 'the
class consciousness of the modern proletariat' (1984b: 366, 924,
65, 98). Thus Weber accepts the thesis on class struggle which is
foregrounded in the *Communist Manifesto* and adapts it with
respect to modern conditions. In his analysis of the proletarianization process he also underlines the same elements as Marx. He
emphasizes for example the separation of the labourer from the
land and the means of production together with the monetary
transformation of these relations. Also Weber's distinction
between precapitalistic and capitalistic class-consciousness is
consistent with Marx's analysis. In the context of the traditional
estate economy class-consciousness could normally only develop
'purely individually in response to the individual lord' (DT, this
volume: 161). It was only the monetary transformation of the
relations, the market and the abolition of the community of
interests which created the preconditions for a class-consciousness
in the modern, abstract sense. If one looks at the categories and
theses applied in their recurrence and interconnection I consider
more justifiable the assumption that Weber has been directly
influenced by Marx than the opposite assumption.

There are, however, in Weber's analysis of the transformation
process, points at which he implicitly dissociates himself from
Marx's conceptions. This holds true above all for the definition of
the reasons for capitalistic development which I deal with in the
following section. But also Weber's emphasis on the differing
institutionalization of power and economy in traditional and
capitalistic estate economy can be interpreted as a questioning of
Marx's idea of a general dominance of the economic in all social
formations. Beyond that Weber also considers the transformation
process from patriarchalism to capitalism as a transition from a
traditional to a capitalist economic ethic. The traditional estate
owner had an 'economically "comfortable existence" '; 'having few
ambitions and hence a low level of economic ability he was
disinclined to systematic exploitation of his position of power'
(DT, this volume: 159). His aim was to meet the requirements for

a *Stand*-related mode of life. 'The low level of commercial ambition among the estate owners was reinforced by the apathetic resignation of the labourer, and together these formed the psychological supports of the traditional form of enterprise and of the political rule of the landed aristocracy' (DT, this volume: 161). The capitalist estate owner, on the other hand, has to organize his estate from a purely economic point of view. According to Weber one of the reasons for their economic decline is the fact that many estate owners did not comply with this necessary rethinking of their behaviour. Thus the 'psyche' and ethos of the persons taking part in the transformation process are subjected to a structural change. Weber's strong emphasis on these factors shows that he had been influenced by the historical *Nationalökonomie* and possibly in particular by Schmoller. I will deal with that in more detail in the following section.

The reasons for the transformation process

Three groups of factors can be distinguished in Max Weber's analysis of the process of transformation from patriarchalism to capitalism. First, he refers to legal measures taken by the state; second, to economic processes and their consequences for material interests; and third, to changes concerning the 'psyche' of rural labourers and estate owners.

The starting point for the development from patriarchalism to capitalism in Prussia was initially the legal reorganization of relations by the agrarian reform legislation of the early nineteenth century. Nevertheless, at first relatively little changed in the organization of the estate economies. At this stage analogous labour relations were established under the new legal conditions on a contractual basis. The legal changes alone do not effect by themselves an alteration in the way of life (*Lebensführung*); they create however, certain preconditions for economic change through the entry of a commercial bourgeoisie into agriculture.

The transformation of the estate owner into a capitalist entrepreneur is a process which forged ahead from the mid-nineteenth century. A threefold competitive situation provokes this process. First, bourgeois strata appear and purchase or rent estates which they run in a rationalized economic manner. Second, the general advance of the bourgeoisie leads to the Prussian aristocracy orienting itself to a bourgeois standard of life, resulting in an increasing need for cash. And third, competition on the world market forces a rationalization of production.[11]

This threefold competition results in the following: abolition of the remaining communal elements in the estate economy, substitution of payment in kind by wages, and intensification of cultivation. The introduction of root crops and of threshing machines results in major seasonal fluctuations in the demand for labour. The groups of labourers which have to be employed and supported throughout the whole year become increasingly unprofitable and day-labourers, that is, particularly migrant workers with seasonal labour contracts, increasingly replace them. Thus the estate owner's economic interest, determined by pressure to rationalize the running of the estate, results in a transformation of labour organization. The economic interests of the rural labourers also play a role in this process of transformation. Thus rural labourers agree in particular to the transformation from an *Instmann* into a free cultivator (*Deputant*) because this gives them independence from incalculable threshing shares and from unpredictable price fluctuations for grain.

In addition to the fact that the behaviour of those involved is massively influenced by material interests, Weber equally emphasizes the importance of psychic factors in the transformation of agrarian relations. For the estate owner this implies his need for 'a status-related way of life' (*Standesgemässe Lebensführung*) which to an increasing extent orients itself to bourgeois living standards in the face of the advancing bourgeois strata. This orientation very often leads to behaviour which is entirely irrational from an economic point of view and in many cases expresses itself in extreme indebtedness. In connection with the disintegration of the estate economy as a community of interests based on natural economic organization the rural labourer develops a desire for personal freedom. This desire leads to the phenomena of migration into towns and industrial areas, emigration overseas, and migrant work in agriculture. In connection with this cash payment develops into a symbol for newly-won individual freedom. In many cases the labourers even accept in exchange a deterioration of their living conditions. The 'psychological magic of freedom', (1984b: 920), often proves to be stronger than material interests. According to Weber, even the phenomenon of local itinerary work results to a great extent from the disinclination to work under the rule of the local estate owner. Thus, for example, a partial exchange of labour from two different regions takes place during harvesting periods, in the course of which the labourers accept a considerable temporary deterioration of their living conditions, although in both regions the level of wages does not differ. Patriarchalism has lost its role not only with respect to the economy but also to 'the psychology of people', (Weber 1984b: 928). Weber considers psychic motives as a behavioural impulse of equal force to that of economic interests.

If we analyse the contemporary economic literature and, setting on one side (indisputable) economic interests, put the emphasis on psychic and ethical motivations, our attention is drawn to Karl Knies and Gustav Schmoller, two economists of the Historical School. In the first edition of Knies's work, *Political Economy considered from the Standpoint of Historical Method* (published in 1853), he already points to the importance of ideal factors. There he writes:

> And here the historical fact must be recalled, that we see in diverse periods of human historical development particular ideas and intellectual tendencies, which while in no way seeming to serve either the economic interests of individuals or of whole peoples, establish themselves with a dominance and often overwhelming force.[12]

In his addenda to the second edition of this work Knies, in addition to his consideration of the influence of different religions on 'economic morale', deals above all with the importance of ethical and psychical factors for the economy, in which he also considers in detail the related writings of Schmoller (1883: 125–41).

In these writings Schmoller emphasizes even more strongly the importance of psychical and ethical motives for conduct, and demands their programmatic inclusion into economics. One has to 'try to recreate the science of economic motives from a psychological and ethical point of view'.[13] The urge for gain represents only one motive among others. Schmoller rejects both utilitarian (John Stuart Mill) and materialistic interpretations (Marx). Marx deduces 'all developed intellectual culture, all political and religious life from the constitution of economic-technological production processes'. In opposition to that, Schmoller writes: 'One cannot dispute links and interactions between the different spheres of life but certainly one can dispute the possibility of giving an exclusive causal explanation of this kind' (1894: 553). It is possible to attribute with great certainty the young Weber's emphasis on ethical and psychical motives for action and their consideration in the *Nationalökonomie* as equal and autonomous with respect to economic interests to Karl Knies and Gustav Schmoller. Biographical findings substantiate this analysis, for at the beginning of his studies Weber attended Knies's lectures on economics in Heidelberg and read his writings (Marianne Weber 1975: 65). In the early 1890s Weber wrote his thesis as an associate of the *Seminar* for state sciences and statistics at the university in Berlin, where not only August Meitzen and Adolph Wagner but also Gustav Schmoller taught. Therefore, in my opinion, Wilhelm Hennis seems to be entirely right when he points out that, with regard to important aspects, Weber is connected to the traditions of historical *Nationalökonomie*. Eberhard Gothein's conception of 'cultural history' from 1889 also points to the central importance of psychical phenomena. Following Jacob Burckhardt and as a counterweight to the writing of political history Gothein sets cultural history the task 'of explaining the change in emotional life of whole generations' and he also concedes that 'psychological and ethical powers have their lawful development'. 'Properly speaking economic life is devoid of ideas; it is only raw material in the shaping of which the other ideas take an active part' (1889: 62). As Gothein attended lectures by Karl Knies in Heidelberg at the end of 1870,[14] his conception could also go back to Knies.

In view of this source material it is indeed difficult to give a final judgement on the issue of whether Weber was influenced more by Knies or by Schmoller, or even by Gothein. Hennis emphasizes the influence of Knies and in doing so makes an important point.[15] Nevertheless, in my opinion Schmoller's influence on Weber is even stronger; in this I refer both to Weber himself and to corresponding opinions expressed by Otto Hinze and Joseph Schumpeter. Hennis underlines that Weber formulated very sharply his criticism of Knies's approach (which was initially planned to be a contribution to the commemorative publication) and clearly dissociates himself from him (Weber 1975). Hennis interprets this psychologically as an affirmation of Weber's dependence. In opposition to that one can state that on a comparable occasion Weber is capable of positively appreciating Schmoller and the interesting thing about this is that he underlines Schmoller's merits with respect to 'psychological analysis'.[16] Otto Hintze, who closely cooperated with Schmoller, expressly points to his importance for Weber and Sombart:

> He who solely judges Schmoller according to his works for the
> development of theoretical *Nationalökonomie* must gain a one-
> sided picture. Without doubt he must be regarded as the
> pioneer of the new 'interpretive sociology' as Max Weber and
> Sombart – both his followers, even though very independent –
> have developed it.
>
> (Hintze 1928: 130)

And Schumpeter, very familiar with the history of economic theory, calls Max Weber, together with Werner Sombart and

Arthur Spiethoff, an outstanding member of the 'Schmollerian School' (Schumpeter 1954: 816–27).[17]

The developmental concept

In his works on rural labour Weber very frequently uses the concept of development, in the sense of the transformation of social conditions. There is nothing striking about this usage as it was current at that time and by no means necessarily implied an evolutionary theory. Characteristic of Weber is, rather, the usage of the term developmental *tendency*, because it contrasts with the concept of developmental *law*. While developmental law stands for a process which of necessity has to happen,[18] in the case of a developmental tendency it is a question of a predictable but probabilistic process. The concept of developmental tendency together with the term 'mass phenomenon' and the 'typical' belong to the language of statistics.

Both the analysis of Roman agrarian history and the capitalist development of East Elbian regions are methodologically based on the concept of developmental tendency, although Weber does not sufficiently explain its logical status. In both cases Weber deduces from the uniform economic structure of the regions in question that the respective observable differences in particular provinces can be explained by the different degree to which the respective development has already gained ground. Thus 'as a tendency' an even process of change is to be expected, which might however be impeded or obstructed by specific historical preconditions and local factors: 'One can state the developmental law to be general in the sense that such "laws" represent tendencies which might encounter locally stronger influencing factors' (1891: 45).

Weber analyses the different provinces of East Elbian Germany as representatives of different stages of development in the process of capitalistic transformation, and he thereby proceeds on the assumption of a general inevitability of this development. He even talks of the 'subconscious teleology' (1984b: 914) of social relations and with this formulation appears to agree with Marx's ideas. On closer consideration, however, he distinguishes himself from Marx in two essential points. First, Weber thinks that the inevitability of the process is not only a result – though this constitutes an important factor – of the economic conditions and the interests institutionalized by them, but also of psychical and ethical changes. Second, while Marx considers capitalist development as a world-historical process of necessity based on natural law, Weber starts on a lower level of abstraction with his analysis of the East Elbian conditions and explicitly rejects all analogies based on natural laws. Thus he formulates with reference to his reform ideas concerning East Elbian Germany: 'Such a suggestion would not make any sense at all if the developmental tendencies outlined above had the character of ruling natural laws. *But this is not the case*, the effects noted can only develop under specific conditions engendered by the distribution of landed property in the east in combination with the political aspirations of a sinking class' (DT, this volume: 182). Consequently Weber rejects all generalizations of capitalist development which proceed on an assumed uniformity of industrial and agricultural development, for this view neglects the different psychical and cultural factors in town and country, in industrial and rural labour. Thus Weber repeatedly points to the fact that economic generalizations, for example the 'iron law of wages', the tendency towards large enterprises, or the free traders' assumption of a general improvement in living conditions related to the free play of market forces do not hold true in agriculture at all. In this respect, Weber follows a strict empirically-oriented approach in the style of Schmoller. Much more than Schmoller, however, Weber aims at conceptualization and at precise, theory-oriented conceptions.

The influence of Meitzen, Sering, and Kaerger

The four preceding partial analyses demonstrated that Max Weber's approach to the study of social development in East Elbian Germany can be interpreted as an attempt to integrate concepts from various writers, such as Otto Gierke, Karl Marx, Carl Rodbertus, and Gustav Schmoller. Looking at these names the question arises why August Meitzen for instance has not been mentioned in this context, and whether the various discussions in which Weber actively took part in the early 1890s are not underestimated here. Justifiable as this criticism might be in this context, the primary objective was to work out basic categories, concepts, and theorems. In so doing we depend on an analysis of Weber's texts, and on comparing them with the texts of other writers. The reason for this is that beyond the congress's records we know precious little about Weber's contacts concerning discussions in the context of the *Verein* and the Evangelical Social Congress. We do know the teachers of the seminar for political sciences and statistics. In respect of the 'Association of Political Science' set up by contemporaries (Weber 1936: 327) we do not even know the names but only have the information that the majority were economists and lawyers. Thus here too we depend above all on textual analyses and comparisons until better information becomes available with the publication of Weber's letters.

With these means let us now analyse the possible influence of August Meitzen on Weber. Primarily this concerns Weber's thesis on *Roman Agrarian History* which he dedicates to Meitzen. In 1889 Weber started to prepare this work. In a letter to Hermann Baumgarten of 31 December 1889 Weber writes: 'Here one is easily pressured to publish; thus e.g. August Meitzen, the well-known historian of agriculture and one of my teachers whom I most like and appreciate is pressing me because of a work concerning Roman land distribution and the *Kolonat* which in my opinion is not yet ripe for the public' (1936: 323). Weber does not mention why he appreciates Meitzen. In the preface to his thesis Weber informs us, however, of the reason for his gratitude towards Meitzen; 'Without any doubt I have the pleasant obligation of acknowledging that my highly esteemed teacher Dr Meitzen, Privy Councellor and Professor, gave me an understanding of a wealth of practical aspects for the investigation of agrarian history through his teaching and since then by the frequent personal contact which I enjoyed' (1891: 4). Consequently Weber owes to Meitzen the 'practical aspects for the investigation of the agrarian history'. As mentioned above, the theoretical idea originated with Rodbertus whom he, despite great reservations, calls a 'major thinker' (Weber 1891: 3). Consequently Meitzen's influence is probably limited to the teaching of techniques and concepts for research in agrarian history and in particular in agrarian statistics. But Meitzen's importance will be illustrated more profoundly than is here possible by the imminent publication of a new edition of the *Roman Agrarian History* by Jürgen Deininger.

If we analyse Weber's texts with a view to the East Elbian rural labour issue the names of two economists emerge with whom Weber had close relations and with whom he obviously also had intensive academic discussions: Max Sering and Karl Kaerger.[19] Both taught at the Agricultural College of Berlin, Sering as professor, Kaerger as *Privatdozent*. Despite their friendship, Weber's relation to Kaerger was marked by a critical, in part polemical, confrontation which essentially concerned political questions. The conservative Kaerger considered the agrarian question on the whole from the aspect (which Weber rejected) of how the great estates might be provided with the necessary labour force (Kaerger 1892; Weber 1893: 74). A certain rivalry might have existed between both men; for Weber, who was five and a half years younger, was given in the context of the *Verein*'s survey the most important region, East Elbian Germany, although Kaerger was actually academically more qualified on account of his book *Die Sachsengängerei* (1890).[20] Weber's monograph was given prominence by Knapp compared to the contributions of the other members, hence also that of Kaerger. And in addition, Weber presented the principal paper to the congress of the *Verein für Sozialpolitik*.[21] Relevant contemporaries estimated Weber's academic performance above that of Kaerger. If one adds to this also that Weber at times addressed Kaerger arrogantly, one can assume that Weber recognized in Kaerger more a partner in political discussion than an academic equal.[22]

The relationship between Weber and Max Sering was entirely different. Weber and Sering, his senior by 7 years, obviously had a relatively close friendship at the beginning of the 1890s.[23] And there are clear signs that they exchanged ideas intensively at that time. This is shown by the fact that in their writings not only identical contents but also partly identical formulations are to be found. Referring to the large estate owners of the German East, Sering writes: 'instead of contenting themselves with the role of a nobility living off rents, like the French nobility, they did not disdain the status of a *Krautjunker* (working farmer)' (Sering 1892: 5). Weber gives them credit because they refused to develop into a *Stand* of rent-consuming magnates (Weber 1984b: 917). Both Sering and Weber allude to Marx's concept of the 'socially necessary' (Sering 1892: 65; DT, this volume: 186) and criticize Marx's writings on the rural question as 'absolutely insufficient' and as 'rather unfortunate' respectively.[24] With reference to that both talk of a 'pattern borrowed from the conditions of the industrial work force' and 'the pattern borrowed from industrial development' respectively (Weber 1984b: 65; Sering 1893: 64). As a student of Schmoller,[25] Sering thinks that the 'final reason for the eastern mass migration is to be found in psychical and ethical motives'; and Weber considers the 'changes relating to popular psychological needs to be almost more important than the transformation of material living conditions' (Sering 1893: 14; Weber 1984b: 920). The obviously close cooperation at the beginning of the 1890s, however, does not tell us very much about the extent and substance of Sering's actual influence on Weber. Schmoller criticized Sering's low philosophical level, explaining that it would be out of the question to offer him a professorship in Vienna as a counterpart to Carl Menger (Lindenlaub 1967: 108). Sering's influence on Weber possibly related more to the field of agrarian policy than to methodological problems or to basic conceptualizations in economics. Weber's relation to Sering has been documented even more poorly than his relation to Kaerger and Meitzen so that especially in this case a clear evaluation has not hitherto been possible.

The theoretical synthesis of the young Weber

The present analysis has led to the conclusion that – irrespective of the influence of academics like Gierke, Knapp, Meitzen, or Sering – Max Weber's early work can be conceptually interpreted as a synthesis, above all, of the approaches of three writers: Karl Marx, Carl Rodbertus, and Gustav Schmoller.[26] While Marx's importance for the early work of Weber is hardly disputed, Rodbertus's and Schmoller's importance has hitherto been largely underestimated or entirely overlooked. As frequently mentioned already, Weber's dependence on them is limited to conceptions and theorems, and does not for example embrace their entire works or even persons; Weber is never a 'pupil'. His relationship to all three writers always remains rather ambivalent.

Weber adopts from Marx central categories for his analysis of the capitalist transformation of East Elbian agrarian relations and he accepts his thesis of the antagonistic constellation of interests between capitalist entrepreneurs and wage labourers.[27] He rejects, however, Marx's economic reductionism and, in accordance with Schmoller, adheres to the independent importance of psychical and ethical moments. Beyond that Weber thinks that historical processes do not take place analogously with natural processes. Thus the same tendencies do not hold true for the capitalist development of industry and agriculture:

> The changes concerning popular psychological needs are almost even greater than the transformation of the material living conditions, and scientifically it would be inadmissible to ignore them. Any purely economic consideration, especially concerning questions of agrarian organisation, would be unrealistic; especially in the agricultural domain and especially now, there are from a purely economic standpoint various possibilities for further development.
>
> (Weber 1984b: 920–21)

Weber adopts from Schmoller the emphasis on psychical and ethical factors as independent moments which influence economic development and determine its course. But while Schmoller thinks that the time for constructing theories in economics has not yet come and consequently gives preference to historical research, Weber insists on a theoretical conceptualization with reference to

Marx and Rodbertus among others.[28] Whereas Schmoller uses for
example the category of the 'enterprise' and traces it from tribes to
the nineteenth century (1890), Weber talks of a specific,
capitalistic development in the nineteenth century which he
contrasts with earlier forms of organization by means of definite
structural features borrowed above all from Marx.

With regard to Weber's theoretical formation, the influence of
the writings of Rodbertus is certainly less important than that of
Schmoller and Marx. Nevertheless, it is not limited to the
adoption of the 'oikos-theory'. Also, in combining the rural labour
question and that of national integration, Weber seems to be
influenced by Rodbertus's analyses concerning the ancient
agrarian problem and to be stimulated to make analogies with
respect to Prussian development. Rodbertus sees the social
problem which primarily contributed to Roman national disintegration and eventually led to Rome's ruin in the class struggle
between large and small estate owners:

> The pressure of large landed property had already extinguished
> any spark of patriotism in small landed proprietors and the
> general flight to the Barbarians forcing their way through the
> borders was an effect of the large estate corruption of the
> contemporary social question which eventually – as the crisis
> could not resolve it – resulted in the doing to death of the state
> and Rome's nationality by its enemies.
>
> (Rodbertus 1885: 14)

Later Rodbertus draws a parallel with contemporary development:
'Contemporary labour with its indifferent patriotism resulting
from the pressure of its situation already seems to give in to
similar international temptations as the Roman small landed
proprietor.'[29] Weber formulates the basic problematic of the East
Elbian rural question very similarly. The patriarchal large
enterprise has conserved the living standard of rural labour and
their military efficiency, but the capitalistically-organized large
enterprise exists at the expense of the standard of living, the
nationality and the military power of the German East (1984b:
917). As in Antiquity, the large landed property of the German
East has a denationalizing effect by importing Polish migrant
workers and in turn motivating German rural labourers to
emigrate or to move away. As in Antiquity, it is thereby a matter
of class struggle; for the recruiting of Polish migrant workers
serves to lower living standards and is consciously used against the
growing consciousness of the German labour force. There is much
to be said for the view point that Weber's uncompromising

placing of the 'national view point' above other factors in the assessment of the East Elbian rural question had been influenced by Rodbertus's analogy between ancient and contemporary development.

If one considers this adoption of theorems and conceptions from such different writers as Schmoller, Marx, and Rodbertus, the impartiality with which Weber proceeds in his theoretical synthesis is striking. Disregarding the writers' respective academic or political affiliations, he draws from their approaches the elements he considers suitable for the analysis of his theme. Here the preponderance of economic writers shows clearly both Weber's own self-conception as an economist and, secondarily, as a lawyer. If one compares Weber's analysis of the transformation from patriarchalism to capitalism with the *Community and Association* of Ferdinand Tönnies (1955) or the 'social differentiation' of Georg Simmel (1890), his national-economic approach clearly differs from their philosophically oriented approach. With his theoretical synthesis Weber ignores the ideological barriers between different economic schools and closes the gap between 'Marxist' and 'bourgeois' approaches, between 'historical' and 'theoretical' *Nationalökonomie*. On the basis of this synthesis Weber develops the essence of his sociology, taking into account the importance of contemporary economic development without lapsing into economic determinism, and uniting historical analysis with precise conceptions. Later Weber calls the conception developed here the 'socio-economic' approach (1949).

On the parallelism of science and politics in Weber's early works

In the above-mentioned analyses concerning Weber's early works his political views and activities were in particular the foci of interest and his academic analyses, especially in the context of the East Elbian rural question, have been considered rather as the outcome of his political convictions. This one-sided consideration has to be supplemented and not replaced by an opposite perspective. For this reason I will try to demonstrate in conclusion that Weber's political conceptions can also be interpreted as realizations of his academic theoretical synthesis. His engagement at the same time in the *Verein*, in the *Evangelisch-Sozialer Kongress*, and in *Alldeutscher Verband* – difficult to understand from today's point of view – as well as his striving for a dialogue with Social Democracy can in my opinion be understood better if one considers the background of his conceptual integration of

Marx, Schmoller, and Rodbertus. This does not by any means
offer an analysis of the complicated interactions between political
conviction and academic conception in the young Weber, but only
points to an aspect to be considered, hitherto neglected in that
context. As already shown above Weber's preference for the
'national view point' was possibly influenced by Rodbertus's
parallelization of ancient and contemporary development. Weber's
membership in the *Alldeutscher Verband* demonstrates a priority of
Staatsraison[30] which he was later to recognize as a faulty
assessment of its real objectives. In addition, however, his
activities in the *Evangelisch-Sozialer Kongress* and his establishment of contacts with Social Democracy aimed primarily at the
realization of this perspective. Marx's influence on Weber's
academic conceptions corresponds politically to his acceptance of
the class struggle, his critique of capitalism, and his expectation
that capitalism as an economic system would inevitably win
through and that the labour force as a whole would obtain
enormous political importance. His contacts with Social Democracy
were especially marked by such views. Schmoller's influence is
reflected theoretically above all in the emphasis on ethical and
psychical moments in the process of economic development. This
theoretical understanding corresponds in particular to Weber's
activities in the context of the Protestant social reform movement
for which, in addition to the economic, the ethical aspect of the
'social question' is also at stake.

Weber's critical statements referring to various political groups
of his time can also be plausibly connected with his academic
ideas. Weber's rejection of conservative positions is especially
harsh and principled. It can be summarized in the following three
theses: first, patriarchalism as a rural system of power has
psychologically become impossible; second, large landed property
acted for a long time as a pillar of the monarchy and served the
national interest while pursuing its own interests; at this stage,
however, the Eastern landed aristocracy maintained itself at the
expense of the nation by importing Polish migrant workers.
Third, that is why in the context of the survey on the rural labour
problem it is by no means a question of how to provide the large
estates with the necessary labour force. The national interest and
the economic interest of the large landed proprietors of the
German East are incompatible and least of all identical. The
rejection of agrarian conservation is based on psychological,
economic, and national arguments, that is, so to speak, 'in the
name of' Schmoller, Marx, and Rodbertus. Weber also criticized
the positions of his 'liberal political friends' (1893: 128) in many
respects. He opposed their ingenuous belief that the capitalist

development of agriculture automatically improves the material living condition of the rural workers. Weber expressly points to the fact that in Silesia, the capitalistically most advanced province, the situation of the rural worker is the most miserable, whereas the comparatively highest living standard can be found in Mecklenburg, a backward, patriarchally organized province. In this context Weber also objects to the thesis that soil quality or the form of management essentially influence the wage level of the workers. On the contrary, the cultural level of the workers is decisive, as is their will and ability to defend it. Weber is negative towards the capitalist transformation of agriculture because it leads to disorganization and disintegration. In the last analysis the demand for Polish migrant workers is produced by the interest-constellation of the large capitalist enterprise. Weber's evaluation of the problematic of capitalist development thus corresponds in essential elements with that of the socialists and the 'socialists of the chair'; respectively, according to the traditions of Marx and Rodbertus.

Weber criticizes in socialist positions the mechanical comparison of industrial with agrarian development, the ignorance of the differing 'psyche' of the rural and industrial labour force as well as their internationalism. In contrast with industrial and urban mentality, in agriculture there prevails an individualist strain (1984b: 921). The objective of the rural labourer is to advance socially to an independent economic existence, which is impossible for him only because of the contemporary structure in the German East. The prospects for the organization of the rural labour force, as sought by Social Democrats, are unpromising because of the geographical dispersion, even on the basis of rights of free association. The rural class struggle is led by the big capitalist enterprises against the German rural labourer, taking the form of importing Polish workers and thus underselling and displacing competition (DT, this volume: 181). Weber considers this ignorance of the connection between rural labour and the national question to be one central error of Social Democracy. Here his criticism corresponds to the conceptions of Rodbertus and Schmoller.

Weber's political attitude (which I do not want to justify here: I only outline the manner in which it corresponds with his academic approach) distinguishes itself from the typical conservative and liberal positions of party politics of his time by the fact that it does not ideologically idealize either patriarchalism or capitalism. While Weber perceives the patriarchal system as anachronistic he criticizes capitalism in so far as it produces undesirable consequences in a national and cultural sense. Thus Weber is neither a 'critic by principle' nor a 'supporter' of the capitalist system; and it is not possible to definitely integrate him within an academic school of thought or a political party. Because of his scientific synthesis and his general political criticism he is, however, capable of a dialogue, and thus interesting for a broad spectrum. Politically liberal social reformers, nationally oriented state socialists, and class-conflictual social democrats can find passages in his rural labour studies whose opinions they share. And within the social sciences, historically and theoretically oriented economists and Marxists can identify themselves at least with some aspects of the work. The positive response to Weber's analyses on rural labour from almost all camps[31] affirms the thesis that his academic and political importance is based above all on his ability to integrate seemingly incompatible perspectives.

Notes

1.   I thank Friedrich W. Graf and Klaus Tanner for intensive discussion about former drafts of this article and Rita Aldenhoff and Gangolf Hübinger for helpful critical advice.
2.   Tenbruck (1989); and in criticism of this, Riesebrodt (1980).
3.   This is also true for Hennis, for while he examines in hitherto unsurpassed detail the early works, he does ultimately interpret them in terms of Weber's 1917 lecture on 'Personality and Life Orders'. This leads to an overemphasis upon a problematic which is undoubtedly present, but subsumes all aspects under this implausible perspective and above all neglects Weber's much more sociological than philosophical method.
4.   Mommsen (1985); Bendix (1966); Dibble (1968); Schluchter (1980); Tribe (1989); Hennis (1988); Scaff (1989).
5.   The following presentation is primarily based upon Weber (1984b); concepts which are mentioned can be traced through the subject index of this work. (Translator's note: a *Gut* is a unit of landholding, sometimes translated into English as 'estate' or 'manor', as would be the case in this instance. A *Rittergut* was a hereditary noble estate, as opposed to the commercially-oriented estates purchased by the new bourgeoisie. Manor is inexact as the medieval manor is not simply a unit of landholding.)
6.   Knapp (1887, 1891). The clear conceptual distinction between *Grund-herrschaft* and *Gutsherrschaft* in agrarian history is owned to Knapp. To this extent Knapp was constantly Weber's model, and Weber recognized the 'painstaking classification, distinct recognition of the significance of law, careful and unambiguous coining of concepts' of Knapp and his school – cited in Hennis (1988: 216, n. 36).
7.   Thus far Lindenlaub's argument that the younger generation in the *Verein* were 'schooled by Marx' is correct; but his further claim that Rodbertus was no longer of any significance is one-sided and wrong, at least for Weber (1967: 280). Heuss has discussed the significance of Weber's work on antiquity in his article (1965).
8.   Schmoller (1890). In other respects I believe that the influence of Gierke upon Weber, especially with respect to the manner in which he constitutes his categories in his sociology of religion, is very great.

9.   Knapp (1891: 62). Scaff misses this material difference, although he rightly emphasizes the centrality of the category of 'labour organization' for Weber's analysis.

10. In a letter to Georg von Vollmar of 13 Dec. 1892 he criticizes Marx's remarks on the agrarian question (Institute for Social History, Amsterdam, Nachlass von Vollmar 2221). See references to Weber's reading of Marx and other socialist writers in Hennis (1988: 209).

11. Cf. my introduction to Weber (1984b) and the literature which is cited there.

12. I here cite Knies according to the second edition of his work, enlarged with additional notes and published under the title *Die politische Oekonomie vom geschichtlichen Standpuncte* (1883: 122).

13. Schmoller (1894: 550). This text can be read as that which Schmoller represented doctrinally in the early 1890s.

14. See A. Bergsträßer, 'Eberhard Gothein', *Neue Deutsche Biographie* Bd. 6, pp. 654–6.

15. I refer here to Hennis's article 'A Science of Man. Max Weber and the Political Economy of the German Historical School', in his (1988).

16. Cf. the cited passage in note 28 below.

17. In his funeral speech for Schmoller Sombart called him 'our master' (*Schmollers Jahrbuch* Jg. 62, 1938, 2 Halbband p. 1). Apart from Max Weber and Sombart, other important members of the younger generation of economists and historians, like Alfred Weber and Kurt Breysig, studied with Schmoller and had their dissertation supervised by him. See the articles on Breysig and Sombart in H.-U. Wehler, *Deutsche Historiker V* (Göttingen 1972).

18. Cf. W. Lexis (1892).

19. See the name index in Weber (1984b: 1022ff.).

20. Kaerger (1890). This book examines the seasonal migration of workers to Saxony for the harvesting of root crops (trans.).

21. See on this my editorial report in Weber (1984b: 28, n. 48).

22. Weber openly distances himself from Kaerger, implies that his statements are not to be taken too seriously, and states: 'He gets carried away – this is our constant point of difference – by the thought of a [patriarchal] relation of domination over men' (*Verein* 1893: 130).

23. Sering was a schoolfriend of Weber's cousin Otto Baumgarten (I would like to thank Karl-Ludwig Ay for the reference to Baumgarten (1929: 34)). On the friendship between Sering and Weber see *Verein* (1893: 81, 159) where they mutually address each other as friends; and also Weber (1936: 351).

24. Sering (1893: 70); Weber in a letter to von Vollmar, see note 11, above.

25. Sering had studied in Strasburg under Knapp and Schmoller and wrote his dissertation there. See von Dietze (1962).

26. This does not represent a claim that no other authorial influence can be demonstrated, particularly with respect to legal literature. Some will also miss a reference to Nietzsche, to whom Scaff refers with requisite care (this volume: 17, 21). While Nietzsche's significance for the later works, especially the writings on the sociology of religion, is undoubtedly great, I remain unconvinced of his relevance to the earlier works. I can only agree with Scaff when he does not trace Weber's rejection of 'eudaemonian' perspectives to Nietzsche, for this could also be found in Rodbertus, for example. See Dietzel (1888: 80).

27. The points made here concerning the influence on Weber of Marx correspond in part with those noted by the Social Democratic periodical *Die Neue Zeit*, which in a review referred to Weber as an 'extremely competent editor' (p. 595) and sees the main thrust of his analyses in the 'clarification of the process of transformation of rural labour organisation' (p. 596) which he evaluates in a

'completely non-partisan' manner (p. 598). *Die Neue Zeit* Jg. 11, Bd. 1 (1892–3) Nr. 19, pp. 594–600.

28. Weber assessed this difference, and also Schmoller's influence, in a letter written 16 years later:

> Whether it is today however time to pay more regard to the theoretical side – that the time could once again come for theoretical work, that an imposing construction full of knowledge and historical penetration, psychological analysis and philosophical formation stands before us, that we of the younger generation might once more attempt to work further with the means of theory construction – all of this we owe ultimately to the incomparable work which you have successfully pursued for decades.

Printed in *Reden und Ansprachen gehalten am 24. Juni 1908 bei der Feier von Gustav von Schmollers 70. Geburtstag*, 1908: 68.

29. Rodbertus (1885: 14, 18). Weber's study of Roman agrarian history closes in an analogous manner with an analysis of the causes of the destruction of national sentiment (1891: 278).

30. It is striking that Weber's emphasis on *Staatsraison* in the debate on the rural labour survey twice coincides exactly with the usage of Adolph Wagner, the economist who stood most closely to the tradition represented by Rodbertus (*Verein* 1893: 128, 187).

31. This judgement is most clearly proved by the fact that both the *Kreuzzeitung* and *Die Neue Zeit* felt able to use Weber to confirm their own opinions. See my introduction to Weber (1984b: 15–17).

References

Baumgarten, O. (1929) *Meine Lebensgeschichte*, Tübingen.

Bendix, R. (1966) *Max Weber. An Intellectual Portrait*, London: Methuen.

Bergsträsser, A. 'Eberhard Gothein', *Neue Deutsche Biographie* Bd. 6, pp. 654–6.

von Brocke, B. (1972) 'Kurt Breysig' and 'Werner Sombart', in H.-U. Wehler (ed.), *Deutsche Historiker*, Göttingen.

Dibble, Vernon K. (1968) 'Social Science and Political Commitments in the Young Max Weber', *Archives Européennes de Sociologie* Jg. 9, Nr. 1, pp. 92–110.

von Dietze, C. (1962) 'Sering', *Staatslexikon* Bd. 7, Sp. 54–5, Freiburg.

Dietzel, H. (1888) *Carl Rodbertus*, Jena.

Gierke, O. (1868–1881) *Das deutsche Genossenschaftsrecht*, Berlin.

Gothein, E. (1889) *Die Aufgaben der Kulturgeschichte*, Leipzig.

Hennis, W. (1988) *Max Weber: Essays in Reconstruction*, London.

Heuss, A. (1965) 'Max Webers Bedeutung für die Geschichte des griechisch-römischen Altertums', *Historische Zeitschrift*, Bd. 201, pp. 529–56.

Hintze, O. (1928) 'Nachruf auf Gustav Schmoller', *Deutsches Biographisches Jahrbuch, Überleitungsband 1917–20*, Stuttgart, pp. 124–34.

Honigsheim, P. (1946) 'Max Weber as Rural Sociologist', *Rural Sociology* vol. 11, Nr. 3, pp. 207–18.

Kaerger, K. (1890) *Die Sachsengängerei*, Berlin.

Kaerger, K. (1892) *Die ländlichen Arbeiterverhältnisse in Nordwest-Deutschland, Schriften des Vereins für Socialpolitik*, Bd. 53, Leipzig.

Käsler, D. (1979) *Einführung in das Studium Max Webers*, München.

Knapp, G. F. (1887) *Die Bauern-Befreiung und der Ursprung der Landarbeiter in den altesten Theilen Preussens*, 2 Bde, Leipzig.

Knapp, G. F. (1891) *Die Landarbeiter in Knechtschaft und Freiheit*, Leipzig.

Knapp, G. F. (1893) in *Verhandlungen des Vereins für Socialpolitik, Schriften des Vereins für Socialpolitik*, Bd. 58, Leipzig.

Knies, K. (1883) *Die politische Oekonomie vom geschichtlichen Standpunkte*, Braunschweig.

Lexis, W. (1892) 'Gesetz (im

gesellschaftlichen und statistischen Sinne)', *Handwörterbuch der Staatswissenschaften*, Bd. 3, Jena, pp. 844–9.

Lindenlaub, D. (1967) *Richtungskämpfe im Verein für Sozialpolitik*, Wiesbaden.

Mommsen, W. J. (1985) *Max Weber and German Politics*, Chicago.

Münch, R. (1980) 'Über Parsons zu Weber: Von der Theorie der Rationalisierung zur Theorie der Interpretation', *Zeitschrift für Soziologie*, Jg. 9, pp. 18–53.

Riesebrodt, M. (1980) 'Ideen, Interessen, Rationalisierung: Kritische Anmerkungen an F. H. Tenbrucks Interpretation des Werkes Max Weber', *Kölner Zeitschrift für Soziologie und Sozialpsychologie* Bd. 32, pp. 111–29.

Rodbertus, C. (1865) 'Zur Geschichte der römischen Tributsteuern seit Augustus', *Jahrbücher für Nationalökonomie und Statistik*, 4. Band.

Rodbertus, C. (1885) *Zur Beleuchtung der socialen Frage, Theil II*, Berlin.

Scaff, L. A. (1989) 'Weber before Weberian Sociology', this volume, pp. 15–41.

Schluchter, W. (1980) 'Der autoritär verfaßte Kapitalismus. Webers Kritik am Kaiserreich', in W. Schluchter, *Rationalismus der Weltbeherrschung*, Frankfurt, pp. 134–69.

Schluchter, W. (1981) *The Rise of Western Rationalism*, Berkeley: University of California Press.

Schmoller, G. (1890) 'Die geschichtliche Entwicklung der Unternehmung', *Jahrbuch für Gesetzgebung, Verwaltung und Volkswirtschaft im Deutschen Reich* 14, Jg. 3, Heft, pp. 1–49.

Schmoller, G. (1894) 'Volkswirtschaft, Volkswirtschaftslehre und-methode', *Handwörterbuch der Staatswissenschaften* Bd. 6, Jena.

Schumpeter, J. A. (1954) *History of Economic Analysis*, London.

Sering, M. (1892) *Arbeiterfrage und Kolonisation in den östlichen Provinzen Preußens*, Berlin.

Sering, M. (1893) *Die innere Kolonisation im östlichen Deutschland, Schriften des Vereins für Sozialpolitik* Bd. 56, Leipzig.

Simmel, G. (1890) *Soziale Differenzierung*, Leipzig.

Tenbruck, F. H. (1989) 'The Problem of Thematic Unity in the Work of Max Weber', this volume, pp. 42–84.

Tönnies, F. (1955) *Community and Association*, London.

Tribe, K. (1989) 'Prussian Agriculture – German Politics: Max Weber 1892–7', this volume, pp. 158–87.

Verein (1893) *Verhandlungen des Vereins für Sozialpolitik von 1893, Schriften des Vereins für Sozialpolitik* 58, Leipzig.

Weber, Marianne (1975) *Max Weber: A Biography*, New York.

Weber, Max (1889) *Zur Geschichte der Handelsgesellschaften im Mittelalter*, Stuttgart.

Weber, Max (1891) *Die römische Agrargeschichte in ihrer Bedeutung für das Staats- und Privatrecht*, Stuttgart.

Weber, Max (1893) 'Die ländliche Arbeitsverfassung', in *Verein* (1893).

Weber, Max (1897) 'Agrarverhältnisse im Altertum', *Handwörterbuch der Staatswissenschaften*, 2 suppl. Bd., Jena.

Weber, Max (1936) *Jugendbriefe*, Tübingen.

Weber, Max (1949) ' "Objectivity" in Social Science and Social Policy', in E. A. Shils, H. A. Finch (eds) *Max Weber and the Methodology of the Social Sciences*, Glencoe: Free Press, pp. 49–112.

Weber, Max (1975) *Roscher and Knies: The Logical Problems of Historical Economics*, New York: Free Press.

Weber, Max (1984a) *Zur Politik im Weltkrieg*, in W. J. Mommsen and G. Hübinger (eds), Tübingen (MWG I/15).

Weber, Max (1984b) *Die Lage der Landarbeiter im ostelbischen Deutschland*, Martin Riesebrodt (ed.), Tübingen (MWG I/3).

CHAPTER 6

Developmental tendencies in the situation of East Elbian rural labourers*

Max Weber
translated by K. Tribe

The *Verein für Sozialpolitik* has completed a survey of the conditions of rural labour, the results of which were published eighteen months ago in three large volumes. The data which is recorded there was collected from enquiries directed to *landowners* – considerations of cost prevented a direct approach to the workers, as in the more recent case of the *Evangelische-soziale Kongress* circular among the rural clergy. The considerable amount of factual material that the investigation collected is therefore certainly one-sided and does not permit definitive conclusions on the actual situation of rural labourers to be drawn. However, the fact that similar surveys were conducted in 1849 and 1873 makes possible something more important from the sociopolitical standpoint: by comparing the results of the three surveys, all of which suffer the same probability of error, it is possible to derive information concerning the *tendencies of development* present in the relations of rural labourers. Instead of posing the question: do *contemporary* workers have a reasonable wage, good accommodation, or not and so on, it is possible to pose a more important one: how does the general development of their position relate to that of the nation, what future do they have?

The publication by the *Verein* of this work offers the possibility of answering this question with some degree of certainty, if not conclusively. Certain basic changes can be detected in the social structure in the labour organization of the large landed properties of the east, changes whose effects (just like in disturbances of the molecular structure of solids) occur slowly but irresistibly, hidden from the eye by its preoccupation with general trends only.

The rearrangement of labour organization and its effects (in so far as they concern us here) cannot however be considered in isolation, for they depend on the general prospects for agriculture in the east and in particular on that of the large agricultural enterprises. It is certainly unjustifiable to consider these charac-

158

teristic large enterprises of the east as forming a homogenous mass without taking into account the substantial differences in their natural conditions; or alternatively to talk in general of the presence, or absence, of a crisis; or attribute such a supposed crisis to a deficiency of capital or of capable management. For in spite of these considerations one factor affects equally all such interpretations of the present situation: the East Elbian estates are not merely economic units, but local political *centres of domination* (*Herrschaftszentren*). Based upon Prussian traditions, they provided the material basis for a stratum of the population which was accustomed to possessing both political authority within the state, and the political and military forces of state power. The dependents of the landed nobility were from the state's point of view qualified for this trusted position (confirmed in Prussian tradition and history) on account of their economically 'comfortable existence'; having few ambitions and a low level of economic ability they were disinclined to systematic exploitation of their positions of power, on which they were in any case not dependent. On this basis the domination of the politically important, yet socially and politically underdeveloped, eastern half of the state could be effected cheaply and without danger of corruption. In brief, the manor houses of the east signified the dispersion of a ruling class throughout the rural areas. They were the points at which the garrisons and administrators of local towns, or even major cities, could find suitable social points of contact; and in addition to that they provided an effective – in fact a decisive – counterweight to the monopoly of political ability by the great bourgeoisie of the cities.

This position itself involved particular aspirations with respect to living standards – for instance with respect to the education of children, the forms of sociability, and in many other ways – all of which had the same principal result, that as the costs of most articles of mass consumption fell, the cost of living constantly increased. The estate owner has to keep up a standard of living on a par with the 'higher' city bourgeoisie, or else he becomes a peasant. For fifty years living standards and expectations have been steadily rising, in particular those of the great bourgeoisie, who were the previous chief competitors with the rural aristocracy for political power. The natural (or unavoidable, given contemporary social relations) attempt to keep in step with this standard of living constitutes for the broad masses of the eastern landed aristocracy a threat to their economic base, quite apart from the effects of foreign competition. The standards that a Prussian knight (*Rittergutsbesitzer*) must maintain – aside from any extravagance – if he wishes to equal the standard of life [English] of a member of the 'ruling class' are not provided by the typical eastern estate, which is clearly far from a 'latifundia'. Five-hundred hectares of average eastern land (more if the land is below average), which is what more than a third of the estates are, no longer supports 'domination', despite improved yields. For this rate of improvement is on average far slower than that of the *average* living conditions of the ruling class, and this ratio has serious consequences. This is often overlooked, since it appears that much of the household requirements of the estate can be met through its own activities and thus present no burden for the budget. This is however an illusion, since modern living requires ever growing disbursements of cash. The changes in modern relations, within which the estate owner has a role to play, oppress at the same time the estate owner who, while possessing a tract of land, cannot realistically farm it independently of other activities. Instead of political power being supported by a secure material base, it is now necessary for it to be put at the service of economic interests. It is only natural that instead of a secure and strong landlord an indigent farmer appears, whose desire for protection from economic forces assumes the form of a petition for charity. This is, within limits, the case apart from any effects of international competition.[1] It is clear that political power cannot be sustained on this basis for any length of time; and the unavoidable consequence is a significant *relative* decline in political and social standing, in so far as this does not interfere with the progress of industrial development.

It is not only the question of revenue from the land that has undermined the attempt of the estate owner to keep up his political standing, but also of the social groups whom he rules and by whom he is at the same time supported. The organization of the large estates perpetuates remnants of the isolated domestic economy. The externalized portion of its activity was indeed greater than that typical of the middle ages, but the growing involvement in a world economy could not and was not planfully directed. Instead the enterprises found themselves partly coerced by these new relations of exchange; partly they ignored them. The typical estate owner continued farming in a traditional manner as though he was producing goods for a local market. The old forms of labour and social relations were maintained by the regulations governing estate workers and *Instleute*.[2] The rural labourer was and remains a smallholder, furnished with land as compensation for subordination to his master and as associate (*Genosse*) sharing in the product of the estate; only during this century did significant money-wages emerge beside, and sometimes in place of, the allocations of land and revenue in labour relations. The estate economy remained however in principle a form of communal economy, patriarchally ruled and directed. The master was not a simple employer, but rather a political autocrat who personally dominated the labour, sharing with him a common interest beyond that to be found in modern relations of employer and worker. Poor harvests, low prices for corn and meat badly affected the budget of an *Instmann*, settled on a piece of land and taking his share of the gross yield, selling his own corn and pigs under conditions often worse than those experienced by his employer. It is obvious that this situation made the worker unconditionally dependent on his master. More important however for the commanding position of the estate owners were those material and resilient bonds which sharply separated the rural worker – or rather in the east the most important stratum, the *Instleute* – from the commercial proletariat. The rural proletariat were able to develop an anti-landlord class consciousness under normal political conditions only in an isolated fashion against *individual* masters, who customarily combined a naive brutality with camaraderie. On the other hand this reflected the fact that the rural labourer was not generally exploited on a purely economic level: he found himself confronted not with an 'employer' but with a small-scale territorial lord. The low level of commercial ambition among the estate owners was reinforced by the apathetic resignation of the labourer, and together these formed the psychological supports of the traditional form of enterprise and of the political rule of the landed aristocracy.

The decay however of this political authority, combined with the threat, or actuality, of dispossession by the wealthy commercial bourgeoisie (*kapitalkräftigere Bürgertum*) – be it in the form of purchase or renting of estates – forced the owners of the large landed estates to become, if they wished to remain owners, what they had not previously been: entrepreneurs working according to *commercial* principles. On the large estates the choice was between this and some degree of break-up into small enterprises. In the first case the land did not 'gravitate to possession by the most suitable' as was claimed, but rather to those landlords with most capital; and this implied that such landlords placed above all else that to which the landed aristocracy ascribed only secondary importance: commercial enterprise. This however dealt the final blow to the isolated estate economy.

The end of the isolation of the estate economies at the same time introduced the necessity of greater compliance with worldwide conditions of production, which now began to rule the enterprises. The necessary consequences for these enterprises differed according to the soil and climatic conditions. Those which were on both counts favoured by nature were able, via increased investment, to adopt more intensive techniques and in this way to engage with international competition. These enterprises intensified production according to established laws on the intensification of capital. In so doing they followed the principle established by Sering[3] according to which there is a tendency for a reduction in the cultivated area of a centrally-run enterprise while increasing its rate of capital investment. From this there also follows, from the point of view of political control, a certain weakening of the power of the estate owner: the dominated territory becomes smaller. While certainly not developing into peasant enterprises, they do become bourgeois-capitalist large enterprises. They therefore merge into ascendant large-peasant enterprises – particularly in the root-growing areas – together with them forming a unified mass of farms run on bourgeois-commercial lines. The other, less favoured, estates become economically worthless and, as large enterprises, can only serve as pasture for extensive cattle-raising. Between these two extremes lie a number of different enterprises with varying qualities of average land, which require with decreasing quality of soil increasing amounts of capital if intensive cultivation is to be adopted. If such investment is not made, the conjuncture in the world market increasingly robs them of the ability to profit from production for the market; if such a course is followed, the enterprise will be brought to the same state as those with the poorest soils, where field crops are no longer a viable proposition. This last case is the most typical of all. The corn duties rise at the expense of the size of the area that can be devoted to cereal production, while the advantages previously enjoyed by beet cultivation and still possessed by potato distilleries make possible cultivation with root crops. On the other hand those sections for which world conditions prescribe total or predominant participation in cattle-raising or market-gardening are in the east not significant. The latter remains small because even a minor increase in the proportion of land devoted to such use would involve a radical alteration in consumption, and in the case of the former because the east lacks (with the exception of the coastal areas of East Prussia and a few other districts) the climatic and other conditions that make England so suitable for intensive cattle raising.[4] Where large enterprises, obeying the dictates of the international division of production, economize on capital and labour and go over to pasture farming, the landlords do not lose political control of an *area* – on the contrary this tends to be greatly extended – they rather lose the retinue that was previously under their domination; under the new conditions a minimal labour force is retained, and also the number of entrepreneurs is reduced as latifundias are built up. Here also then the estate (*Stand*) as such forfeits its political influence.

Everywhere we find a common phenomenon as the outcome of this situation: where after a time neither fragmentation into small farms nor the desolation of pasture-farming can be observed, the necessity emerges of increasing the outlay of capital and farm management on business-like lines unknown to the traditional landlord of the east. In other words: in place of the landed aristocracy there necessarily enters – with or without a change of person – a class of agricultural entrepreneurs, who are in principle no different to commercial entrepreneurs in their social characteristics.

This transformation in the general type of rural employer has significant consequences for the position of the labourer. In all major respects the complexity of labour relations and the purely individualized situation of the solitary labourer is a concomitant of the patriarchal estate economy, as in the estate organization of feudality. At that time estate labour relations were not arranged according to commercial principles and with the objective of profitability, but rather developed historically as means of affording the landlords a suitable existence. Under these conditions as little deviation as possible was made from the natural and communal economic foundations of this order. Thus a rural working class with *common* economic interests could not and did not exist in the principal regions of the east.

Modern development seeks initially to introduce the principle of *economic rationality* into the wage-forms within this natural economic order. Accordingly the communal remnants (plots of land, threshing shares, grazing rights) are initially abolished. These rights to a share of the revenue decay of necessity, since they are implicated in relations which presuppose the isolation of the individual estates from the wider economy. Under the old system, which did not require special use of machinery, fertilizer, drainage, and so forth, the landlord could effectively claim that the revenue produced was the result of his workers' labour and nothing else. Such a claim disappears with each investment of capital: the gross product of those estates under the influence of the national economy is no longer the labour product of a communal association of labour. Instead, the compensation for the use of the products of alien labour appears (on the basis of capitalist organization) implicitly or explicitly as rent of capital, having a prior claim on the revenue. With this the wage forms based on share-rights disappear, all the more quickly where their existence was in the main the outcome of a deficiency of capital on the part of the entrepreneur and his consequent inability to pay

money-wages. In fact the money-wage is the eventually indispensable correlate of any economic system based on purely
commercial foundations, coercing also agricultural enterprises,
where the particular form in which it appears is that of a piece-
work system where payment is calculated according to performance.

If we wish to understand the full meaning of this slow but
unavoidable transformation, we have to consider more closely the
characteristics of eastern rural labour organization. This involves,
as with the labour relations of any large estates, the manner in
which the most important problems of labour organization in
agricultural enterprises are solved. The fundamental problem is
that in any particular course of cultivation – although far less so in
cattle-rearing – the requirement for labour power during the
different seasons fluctuates considerably. On this basis the
distinction of *permanent* from *seasonal* agricultural workers arises.
From time immemorial the first have been paid mainly in kind,
bound by a contract, and housed on the estate. The latter are paid
principally in money – by day or piece – and customarily brought
in as 'outside' labour and then dismissed. Only in a very large
enterprise can the harvesting be performed with the available
permanent labour (augmented by wives, etc.). No means exist, in
particular no machinery, to redress this differential; indeed the
machinery most often in use, such as threshing machines,
exacerbates it. This is also the case with the increase in intensity of
cultivation, where root crops especially promote seasonal fluctuations of labour-use.

The alteration in labour relations that recent reorganizations of
farm management have given rise to affects both the composition
of the labour force as a whole and the individual categories of
work. The ratio of permanent to seasonal labour is changed, and
in addition to this the complexion of the permanent labour force is
altered to a greater extent than that of the seasonal.

According to the customary arrangements of the farm, the cattle
were tended by unmarried servants, who were also expected to
take some part in work in the fields. In general the need for
permanent field-workers was met by *Instleute*. In payment they
received the shares outlined above from mowing and threshing
(Fifteenth and threshed measure), land in the form of a garden
plot and an allotment in the estate's rotating 'Morgen', and
pasture. They do not possess an individual contractual relation to
the landlord, the family of the labourer is instead subordinated to
his rule and bound as a whole to work with all the means at its
disposal howsoever the lord wishes. At least two workers are
required, such that in the absence of grown children the *Instmann*
had perforce to hire an additional hand. Written contracts and

rights concerning security of work did not originally exist, and the money payments made were for periods outside those of harvest and threshing and were more in the nature of pocket money. It was therefore a purely one-sided relation of subordination in which the working families accommodated on the estate were formally at the unconditional disposition of the landlord. According to some provincial regulations the *Gesindeordnung*[5] was applicable to the *Instleute*, adding to the restrictions on free movement the ability of the landlord to compel the return of any who left without permission. Rights of association are also completely absent.

So much for the permanent labour force. In contrast seasonal labourers were brought in from neighbouring peasant villages wherever the harvest labour of the wives of the *Instleute* was insufficient, and paid money wages under fixed contracts. In earlier times the reapers were also occasionally paid by the piece. They usually did not live on the estate, and their rights at that time approached those of industrial workers. All the other varied categories of estate labour were specific to the northern provinces (others even earlier in Silesia) or arose from local rearrangements or combinations.

This form of labour organization however is now declining. The share-payments described above, and the payments in kind, predominate now only in the northern half of the east: Prussia, Pomerania, Mecklenburg, North Brandenburg, Posen – and are also here disappearing. The type of permanent labour that modern development appears to favour on the large eastern estates is that of the '*Deputant*'. In this case the labourer is bound to work for the whole year, and is housed on the estate either free or for a small rent. In payment he receives a small cash wage, calculated by number of days worked or like the *Gesinde* payment as a fixed yearly sum, and also a so-called '*Deputat*', that is, food in kind corresponding to the board received by the farm-servant. This portion of his pay is reckoned as a sum sufficient to cover the food required by the labourer and his family, for the latter are frequently called upon to provide additional labour.

The contrast with the *Inst* relations consists in the disappearance of the share-rights and their replacement by *fixed* incomes – corresponding to the general features of development outlined above. The rise of the *Deputant* is at the cost of the *Instmann* and of the unmarried farm servant.

However the steady growth of labourers paid entirely or mainly in money eclipses that of the *Deputanten*. At the beginning of the century they did not exist to any notable extent. By 1849 they were nevertheless the fastest growing category of labourers, and this has remained the case. The increase in the demand for labour engendered by the switch to intensive cultivation was not usually met by the engagement of *Instleute*; the landlords sought rather to avoid this, since to employ more such labourers would have involved allotting portions of his land to them at the same time as the value of this land was rapidly rising. A further consideration was that the prosperity of agriculture from the early 1870s made the payment of money wages easier. The landlord also generally lacks the capital these days necessary for the construction of housing suitable to the rising standards of today. As a consequence of these factors, and others concerning the shift of labour-requirements that will be discussed below, there is a *relative* decline in the significance of labourers paid in kind.

The 'free labour contract' thus arrived in the countryside, with a worker paid in money living either in his own or rented property. What are the consequences of this?

The advantage of the married *Deputatknechte* or *Deputat* day-workers supported by payment in kind from the estate was that *additional* labour could be called upon from the single household of the worker. On the one hand they could be cheaply supplied by using the ability of the larger estate to produce objects of consumption without the intervention of intermediaries, and on the other the advantages of the family as a consuming unit could be realized. The advantages of payment in kind can partially be developed further (particularly in the northern provinces), since the supply of goods can take on many different forms. In parts of Silesia the *Deputatknechte* regularly receive, weekly or monthly, portions of meat, potatoes, bread, salt, milk, and linen. They receive also other objects of need – if the expression can be permitted – in the form of manufactured or semi-manufactured consumer goods. With respect to these goods they are consumers in a fashion little different from that typical of servants in receipt of full board. The reason for this is that in Silesia the tendency towards the concentration of land has absorbed the holdings of the one-time bonded subjects, or alternatively prevented them from being founded. In the northern provinces it is usually quite different. Grain is given unmilled and unbaked as *Deputat*, while potatoes only form a part which is made up by the *Deputant* growing his own on land supplied for the purpose. Sometimes he is given seed, at others this has to be individually saved, and even manure has to be found by the *Deputant*. It is just the same with flax: where the old relations still persist, he both sows and harvests it, he also shears the wool from his own sheep grazed on land placed at his disposal, obtains milk and butter from his own cow (which itself is pastured and fed on the estate), has meat from his own pig which in turn is fed out of his payment in kind, and then during the winter the family occupies itself with spinning and weaving. In other words, a substantial part of the process of producing the *Deputant*'s needs is shifted from his master's to his own shoulders, using his own free time (evenings, Sundays, and quiet winter months) and that of his family. The labourer's family thus becomes indispensable for the reproduction of the labour force, and the family community becomes in this way useful to the landlord not only as an association of consumers, but also as an association of producers. If we for a moment disregard the social aspects of the question, the principle of economic rationality appears as follows: it permits the reduction of the costs of maintenance and reproduction of the labour force to a minimum, presenting a much better outcome for the landlord than that which can be found in Silesia. For the same given standard of nutrition, the landlord in the northern provinces has considerably less work to do, since apart from supplying a house all other factors are either in the form of raw materials or natural forces – the production and processing of a satisfactory level of food and other goods is then left to the labourer.[6] Or to put it in another way: with the same (or less) expense he makes it possible for the family of the labourer to enjoy a relatively higher standard of living. The landlord is thus able to stretch his labour power to the ultimate conceivable extent, and under the same conditions this clearly does not happen in Silesia. This has nothing to do with the menial cultural level of the Polish working population in Silesia, but rather is caused by the neglect of the potential productive powers of the purely consumer domestic economy.

This divergence in the condition of the north-eastern estate labourer from that of the Silesian certainly does not result from considerations of economic rationality. The difference arises instead on historical grounds.

The Silesian *Deputatknecht* has clearly visible origins, placed as he is in the position of a modified house servant. His household is barely separated from that of the estate, his situation approaches that of a boarding servant. This is shown by the fact that it is usual for the *Deputatknecht* and his wife to have separate contracts in which separate amounts of payment and produce are specified, but which when taken together add up to the typical requirements of a worker's family and its children. The Silesian *Deputant* is a product of the beginning of the emancipation of the house servant from the patriarchal household.

In the north the situation is different. Here the *Deputant*-form for the remuneration of permanent labour developed very slowly and is not yet generalized; and in any case it is likely that the present changes in labour organization will lead to the establishment of *purely* monetary conditions. The northern *Deputant* is far from a servant emancipated from the master's kitchens. The form of remuneration is adapted from that of estate officials: bailiffs, chamberlains, attendants, and so on were always maintained in this fashion. The majority of the *Deputanten* in the north developed from the independent cultivators bound to particular services – the modern *Deputant* stands at the end of a process that has its origins in the antiquity of modern agricultural estates. At that time the situation existed (although evidence is only local) whereby labour was not performed for the lord, but rather produce was delivered to defray the costs of his household. The manor (*Grundherrschaft*) corresponded to the household of the lord (but not to an estate economy), the lord, on the basis of political domination, drawing his subsistence from the dependent holdings; and it was the latter which were the sole agricultural producers. On this basis there developed, as in England, the other elements of the patriarchal economy: lord and subjects worked the dependent holdings supplying at the same time the labour for the estate economy. In England this remained a transitory phase, the lord soon returning to the use of his subjects as independent small producers owing him tribute, with the difference that instead of receiving produce he received money rents. By contrast, in eastern Germany the natural-economic foundation of the landlord developed further, on account of the backwardness of monetary relations, at the expense of his subjects. Only a few of the latter managed to escape with some land from the oppressive embrace of the manor, taking advantage of any opportunities that arose. In general however the earlier conditions returned, the lord becoming a solitary entrepreneur, his subjects, instead of him, drawing their subsistence from the estate.

This process is, as emphasized, not yet complete in the north, mostly on account of the economic weakness of the landlords. Their lack of capital saved those peasants trapped by by-laws and regulations. Otherwise, if the landlords had possessed enough resources to farm larger areas, large sections of the peasantry might have disappeared as they were bought out. A shortage of capital and the consequent inability to pay wages in cash prevented the complete proletarianization of those peasants and rural workers who were forced to the margins, or slowly dispossessed. Remuneration in the form of product-shares, allotments, and grazing rights had to be retained, since these were the only forms of payment that the landlords could afford. In this way a respite was given to hundreds of thousands of hybrid independent holdings in the east – the *Inst* holdings (in the restricted sense, excluding *Deputanten*). The dual nature of these labourers who both were supplied with land and shared in the produce of the estate, part small cultivators, part shareholder in the lord's economy, has been discussed above. It is characteristic of this relation that the complete subordination of the worker to the will of the landlord is combined with a common economic interest. The *Deputanten*, combining with and replacing the *Instleute* as the value of the land rises and intensive cultivation is adopted, find with the replacement of product-shares by fixed payments and the withdrawal of allotments that the risks previously affecting labourers are reduced, and that there is in some respects an improvement in their position. Simultaneously their budget is more sharply detached from that of the estate economy and the *Deputanten* are in this way made more independent. Any further pruning of the *Instmann*'s 'petty entrepreneur' status, and every increase in the relative significance of money payments, has the same effect, appearing as an improvement on the position of the older form of *Instmann*. This decline of 'petty entrepreneurship' does not stop with the *Deputanten*. The principal strong point of payments in kind – as we saw – was that the individual household supplied to the estate *multiple* labour power. The workers are however increasingly unable to supply such a number of hands. After their period of military service their own children tended to remain away, and only the lowest strata become the hirelings (*Scharwerker*) of the *Instmann*. It is certain that the days of such employment are numbered.

The result of this however is that the advantages to the landlord of rendering payment in kind dissolve – he cannot afford to supply the goods needed by a whole family and only receive half the labour, so he reduces the amount and leaves the family short of its requirements. On both sides then money payments become necessary. The money payment has apparently the great advantage of the worker knowing precisely what he receives; the value tendered by the landlord, always problematic in the case of payment in kind, is made absolutely clear.

It is however not always the case that the legal and formal fixing of payment-levels leads to an improvement in the situation of the workers. This is shown clearly in the case of developments in Silesia.

In Silesia, especially Middle and Lower Silesia, economic enterprises had taken on a commercial-capitalistic character earlier than in the north, and at the same time the legal relation of the labourers to the estate was more well-defined than in the north. We find here even in the first half of the century a category of labourers involved in threshing whose economic position fully corresponds to that of the *Instleute*. The difference in their situation was twofold. Firstly they possessed (in contrast to the '*Robotgärtner*'[7] of Upper Silesia) inherited property rights with rights and duties that imposed legal boundaries on the ability of the landlords to control them. On the other hand the economic domination of the Silesian magnates was incomparably greater than that of the northern landlords. Put together, these two factors had serious consequences. The relation was not so flexible as that of the *Instleute*, and the constitution of the estate economies as the sole and rational property of the landlord therefore shattered it. The landlords forced the dissolution of labour-duties and also product-shares, and the threshers were made into formally-free smallholders no longer bound to work on the estate, but also no longer entitled to a share in its product, and thus still dependent on working for the estate. The increased need for labour was covered by the landlords by introducing equivalents of *Instleute*, called '*Lohngärtner*' who were housed next to the previous threshers in newly-built family cottages with small allotments. Depending on the capitalization of each landlord, the labour relations were calculated on a monetary basis; the smallholder received from the beginning usually only a money payment, while the *Lohngärtner* also had land and grazing – but in both cases in far smaller proportions than those enjoyed by the northern *Instmann*. It is typical of the traditional rural wage structure that the smallholder receives after his conversion to money payment little more than that received by the *Instmann* in addition to payment in kind, and has as a money wage the same as that received by a fieldworker or other propertyless labourer, who in addition has a secure domicile and allotment.

The landlords have come to think that they advance housing and land to the propertyless workers gratis. Historically and economically quite the reverse is true: the piece of land and the house (which is in any case not guaranteed by the landlord but possessed by the labourer) advanced to the smallholder is *offset against his wage*. This corresponds to the manner in which landlords have come to regard the wage question. If when talking with landowners from Saxony for instance (where the employment of landed workers from villages is growing) the previously typical wage of one Mark is criticized, the immediate response is: since the workers have their own land they are not dependent on this wage. This shows how irrelevant juridical forms are when faced with the overwhelming power of traditional economic relations. The work performed in the fields is not the standard for the payment of wages, but rather the minimum needs of the worker under a traditional style of life. This is as true for the *Deputanten* as for the pure wage-labourers – the levels of remuneration are from district to district quite diverse, and are based on historical, gradually developing levels of subsistence. It is this that determines the wage, and not vice versa. Because of this the treatment of the *Instleute* as bonded associates in the northern patriarchal form, rather than as free labourers, was from the point of view of the worker a distinct advantage. It can be said that precisely because of the formally limitless powers of the landlords the constancy of the traditional skills of the labourers enabled them to improve their material position in terms of subsistence with the gradual rise in gross output. Only on a much weaker level can the same be said for the payments to the *Deputanten*.

In the system of money payments things are quite different. The payments in kind to the *Instleute* and to a lesser extent to the *Deputanten* were met from the rising gross revenues consequent on switching part of the risk and part of the production process to the responsibility of the labourer; while the money payments were met from falling net revenues without a corresponding change. This ensured the collapse of the purely economic advantages mentioned above. The fact that a section of the labourers possessed their own land had nearly uniformly unfavourable effects, since their immoveability and the corresponding influence on the calculation of wages squeezed wages generally. The smallholder was barred from the communal economy of the estate; unlike the corn-selling *Instmann*, he possessed no interest in common with the landlord, but on the contrary was involved in a conflict of interest with him over the sale of bread. It was not in the latter's material interest however to create a formal juridical barrier (which would be resistant to alteration by the exercise of economic power) in the form of a grant of property to the worker. For this reason the formal and complete power of disposition given to the landlord in the patriarchal relations of domination transformed into a commercial form. For the labourer then the possibility of brutal personal domination that could be only escaped by flight gave way to commercial exploitation which, arising almost unnoticed, was actually much harder to evade and which as a smallholder he was not in a position to do. Formal equality then placed the labourers in a struggle of interests for which, dispersed far over the land as they were, they lacked the means of resistance.

If we refer to the *Inst* relation here as 'patriarchal' and characterized by a 'community of interest' between the labourers and the landlords, this should not be taken to mean that there was as a consequence of this an atmosphere of personal trust. All that is being claimed is that a secure common bond of interest tied labourer and landlord into a relation where patriarchal direction of the communal economy was effective, whereas the displacement of this relation through money-wages abolished the common interest and rendered such direction ineffective. The patriarchal system of labour relations expressed honestly the fact that the rural labourer did not stand in a contractual relation, but one of personal subordination to the landlord. *This honesty is its strength*. This does however presuppose a resigned, unemancipated working population like the eastern *Instleute*, and such conditions are fast disappearing. Not only the employer but also the labourer prefers a position as *Deputant* instead of one as *Instmann*, money payments instead of payment in kind, and lack of legal restraints instead of contractual relations. With this transformation a necessary condition of the patriarchal relation collapses: the connection to *one particular* estate. The differentiation between various categories of labour are reduced, and the employer becomes as 'fungible' for the rural worker as he already is for the industrial labourer. In other words, this process of development brings the rural labourers steadily closer to the form of a *unified* class of a proletarian type in its material conditions of life, a state already attained by the industrial proletariat.

For the reasons indicated above, capitalist enterprise struggles to detach itself from the system of payment in kind, despite its economic advantages – the labourer seeks money wages which free him from the dependence and good will of the landlord despite the economic decline that is a result. Just as money rent appeared to the medieval peasant as the most important sign of his personal freedom, so does the money wage appear to today's worker. The rural workforce forsakes positions that are often more favourable, always more secure, in a search for personal emancipation. This decisive psychological factor is quite unconscious, but all the more effective for it. This labour force, whose ambitions to climb into the position of the employer are normally as feeble as those of the industrial workers, conceives this transformation as the stage preparatory to a *class struggle*. But it is also evident that the landlords have begun to change into a more or less uniform class of commercial entrepreneurs. So here as well the process of modern development replaces the personal relations of domination with impersonal class-rule, with all its psychological consequences.

What will the result of this be? Will the struggle develop in a manner similar to that in industry? Is there a possibility that over a period the organization of workers will create a rural labour aristocracy as has emerged in England, whereby thorough proletarianization engenders in turn a movement made up of the highest levels of the workers?

Unfortunately the prospects of rural class struggle are not as bright as this.

If we try to outline the effects on the general situation of the rural working population of the reorganization of economic activity in accordance with the imperatives of international competition, we find at once that an 'average enterprise' does not exist. Forty or fifty years ago an eastern estate of 500 hectares or more with average sandy soil could be taken as typical, but no more: machinery, intensive cattle-rearing, and a reliance on root crops on the one hand, emancipation from three-field systems and extensive pasture on the other, have altered matters. No longer does intensive grain cultivation and moderate cattle-rearing rule the farming enterprise. We will now try to show how the transformation of the enterprise according to commercial principles influences the aspects that interest us here.

This question is simple if we are dealing with a transition to exclusive (or predominant) cattle-rearing. The result in this case is a marked *reduction* in the labour force. This is particularly true of Germany, since the English intensive system has not been adopted, but rather a comparatively extensive form of pasturing requiring a minimum of labour. This has particular repercussions on the seasonal workers employed during the summer and harvesting.

The consequences for intensive cultivation (drilling of cereals, heavy use of artificial fertilizer, use of threshing machines, general application of machinery, intensive root cultivation, etc.) are more interesting and in comparison with more traditional methods not so straightforward. First, the particular forms in which this transition is expressed are not equivalent in their effects. But they do have one thing in common: the significant increase of *summer* work in relation to *winter* work, combined with the absolute increase of labour requirements *in general*. This latter aspect was the first to develop, followed later by the former. The intensity of cultivation and the proportion of permanent workers to the cultivated area began to rise slowly at first; while the proportion of seasonal workers increased more rapidly. As the trend developed or a faster transition to intensive cultivation took place the increase in seasonal workers predominated, in cases of rapid change being accompanied by a relative or even absolute decrease in the permanent labour force. This last case, where the number of permanently employed workers decreases – not a general phenomenon, but predominating in those areas where migrant labour was regularly employed – might appear surprising. The reason for this development is, as will be discussed in more detail below, related to the mode of organization of the enterprise. Traditionally this was aimed at minimizing the seasonal differences in the distribution of work, attempting to keep the available labour permanently occupied and thus as far as possible moderating the seasonal character of agriculture. The object was thus to distribute the necessary work as far as possible through the year. On the other hand it was just as simple to do the reverse, altering the disposition of labourers rather than that of work: for example, work normally carried out during the winter months could be transferred to summer and autumn workers. This had the effect of *emphasizing* the seasonal character of agricultural enterprise and reducing not inconsiderably the need for permanent labour. The condition for this course was naturally that seasonal workers were freely available, which was not the case in the traditional organization of farming.

Things turned out differently if intensive cultivation was adopted. Here the need for seasonal labour was reinforced and was met by the increase of seasonal money wages. This gave rise, when combined with modern means of travel, to a new class of workers: migrant workers, who were exclusively *seasonal* agricultural labourers. They came first from overpopulated or extensively farmed areas, and represented a surplus population. After a time however such migrant employment was adopted by increasing sections of rural labour, this newly created seasonal workforce being heavily drawn on by the intensive enterprises. Piece rates increase performance, but the workers are themselves more willing to work; Polish girls who at home have no such wages to spur them on here work exceptionally hard. The migrant worker, torn from his family and usual environment, is regarded as simple labour power both by the landlords and by himself. The barracks of the migrant workers are the money-economy equivalents of the slave barracks of antiquity. The estate owner saves on workers' housing, since accommodation for the migrant costs little or nothing. He also has no need to allocate plots of land, but above all he is not regulated by laws governing conditions of work and pay. Thus while the seasonal wage rates are higher, taken over the year the employer lays out no more, usually less, than he used to for a resident worker through the year. The disadvantages of the money-wage from the point of view of economic rationality are in this way more than balanced. In some parts of Silesia these migrant workers are regarded as the core of the working population.

What are the reasons from the worker's point of view for the adoption of migration? The prime cause appears to be the difference in the level of wages. However the surveys of the *Verein für Sozialpolitik* and the Protestant Social Congress show that where such differences, or related factors, do not arise, migration still takes place, neighbouring districts exchanging labourers either directly or indirectly. A combination of economic and psychological factors explains this. The migrant would not accept at home the kind of living conditions (and diet is not the only, or even principle, factor here)[8] that are offered to him by a distant place of work. Because of this lower standard and because of the lack of the usual additional tasks that face him in his home he is able to save significant amounts from his wages even when they are no higher than the local rates, something that would not have been possible had he not migrated. In addition to this he can, during the workless winter months, have a 'holiday'. But above all, migration removes the necessity of seeking work from the local *estate* owners. Local employment is historically and mentally associated with traditional power relations – it is the urge for personal freedom that drives the worker to employment away from his home. They sacrifice their accustomed conditions in their aspiration for emancipation: their apathy is shattered. The oft lamented 'mobilization' of the rural labourer at the same time sets in motion the beginnings of class struggle.

We can see that the consequences of a calculated 'involvement in the world economy' on the part of eastern agricultural enterprises of a size – those particularly large estates – which prevents a transition to intensive cattle-rearing are substantial for the local class structure. If extensive cattle-rearing is adopted at the behest of the international division of production the value of agricultural products and the population figures fall. If they adopt intensive arable cultivation the relative, and sometimes absolute, significance of permanent workers declines, promoting on the other hand fluidity in the working population and thereby threatening the stability of the population structure through a modern nomadism. It is clear then that the competitiveness of foreign producers rests on their *lower* cultural level, on unimpaired natural forces and the absence of the direct social costs that the population density and standards of an older culture create. If the agricultural enterprises of the east, based as they are on land that is of no particular quality, wish to remain competitive then they have to step down the cultural ladder, in cultivation as well as in the social level of the worker and employer.

This fateful situation has momentous significance for the material situation of the rural labourer (i.e. their provisions) when free competition appears for the first time as the organizing principle of the rural labour market. The traditional mode of calculating wages in the lowlands involved only partially and indirectly a purely economic assessment of the income and subsistence relations of the worker, and was on the contrary determined by those factors that shook the traditional rural relations themselves. This is the case with each of the changes introduced by the management of modern enterprises.

Consider the most important of these factors which can possibly have an influence of the situation of the labourer – they are:

(1) the differing *sizes* of the individual enterprises;
(2) the varying qualities of the soil;
(3) the differing intensities of cultivation;
(4) the distribution of landed property.

With respect to the first of these, it appears simple to state that: the larger the enterprise, the fewer permanent labourers are needed in proportion to the cultivated area. A reduction in the number of permanent labourers in relation to *cultivated area*, given constant quality of land and intensity of cultivation, appears in addition to be regularly associated with an improvement in their position.[9] This is analogous to industrial experience, and is natural since in these cases all that is involved is a more rational disposition of the available labour force and the saving of unproductive dependents. Following from this – and corresponding to experience – the position of the workers in large enterprises is better than that of those in smaller, all other things being equal. This principle ceases to be true however as soon as an attempt is made to compare differing intensities of enterprise, in particular if one considers estates from different areas not directly neighbouring each other which possess a range of labour relations and workers with different cultural levels. Comparability exists only for local districts with similar traditional relations. And it is yet another question if we consider how the situation of workers on peasant farms relates to that of those who work on large estates. Enterprises can only be directly compared with each other which possess similar social characteristics.

It is the same in the case of quality of land. The better land requires during the harvest period a greater amount of labour, although in general the increase in permanent labour required rises more slowly than the yield. There is also an effect on the shares of the *Instmann* which, other things being equal, tends to raise his income; this is also to some extent the case with the *Deputanten*. As far as money payments go, there is no certain connection of its level with the qualities of land in immediately neighbouring districts, local factors predominate here like the isolation of the estate. If regions of four or five districts with similar conditions of land and types of cultivation are taken, a clearer relation between wage-rates and quality of land can be detected.[10] This relation ceases as soon as the provincial level is considered, and in fact it goes into reverse if the net yields of Silesia are compared with those of the north. The reason for this is contained in the relations and organization of labour.

Both of the factors that have just been discussed are of far lesser significance than the form of labour relations and the nationality of the worker. Let us now consider the influence of the third factor mentioned above: the rising or falling intensity of cultivation. A reduction of intensity – whether of labour or capital – is for the remaining large enterprises in the east identical with the displacement of field-labour by cattle-rearing; whereas on the other hand an increase compared with the traditional method of cultivation can take the form of intensive cattle raising – this is associated with increased capitalization of the enterprise – or of intensive arable cultivation – in which case the intensity of capital and labour is increased.

The transition to exclusive (or predominant) cattle-raising in large enterprises seems, where there is a sharp reduction in the number of workers, in fact to make the situation of the workers more favourable, as long as this transition is principally engendered by climatic considerations.[11] The data on this question is not available, and it does not really concern us here: there is the notable and interesting effect however that the increase of cattle-rearing at the expense of arable significantly *reduces* the number of workers and consequently the lowland population.

The intensive arable cultivation that concerns us here does not lead to such a reduction in the labour force, since the replacement of human by mechanical labour plays a much smaller role in agriculture than in industry. It leads more at first – as shown already above – to a displacement within the working population, reducing the proportion of permanent workers in relation to the total numbers of workers employed. A discussion of the manner in which material and social conditions affect the permanent and seasonal workers remains for our consideration.

Intensive agricultural cultivation clearly implies a tendency toward the improvement of the cultural level and living standards of the population. Where a majority of the smallholders achieve the benefits of rising yields in full the result must be a hesitant rise in the aspirations of all levels of the population, including the labourers. The question is problematic however for the labourer under the domination of the large estate. Where the worker under secure labour relations has grown used to high levels of subsistence such aspirations can meet with satisfaction. This is the case in Mecklenburg, East Holstein, and sections of Pomerania. The possibility of the contrary is shown by the poor position of labourers in the parts of Silesia that are intensively cultivated, the relations obtaining here having already been discussed above, and where also of course the labourers are partly of foreign nationality. The higher or lower intensity of cultivation, like the quality of the soil, can thus be seen as having in itself beneficial consequences, but these can only be decisive via the social division of the labour force and its customs (*Rassengewohnheiten*). It is the *organization* of *labour relations*, that is the social division and grouping of the rural labour force, which decides their material situation; but as we have seen, the monetary restructuring of these relations threatens the material situation of the labourer. The reorganization of the enterprise, which these monetary relations more or less completely engenders, contains the same danger. In the case of intensive farming this is indeed the case.

It was emphasized above that so long as the labour relations remained unaltered in principle, then for intensive arable cultivation there was at first a relative increase in the proportion of permanent labourers in relation to the land. Under the same assumption their incomes increased as well. Since the old *Instmann* was paid by shares, his earnings rose, all other things being equal;[12] and this did not necessarily change even though general agricultural improvements resulted in a consistent decline in the share-rate (this is always so with the introduction of mechanical threshing).[13]

Later, as we saw, the share relation was displaced completely and a fixed *Deputat* put in its place. With this the participation of the labourer in rising yields ended, but this did not automatically signify a worsening of the situation either from the general point of view, or from that of subsistence. On the contrary, initially there was often an improvement by virtue of the security and regulation of a set amount of necessary goods. It did mean however that the removal of a share of corn from the threshing led to a shift towards potatoes at the expense of cereals in the worker's budget, and this can be seen clearly in the reports. Together with this there was a general trend from payment in kind to payment in money, a step therefore on the road to proletarianization, which meant above all a break with the traditional means of subsistence.

One hundred years ago the typical diet of the rural worker consisted of cereals and milk, with meat on rare occasions. Since then potatoes have taken the place of the 'daily bread', and this is not so unimportant as it might seem. It is not a question of whether the relative increase in the place of potatoes in the popular diet in itself was a bad thing. On the contrary, the need to feed so many mouths from the same piece of land determined the food to be grown. What is important from the point of view of the general level of nutrition is what is eaten in addition to potatoes, since they have the characteristic of filling the stomach and giving the sensation of physical satisfaction, without giving the body the protein (*Eiweißstoffe*) that it needs.

Since the Middle Ages we have experienced an alteration in nutrition whereby the increase in meat consumption at the expense of cereals has accompanied cultural development. The virtually exclusive cereal diet of the rural population was perhaps one of the major contributing physiological factors of their psychic nature – apathy and tractability. In this century the consumption of meat began again to be a cultural measure, and the typical diet of the rising modern proletariat is increasingly based on meat and potatoes – apart from schnapps, of course. The last replaces only too easily, although only apparently, the nutritive value needed above that given by potatoes. It is on the whole decisive for popular nutrition then whether an appropriate protein intake (be it meat or milk) balances the increased consumption of potatoes. In the case of the rural labourer, the fate of his livestock is of great significance from the point of view of both social standing and suitable nutrition. This is the objective and subjective centre of his household, the basis of useful work on the part of the wife and children *within* the household in the general interest of the family. But this is precisely what is most sharply attacked by the switch to intensive arable cultivation, the rising value of the land leading to the ploughing-up of meadowland and pasture.

We find thus in some areas, but especially where root crops and livestock farming predominate, first the restriction and then the disappearance of individually held geese, sheep, and cows. Only pigs remain. This overthrows the old forms of provisioning the family from the estate, serving now only consumption and not family production. The labourer becomes then a proletarian, and for the sake of his freedom he needs a money wage. For this reason also there is a necessary progression beyond the present circumstances, as in the case of Silesian *Lohngärtner*, since a proletarianized, propertyless labourer cannot afford to accept the position of *Instmann*. The extent of his own possessions (furnishings, livestock, etc.) and the significance of his own holding are inversely related, as can be seen from the insurance statistics for Mecklenburg wage-labourers compared with those in Silesia. It is also for this reason that the number of 'free' labourers paid entirely in money who replace the *Instleute* as permanent workers is declining. For them potatoes are the main item of diet, **grain** and meat consumption being very low. While it is reported everywhere that the material conditions of the free labourers are inferior to those of the *Instleute*, it is on the other hand clear that they form an ever-growing section of the permanent labour force. The demand for such labourers has grown rapidly in the last few years for the reasons outlined above, and the wages paid to them in money risen while the payments in kind to contract labourers have remained steady. These 'free' labourers were previously inhabitants of villages who earned a little on the side, a numerically large and at the same time lowest section of the population, even in 1849 occasional receivers of alms and finding work both within and without agriculture. They are now a group whose relative significance is steadily rising. The levels of wages paid to them are tending to be equalized in the larger districts with comparable labour relations, on the basis of a level typical in 1873 only of the richer areas. In contrast the transformation of *Instleute* into *Deputanten* regularly levelled out the rate of payments to the contract labourers at a sum similar to, but not much greater than, that paid in the *least favourable areas* (although not the worst); frequently because of the removal of livestock it was pushed below it. The increased wages of the free labourer produced only in the most favourable cases a material situation which was equivalent to the total income of the *Deputanten*, at whose cost their numbers increased.

A general result which we have noted for those areas in which patriarchal labour relations prevail is a depression of the standard of living of the rural labourer to a level previously enjoyed by their proletarian social inferiors, combined with a declassing of their highest levels and an increasing separation from connections with smallholding. We have in addition noted a steady emergence of capitalist labour relations, and where these have existed for some time (for example in Silesia) we find the lowest wages and the poorest material and social living conditions, both developed to a pitch to which the workers are resigned. In contrast then to the tendency to the emergence of a labour aristocracy as in highly capitalized English industry, capitalist development here creates a homogenous proletarian mass among the permanent workers. It would indeed be curious if any other consequence followed, since the most intensive cultivation (beet) requires large amounts of unqualified labour, and the demand for skilled labour, while not being completely absent from modern agricultural production, is in no way as significant numerically as in industry at a high level of technical development.

These circumstances are most decisive for the growing body of migrant labour, highlighting the national contradictions of the east.[14] Since the abolition of the ban on Polish migrants (1890) there has not only been a movement from Prussia to Saxony (*Sachsengängerei*), but in addition to the eastern provinces from Russian Poland and Galicia and even further afield – some from as far as Wetterau! These foreign nomads numbered recently – contemporary figures are not available – around 30,000 per year in the four border provinces. It is particularly the cultivation of sugar beet, requiring little in terms of the quality of labour, which has attracted them.

It is not those workers with the higher living conditions that are favoured, but those with the lowest. This situation is not solely produced by the purely economic interests of the estate owners, but is bound up indirectly with their local authority. The control over the Poles is limitless: one nod, and the local administrator – who is also an estate owner – sends him back to Poland. The introduction of Poles is here a weapon in the anticipated class struggle which is directed against the growing consciousness of the workers, and it is obvious that in this connection it is a very effective weapon. The argument over whether domestic migration has given rise to emigrant workers, or vice versa, will never end; but in any case the result is the same in both cases, since both increase in relation to each other being as they are weapons in a struggle between property and labour. Migration is a tacit strike, and the inflow of Poles a means of combating it.

In this struggle the *distribution of landed property* in the east takes on a fateful role. Those categories of holding which have a deficit of labour are naturally those which employ foreign labour – partly large peasants, but increasingly the estates of the nobility (*Rittergüter*). The peasant is of course not in a position to plan the import of Poles, but the estate owner is; and if he wishes to farm on an intensive basis he is forced to do so. He cannot even satisfy his need for harvest workers out of the local labour available to him, and this is because his neighbouring district is made up of estates that do not 'produce', but rather 'consume', labour power – or in other words, because of the absence of villages. The average population density in the estate districts is only a portion of that usually prevailing in rural areas, which is to be expected since such estates do not feed a local, but a foreign market. Where a policy of deliberate interior colonization has led to the formation of a strong peasant strata (as in Mecklenburg), there are few complaints of labour shortage and migration is low. In those areas where the estates have destroyed the peasantry, this history is avenged by the absence of a labour force. It is no accident that it is in the east where large estates predominate that the figures for debt are highest and there is the greatest deficiency of labour. The 'Sins of the Fathers' are visited on contemporary estate owners and threaten us all with a Slavic invasion (*slavische Überflutung*) which could mean a cultural regression of major proportions.

In this can be seen the hopelessness of the struggle for both parties. The class struggle in eastern agriculture is a vain and hopeless combat in which both property and labour will suffer. This is all the more certain on the part of labour, since even after the abolition of proscriptions on unionization it will of necessity remain unorganized. The right of association, which for the workers offers only formal legality, will apart from local cases not serve as a means of struggle because their dispersion permanently obstructs constructive use of such a right. Even after the present ongoing process of proletarianization has reduced them to equality, there is no possibility of a general union on the basis of common interests of groups with divergent interests.

The fact that in the countryside the income of the workers has in many cases increased, sometimes considerably, will serve as consolation only for do-gooders and the representatives of the landlords' interests. In fact the situation will in time become as bad in such areas in terms of class contradictions as it is in industry, and the growing problems are not confined to a simple 'shortage of labour'. There is as major a transformation taking place in the character of the landowner as in that of his workers in which the state has to defer to both, while stripping the first of their status as trustees. This transformation involves a major relocation of the population and cultural dangers for both production and the workers, and these consequences are not from the purely political viewpoint insignificant.

The establishment of these unhappy circumstances might be nothing more than an expression of a sociopolitical Jeremiad of a sort so fashionable these days, if the developmental tendencies outlined above had the character of ruling natural laws. *But this is not the case*, the effects noted can only develop under specific conditions engendered by the distribution of landed property in the east in combination with the political aspirations of a sinking class. Otherwise these factors should appear in the west where the form of landholding is the same, and this has not happened – which is not to say that in similar areas of the south and west there are no problems to be found. For the economic changes that have been presented here it is not a matter of indifference, or of slight numerical significance, if the large estates occupy either 20 per cent or 50 per cent of the land-area: *it is rather quite the opposite*. In the period of crisis that now prevails in agriculture as a result of competition, one hundred thousand peasants relate to their home soil in a different way to one hundred thousand workers.

The precondition for the state's intervention in the cultural question that has appeared – I do not believe that this phrase overestimates the significance of the conditions of the rural workers – is to abandon the notion that the present distribution of landed property in the east is the untouchable basis of a political and social order within which *radical* interventions cannot be contemplated. The dangers of intensive cultivation, and of the state of the world market in so far as it does not favour intensive cultivation, relate in the east the fate of our culture with the present distribution of landed property. The typical and average 'sandy soils' of the east, excluding perhaps areas of the best and the worst soils, finds itself, to the disadvantage of cultivation and the cultural level of the workers, trapped in these property relations and held together by the golden hooks of mortgage debts.

The organization of labour can also not be changed without a corresponding alteration in the distribution of property. As Kaerger has shown quite convincingly, good labour relations are to be found at present among the hired workers in Westphalia and among the farmworkers of Eastern Holstein. In both cases there can be found a combination of allotments with labour contracts. The labourers receive land and pasture for rent from the estate for a specific sum; they work on the estate for day wages, the claims and debts of each being reckoned together. Here we have the *Inst* relation, but with security of tenure and without the bonds that the *Instmann* suffers – free labour contracts in addition to a smallholding for the labourer. While it might happen in places that the labourers in the east under the present system of property resolve to adopt the position of the smallholder, it would be an illusion to think that this could occur in general. Knapp emphasized quite rightly that the process of development was in general taking the contrary course. It is obvious from the position of the labourer. Intensive cultivation has had *one* benefit for him, but a cultural one that is not in itself material: he has tasted *freedom* and he increasingly inclined to sacrifice his material welfare in his aspirations towards this end. Under the present division of property he cannot entertain the prospect – and it is this rather than the objective possibility which is critical – of improving himself while living in his home district. Under such conditions he draws the following unconscious, but certain, conclusion: under the rule of large estates and farms in the countryside homelessness and freedom are the same thing.

The most important problem then is thus interior settlement, from the point of view of the rural labour question as well.

This is today in the hands of two bodies: the Settlement Commission established by the state; and the General Commission, which negotiates between private landowners the pruning of their estates. The Settlement Commission has already settled around 1,500 peasants, whereas the General Commission has dealt with around 6,000. This numerical superiority of private settlement has however two hidden aspects. First, it creates mostly dwarf holdings. It is these that can most easily bear the pressure today on prices, since they for the most part consume their own product and suffer no shortage of labour, since they do not employ wage-labour. There is nevertheless the danger that this section of the population will settle for the lowest possible cultural aspirations, creating in this way that horror of horrors – a landowning *proletariat*. The second problem is that the General Commission does not possess the means to equip the new settlements adequately. For the smallholders this is a critical matter.

It is thus essential that the state concern itself directly in these problems, taking up again the project abandoned in the 1870s of settling the state-owned lands.

On the other hand no one who appreciates the situation would wish for a diminution of state lands and the consequent deprivation of an important means of regulation in the agricultural sector.

Only the most foolish fear of 'Expropriation' prevents more people from expressing what everyone is thinking anyway: that a major part of large landed property in the east cannot be maintained in private hands. It would be possible through state agencies, not precipitately but rather systematically and gradually, to *buy up* this property and transform it into state property, to rent it out to wealthy farmers and furnish them with loans for improvements. In this way that which was laid out on the one hand is got back with the other, and *over a period* this would be to the good of the state's financial interests. This is clearly a major task, which has never been approached in *this* form. It is not possible to entrust this task to just any State Land administration. I do not believe one can be suspected of flattery however if one recognizes that German administrations – not only in Prussia, but also Mecklenburg and Baden – have shown their preparedness for assuming the task which in the highest interests of the nation would be given to them. It is to be hoped that the future fulfils the promise of the past.

Notes

* Translator's note: this is a translation of the version of 'Entwickelungs-tendenzen in der Lage der ostelbischen Landarbeiter' that appears in Weber's *Gesammelte Aufsätze zur Sozial- und Wirtschaftsgeschichte* (1924) pp. 470–507; which is a revised version of the original article that appeared under the same title in *Archiv für soziale Gesetzgebung und Statistik* Bd. 7, 1894, pp. 1–41. The revisions that were made were relatively minor: discussion and criticism of the other *Verein* reports was excluded, the introduction altered, and the five-paragraph section on interior colonization was added to the end of the original.

As other translators have noted, rendering Weber into clear and consistent English is not always an easy task; in some instances ambiguous phrasing has been allowed to stand, in others it has been altered to suit the drift of the narrative. However, the construction of a well-ordered narrative was not Weber's strong point, so that rambling sentences are often followed by a series of short, pithy ones which, however, are not designed to emphasize any particular point, and which frequently present statements at random. Steps have therefore been taken to both break up some of the overlong, and obscure, sentences and paragraphs, while at the same time amalgamating shorter sentences.

In addition to these stylistic considerations, the terminology used by Weber presents some difficulty. Some of the categories of labour that he uses have been adopted unaltered and explained in the notes; in general '*Arbeiter*' has been rendered as 'labourer' rather than 'worker' because of the context. There is some difficulty with the term '*Arbeitsverfassung*' which is frequently used by Weber, and is variously translated here as 'labour relations' or 'organization of labour'. The problem here is that '*Verfassung*' means literally 'constitution' as in the 'British Constitution', and is used by Weber and others to denote the ensemble of legal, economic, and political conditions governing the employment of labour and the relation of labourers to specified persons. Since there is no obvious term or phrase in English for this, it has been translated as indicated, although the reader should note the deficiency of this rendering.

1. Translator's note: international competition plays a major part in the analysis conducted by Weber here, for in grains and dairy produce Germany was being seriously affected at this time by the restructuring, and creation, of new markets. For an analysis of the relation of political and economic problems involved which coincides in some measure with that of Weber, see Alexander Gerschenkron: *Bread and Democracy in Germany* (1966, University of California).

2. Translator's note: *Instmann*, plural *Instleute*, also *Instverhältnisse* rendered here as '*Inst* relations'. While the dependent status of these landless labourers, hired by the year and paid partly in kind and partly in money, and for this period allotted a strip of land, might appear to be semi-feudal, it would be inaccurate to translate this category with one drawn from English feudality. Weber goes on to argue in fact that this form of labour is not a *relic*, but a creation of the changes taking place in agriculture. Likewise with *Deputant*, plural *Deputanten*, who are paid in the form of a *Deputat*.

3. Translator's note: the reference here is to Max Sering, German agronomist and member of the *Verein*.

4. A good number of the cases where there has been a transition to exclusive or predominant livestock rearing on good soil have been prompted not by market conditions but rather by a shortage of labour – even in the instances where the enterprise is run on intensive lines.

5. Translator's note: the *Gesindeordnungen* were introduced in 1810, enabling

the landlords to retain the use of the families of their ex-serfs and bringing the labourer under the laws governing domestic servants. In particular, the labour of the wife and children could be used by the landlord in his house or on the estate without payment. Rights of association were expressly denied by these regulations.

6.   Even the seemingly anachronistic production-form of domestic spinning and weaving arises in this case on principles of economic rationality. Although the labour expended in the creation of clothing here is many times that 'socially necessary', it would otherwise be unemployed during the winter months.

7.   Translator's note: 'Robot' here is a term derived from the Slavic word for work; its use here implies both overwork and the unGerman character of the worker.

8.   It should not be thought here that reference is being made to cases of migration from the semi-barbarian regions (Upper Silesia) to those with the highest level of culture (Saxony). The statistics show that it is in cases of internal migration in the east that the subsistence of the worker is by far the worst – although there are exceptions.

9.   An example: according to a careful survey conducted by the Protestant Social Congress which drew on material from workers and estate account books in the Königsberg area, there is one district where the land-relations are particularly influential because of the nature of the district. Here there is apparently a great similarity in the intensity of cultivation, and if monetary calculations are made, then the net income of the *Inst* families on several neighbouring estates appears as follows (aside from payments to helpers):

1.   For 1 *Instmann* on 35 hectares, 525.35 Mark.
2.   40   742.50 Mark.
3.   43   752.50 Mark.
4.   53   803.63 Mark.

The proportionality is apparent. In a fifth case the income is as follows:

5.   For 1 *Instmann* on each 57 hectares, 645.00 Mark.

Here threshing machines were reportedly in use; and the difference between cases 1 and 2 can be accounted for in the same way, so that 1 and 5 do in fact follow the rule. It can be seen that comparisons are only possible between enterprises organized in similar ways. (In this instance the intensity of labour does not depend on the size of the enterprise.)

10.   Some examples: the wage relations in East Prussia, where highly intensive cultivation (e.g. beet) was not widespread on the better grades of land, but where on average the level of intensity depended on the differing quality of soil. According to the very rough, but for these purposes sufficient, summaries in the survey the following correspondence appears:

Königsberg Region	Average revenue from rent per ha.	Average male day wage per year	Gumbinnen Region	Average revenue from rent per ha.	Average male day wage per year
Ortelsburg District, Neidenburg	4.31	1.10	Southwest Masuren	5.49	1.10
Ermland	8.71	1.21	Upper Masuren District	6.25	1.11
Mohrungen District Pr. Holland	9.92	1.32	Southern Littau	9.40	1.25
Osterode Samland and Natangen	13.12	1.50	Eastern and Northern Littau	10.83	1.28

11.   In the relatively intensive pasture farms in Fischausen, where the climate especially favours livestock rearing, the workers are better off according to the

reports than those in grain growing farms. Where the climatic advantage does not exist, the reverse is the case, as for instance in Filehne.

12. Where the shares have remained more or less constant, revenues from threshing have in more fertile areas increased greatly – up to 120 bushels of different grains on average per year on some parts of Königsberg according to the data provided by the Protestant Social Congress's survey.

13. In East Prussia 10 to 11 bushels is usual, farther west 15 to 18 was for a long time customary; on better land and with mechanical threshing the share, where it remains, rises to 33 bushels and then has the form of a percentage. The harvest share has been abolished now everywhere.

14. The domination of the large estates exacerbates in itself only class differences. The *material* situation of the worker, as long as a secure and customary organization of labour is maintained, can improve on account of the greater demand for labour by the large estates. This was the case in New Pomerania because of the high standard of living which was inherited from the past. It is the reverse in Silesia, where the Polish workforce faces powerful magnates.

CHAPTER 7

The national state and economic policy

Max Weber
(Inaugural lecture, Freiburg, May 1895)
translated by Ben Fowkes

The title I have chosen promises much more than I can achieve today, or wish to achieve. What I intend is first of all this: to use a *single example* to make clear the role played by racial differences of a physical and psychological nature, as between nationalities, in the economic struggle for existence. I should then like to add some reflections on the situation of a state which rests on a national basis – such as our own – within the framework of a consideration of economic policy. I am choosing for my example a set of events which although they are occurring a long way from us have repeatedly come to the notice of the public in the last ten years. Allow me, then, to conduct you to the eastern marches of the *Reich*, to the open country of the Prussian province of *West Prussia*. This setting combines the character of a national borderland with some unusually sharp variations in the conditions of economic and social existence, and this recommends it for our purpose. Unfortunately I cannot avoid calling on your forbearance initially while I recite a series of dry data.

The rural areas of the province of West Prussia contain three different types of contrast, as follows. First, extraordinary variations in the *quality of agricultural land*. From the sugar-beet country of the Vistula plain to the sandy uplands of Cassubia the estimates of the gross tax yield vary in a ratio of 10 or 20 to 1. Even the average values at district level fluctuate between 4.75 and 33.66 marks per hectare.

Then there are contrasts in the *social stratification* of the population which cultivates this land. As in general in the East, the official statistics refer alongside the 'rural parish' (*Landgemeinde*) to a second form of communal unit, unknown to the South: the 'estate district' (*Gutsbezirk*). And, correspondingly, the estates of the nobility stand out in bold relief in the landscape between the villages of the peasants. These are the places of residence of the class which gives the East its social imprint – the Junkers. Everywhere there are manor-houses, surrounded by the single-

storey cottages the lord of the manor (*Gutsherr*) has allotted to the
day-labourers, plus a few strips of arable land and pasture; these
people are obliged to work on the manor the whole year round.
The area of the province of West Prussia is divided between these
two categories in roughly equal proportions. But in particular
districts the share of the manorial estates can vary from a few per
cent to two-third of the whole area.

Finally, within this population which is subject to a twofold
social stratification, there exists a third contrast; it is between the
nationalities. And the national composition of the population of the
individual communities also varies from region to region. It is *this
kind of variation* which is of interest to us today. In the first place,
the proportion of Poles is naturally greater as you approach the
boundary of the *Reich*. But this proportion of Poles also *increases*
as the quality of the soil *deteriorates*. Any language-map will show
that. One will at first wish to explain this historically from the
form taken by the German occupation of these lands, which
initially spread over the fertile plain of the Vistula. And this would
not be entirely incorrect. But let us now ask the further question:
what *social strata* are the repositories of Germanism (*Deutschtum*)
and Polonism (*Polentum*) in the country districts? In answer to this
question, the figures of the most recently published population
census (that of 1885)[1] present us with a curious picture.
Admittedly we cannot directly extract the national composition of
each parish from these figures, but we can do this indirectly,
provided we are content to achieve only approximate accuracy.
The intermediate step is the figure for religious affiliation, which,
for the nationally mixed district we are concerned with, coincides
to within a few per cent with nationality. If we separate the
economic categories of the peasant village and the manorial estate
in each district, by identifying them with the corresponding
administrative units of the rural parish and the estate district,[2] we
find that their national composition is related *inversely* to the
quality of the soil; in the fertile districts the Catholics, i.e. the
Poles, are relatively most numerous on the *estates*, and the
Protestants, i.e. the *Germans*, are to be found in greater
proportions in the *villages*. In districts where the soil is inferior the
situation is precisely the opposite of this. For example, if we take
the districts with an average net tax yield of under 5 marks per
hectare, we find only 33.5 per cent Protestants in the villages and
50.2 per cent Protestants on the estates; if on the other hand we
take the group of districts which provide an average of 10 to 15
marks per hectare, we find the proportion of Protestants rising to
60.7 per cent in the villages and falling to 42.1 per cent on the
estates. Why is this? Why are the estates the reservoirs of

Polonism on the plain, and the villages the reservoirs of Polonism in the hills? One thing is immediately evident: *the Poles have a tendency to collect together in that stratum of the population which stands lowest both economically and socially.* On the good soil, like that of the Vistula plain, the peasant's standard of living has always been higher than that of the day-labourer on an estate; on the bad soil, which could only be rationally exploited on a large scale, the manorial estate (*Rittergut*) was the repository of civilization and hence of Germanism; there the miserable small peasants still live *below* the level of the day-labourers on the estates. If we did not know that anyway, the age-structure of the population would lead us to that presumption. If we look at the *villages* we find that as one rises from the plain to the hilltops, and as the quality of the soil deteriorates the proportion of children under 14 years old rises from 35–36 per cent to 40–41 per cent. If we compare the *estates*, we find that the proportion of children is higher on the plain than in the villages, that it increases as the height above sea-level increases, though more slowly than this happens in the villages, and finally that *on* the hilltops the proportion is lower than the proportion in the hilltop villages. As usual, a large number of children follows hard on the heels of a low standard of living, since this tends to obliterate any calculations of future welfare. Economic advance (*wirtschaftliche Kultur*), a relatively high standard of living and *Germanism* are in West Prussia identical.

And yet the two nationalities have competed for centuries on the same soil, and with essentially the same opportunities. What then is the basis of the distinction? One is immediately tempted to believe that the two nationalities differ in their *ability to adapt* to different economic and social conditions of existence. And this is in fact so – as is proved by the tendency of development revealed by shifts in the population and changes in its national composition. This also allows us to perceive how fateful that difference in the ability to adapt is for the Germanism of the East.

It is true that we only have at our disposal the figures of 1871 and 1885 for a comparative examination of the displacements which have occurred in the individual parishes, and these figures allow us to perceive only the indistinct beginnings of a development which has since then, according to all indications, been extraordinarily reinforced. Apart from this, the clarity of the numerical picture naturally suffers under the enforced but not entirely correct assumption of an identity between religious affiliation and nationality on one side, and administrative subdivisions and social structure on the other. Despite all this, we can still gain a clear enough view of the relevant changes. The rural population of West Prussia, like that of large parts of the whole of eastern Germany, showed a tendency to *fall* during the period between 1880 and 1885; this fall amounted to 12,700 people, i.e. there was a decline of 1.25 per cent, while the overall population of the German *Reich* was increasing by about 3.5 per cent. This phenomenon, like the phenomena we have already discussed, also occurred unevenly: in some districts there was actually an increase in the rural population. And indeed the *manner in which* these phenomena were distributed is highly characteristic. If we take first the different soil qualities, one would normally assume that the decline hit the *worst* land hardest, for there the pressure of falling prices would be first to render the margin of subsistence too narrow. If one looks at the figures, however, one sees that the *reverse* is the case: precisely the most well-favoured districts, such as Stuhm and Marienwerder, with an average net yield of around 15–17 marks, experienced the greatest *population loss*, a loss of 7–8 per cent, whereas in the hilly country the district of Konitz and Tuchel, with a net yield of 5–6 marks, experienced the biggest *increase*, an increase which had been going on since 1871. One looks for an explanation, and one asks first: from which social strata did the population loss originate, and which social strata gained from the increase? Let us look at the districts where the figures demonstrate a great reduction in population: Stuhm, Marienwerder, Rosenberg. These are without exception districts where *large-scale landownership* predominates particularly strongly, and if we take the *estate districts* of the whole province together, we find that although in 1880 they exhibited a total population two-thirds smaller than the villages (on the same area of land) their share in the fall of the rural population between 1880 and 1885 comes to over 9,000 people, which is almost three-quarters of the total reduction over the whole province: the population of the estate districts has fallen by about 3.75 per cent. But this fall in population is also distributed unevenly *within* the category referred to: in some places the population actually increased, and when one isolates the areas where the population was sharply reduced, one finds that it was precisely the estates on *good* soil which experienced a particularly severe loss of population.

In contrast to this, the *increase* of population which took place on the bad soils of the uplands worked chiefly in favour of the *villages*, and indeed this was most pronounced in the villages on *bad* soils, as opposed to the villages of the plain. The tendency which emerges from these figures is therefore towards a *decrease in the numbers of day-labourers* on the estates situated on the *best* land, and an *increase in the numbers of peasants* on land *of inferior quality*.

What is at stake here, and how the phenomenon is to be explained, becomes clear when one finally asks how the *nationalities* are affected by these shifts in population.

In the first half of the century the Polish element appeared to be in retreat, slowly but continuously. However, since the 1860s, as is well known, it has just as continuously, and just as slowly, been advancing. Despite their inadequate basis, the language data for West Prussia make the latter point extremely plain. Now a shift in the boundary between two nationalities can occur in two ways, which are fundamentally distinct. It may on the one hand happen that the language and customs of the majority gradually impose themselves on national minorities in a nationally mixed region, that these minorities get 'soaked up'. This phenomenon can be found as well in eastern Germany: the process is statistically demonstrable in the case of Germans of the Catholic confession. Here the ecclesiastical bond is stronger than the national one, memories of the *Kulturkampf* also play their part, and the lack of a German-educated clergy means that the German Catholics are lost to the cultural community of the nation. But the second form of nationality-displacement is more important, and more relevant for us: *economic extrusion*. And this is how it is in the present case. If one examines the changes in the proportion of adherents of the two faiths in the rural parish units between 1871 and 1885, one sees this: the migration of day-labourers away from the estates is in the lowlands regularly associated with a relative decline of Protestantism, while in the hills the increase of the village population is associated with a relative increase of Catholicism.[3] *It is chiefly German day-labourers who move out of the districts of progressive cultivation; it is chiefly Polish peasants who multiply in the districts where cultivation is on a low level.*

But both processes – here emigration, there increase in numbers – lead back ultimately to one and the same reason: *a lower expectation of living standards*, in part physical, in part mental, which the Slav race either possesses as a gift from nature or has acquired through breeding in the course of its past history. This is what has helped it to victory.

Why do the German day-labourers move out? Not for material reasons: the movement of emigration does not draw its recruits from districts with low levels of pay or from categories of worker who are badly paid. Materially there is hardly a more secure situation than that of agricultural labourer on the East German estates. Nor is it the much-bruited longing for the diversions of the big city. This is a reason for the planless wandering off of the younger generation, but not for the emigration of long-serving families of day-labourers. Moreover, why would such a longing arise precisely among the people on the big estates? Why is it that the emigration of the day-labourers demonstrably falls off in proportion as the *peasant village* comes to dominate the physiognomy of the landscape? The reason is as follows: there are only masters and servants, and nothing else, on the estates of his homeland for the day-labourer, and the prospect for his family, down to the most distant of his progeny, is to slave away on someone else's land from one chime of the estate-bell to the next. In this deep, half-conscious impulse towards the distant horizon there lies hidden an element of primitive idealism. He who cannot decipher this does not know the magic of *freedom*. Indeed, the spirit of freedom seldom touches us today in the stillness of the study. The naive youthful ideals of freedom are faded, and some of us have grown prematurely old and all too wise, and believe that one of the most elemental impulses of the human breast has been borne to its grave along with the slogans of a dying conception of politics and economic policy.

We have here an occurrence of a mass-psychological character: the German agricultural labourers can no longer adjust themselves to the *social* conditions of life in their homeland. We have reports of West Prussian landowners complaining about their labourers' 'self-assertiveness'. The old patriarchal relationship between lord and vassal is disappearing. But this is what attached the day-labourer directly to the interests of the agricultural producers as a small cultivator with a right to a share in the produce. Seasonal labour in the beet-growing districts requires seasonal workers and payment in money. They are faced with a purely proletarian existence, but without the possibility of that energetic advance to economic independence which gives added self-confidence to the industrial proletarians who live cheek by jowl in the cities of the west. Those who replace the Germans on the estates of the east are better able to submit to these conditions of existence: I mean the itinerant Polish workers, troops of nomads recruited by agents in Russia, who cross the frontier in tens of thousands in spring, and leave again in autumn. They first emerge in attendance upon the sugar-beet, a crop which turns agriculture into a seasonal trade, then they are everywhere, because one can save on workers' dwellings, on poor rates, on social obligations by using them, and further because they are in a precarious position as foreigners and therefore in the hands of the landowners. These are accompanying circumstances of the economic death-struggle of Old Prussian Junkerdom. On the sugar-beet estates a stratum of industrial businessmen steps into the shoes of the patriarchally ruling lord of the manor, while in the uplands the lands of the manorial estates crumble away under the pressure of the crisis in the agrarian economy. Tenants of small parcels and colonies of small peasants arise on their outfields. The economic foundations of the power of the old landed nobility vanish, and the nobility itself becomes something other than what it was.

And why is it the *Polish* peasants who are gaining the land? Is it their superior economic intelligence, or their greater supply of capital? It is rather the opposite of both these factors. Under a climate, and on a soil, which favour the growing of cereals and potatoes above all, alongside extensive cattle-raising, the person who is least threatened by an unfavourable market is the one who brings his products to the place where they are least devalued by a collapse in prices: his own stomach. This is the person who produces *for his own requirements*. And once again, the person who can set his own requirements *at the lowest level*, the person who makes the smallest physical and mental demands for the maintenance of his life, is the one with the advantage. The small Polish peasant in East Germany is a type far removed from the bustling peasant owner of a dwarf property, whom one may see here in the well-favoured valley of the Rhine as he forges links with the towns via greenhouse cultivation and market-gardening. The small Polish peasant gains more land, because he as it were eats the very grass from off of it, he gains not *despite* but *on account of* the low level of his physical and intellectual habits of life.

We therefore seem to see a *process of selection* unfolding. Both nationalities have for a long time been embedded in the same conditions of existence. The consequence of this has *not* been what vulgar materialists might have imagined, that they took on the same physical and psychological qualities, but rather that one yielded the ground to the other, that victory went to the nationality which possessed the greater ability to adapt itself to the given economic and social conditions of existence.

This difference in the ability to adapt seems to be present ready-made, as a fixed magnitude. The nations' respective abilities to adapt might perhaps undergo further shifts in the course of many generations, through the millennial process of breeding which no doubt originally produced the difference, but for any reflections on the present situation it is a factor with which we have to reckon, as given.[4]

The free play of the forces of selection does not always work out, as the optimists among us think, in favour of the nationality which is more highly developed or more gifted economically. We have just seen this. Human history does not lack examples of the victory of less developed types of humanity and the extinction of fine flowers of intellectual and emotional life, when the human

community which was their repository lost its ability to adapt to
the conditions of existence, either by reason of its social
organization or its racial characteristics. In our case it is the
transformation of the forms of agricultural enterprise and the
tremendous crisis in agriculture which is bringing to victory the
less economically developed nationality. The rise of sugar-beet
cultivation and the unprofitability of cereal production for the
market are developments running parallel and in the same
direction: the first breeds the Polish seasonal worker, the second
the small Polish peasant.

On looking back at the facts presented here, I am in no
position, as I shall willingly concede, to develop theoretically the
significance of the various general points which may be derived
from them. The immensely difficult question, certainly insoluble
at present, of *where to place the limit* of the variability of physical
and psychological qualities in a population under the influence of
its given conditions of existence is something I shall not even
venture to touch on.

Instead of this, everyone will automatically want to ask, above
all else: what can and should be done in this situation?

You will however permit me to abstain from an exhaustive
discussion of this on the present occasion, and to content myself
with briefly indicating the two demands which in my view should
be posed from the standpoint of Germanism, and are in fact being
posed with growing unanimity. The first is the demand for the
closing of the Eastern frontier. This was accomplished under
Prince Bismarck, and then reversed after his resignation in 1890:
permanent settlement remained forbidden to the aliens, but they
were permitted entry as migratory workers. A 'class-conscious'
landowner at the head of the Prussian government excluded them
in the interests of the maintenance of our nationality, and the
hated opponent of the Agrarians [Caprivi] let them in, in the
interests of the big landowners, who are the *only people* to gain
from this influx. This demonstrates that the 'economic class-
standpoint' is not always decisive in matters of economic policy –
here it was the circumstance that the helm of the ship of state fell
from a strong hand into a weaker one. The other demand is for a
policy of systematic land purchase on the part of the state, i.e. the
extension of crown lands on the one hand, and systematic
colonization by German peasants on suitable land, particularly on
suitable crown land, on the other hand. Large-scale enterprises
which can only be preserved at the expense of Germanism deserve
from the point of view of the nation to go down to destruction. To
leave them as they are without assistance means to allow unviable
Slav hunger colonies to arise by way of gradual fragmentation of

the estates into small parcels. And it is not only our interest in stemming the Slav flood which requires the transfer of consider- able parts of the land of eastern Germany into the hands of the state, but also the annihilating criticism the big landowners themselves have made of the continued existence of their private property by demanding the removal of the risk they run, their personal responsibility for their own property, which is its sole justification. I refer to the proposal for the introduction of a corn monopoly [the Kanitz proposal of 1894 for a state monopoly on the import of corn into Germany] and the granting of a state contribution of half a billion marks a year.[5]

But, as I said earlier, I would prefer not to discuss this practical question of Prussian agrarian policy today. I would rather start from the fact that such a question arises at all, the fact that we all consider the German character of the East to be something that *should* be protected, and that the economic policy of the state *should* also enter into the lists in its defence. Our state is a *national state*, and it is this circumstance which makes us feel we have a right to make this demand.

However, how does the attitude assumed by economics relate to this? Does it treat such nationalist value-judgments as prejudices, of which it must carefully rid itself in order to be able to apply its own specific standard of value to the economic facts, without being influenced by emotional reflexes? And *what is* this standard of value peculiar to economic policy (*Volkswirtschaftspolitik*)? I should like to try to get closer to this question by making one or two further observations.

As we have seen, the economic struggle between the nationalities follows its course even under the semblance of 'peace'. The German peasants and day-labourers of the East are not being pushed off the land in an open conflict by politically superior opponents. Instead they are getting the worst of it in the silent and dreary struggle of everyday economic existence, they are abandon- ing their homeland to a race which stands on a lower level, and moving towards a dark future in which they will sink without trace. There can be no truce even in the *economic* struggle for existence; only if one takes the semblance of peace for its reality can one believe that peace and prosperity will emerge for our successors at some time in the distant future. Certainly, the vulgar conception of political economy is that it consists in working out recipes for making the world happy; the improvement of the 'balance of pleasure' in human existence is the sole purpose of our work that the vulgar conception can comprehend. However the deadly seriousness of the population problem prohibits eudae- monism; it prevents us from imagining that peace and happiness lie hidden in the lap of the future, it prevents us from believing that elbowroom in this earthly existence can be won in any other way than through the hard struggle of human beings with each other.

It is certain that there can be no work in political economy on any other than an altruistic basis. The overwhelming majority of the fruits of the economic, social, and political endeavours of the present are garnered not by the generation now alive but by the generations of the future. If our work is to retain any meaning it can only be informed by this: concern for the *future*, for *those who will come after us*. But there can also be no real work in political economy on the basis of optimistic dreams of happiness. Abandon hope all ye who enter here: these words are inscribed above the portals of the unknown future history of mankind. So much for the dream of peace and happiness.

The question which leads us beyond the grave of our own generation is not 'how will human beings *feel* in the future' but 'how will they be'. In fact this question underlies all work in political economy. We do not want to train up feelings of well-being in people, but rather those characteristics we think constitute the greatness and nobility of our human nature.

The doctrines of political economy have alternately placed in the forefront, or naively identified as standards of value, either the technical economic problem of the production of commodities or the problem of their distribution, in other words 'social justice'. Yet again and again a different perception, in part unconscious, but nevertheless all-dominating, has raised itself above both these standards of value: the perception that a *human* science, and that is what political economy is, investigates above all else the *quality of the human beings* who are brought up in those economic and social conditions of existence. And here we must be on our guard against a certain illusion.

As a science of explanation and analysis political economy is *international*, but as soon as it makes *value judgments* it is bound up with the distinct imprint of humanity we find in our own nature. We are often most bound to our own nature on precisely those occasions when we think we have escaped our fleshly limitations. And if – to use a somewhat fanciful image – we could arise from the grave thousands of years hence, we would seek the distant traces of our own nature in the physiognomy of the race of the future. Even our highest, our ultimate, terrestrial ideals are mutable and transitory. We cannot presume to impose them on the future. But we can hope that the future recognizes in our nature the nature of *its own ancestors*. We wish to make ourselves the forefathers of the race of the future with our labour and our mode of existence.

The economic policy of a German state, and the standard of value adopted by a German economic theorist, can therefore be nothing other than a German policy and a German standard.

Has this situation perhaps changed since economic development began to create an all-embracing economic community of nations, going beyond national boundaries? Is the 'nationalistic' standard of evaluation to be thrown on the scrapheap along with 'national egoism' in economic policy? Has the struggle for economic survival, for the maintenance of one's wife and children, been surmounted now that the family has been divested of its original function as an association for production, and meshed into the network of the national economic community? We know that this is *not* the case: the struggle has taken on *other forms*, forms about which one may well raise the question of whether they should be viewed as a mitigation or indeed rather an intensification and a sharpening of the struggle. In the same way, the world-wide economic community is only another form of the struggle of the nations with each other, and it *aggravates* rather than mitigating the struggle for the maintenance of one's own culture, because it calls forth in the very bosom of the nation material interests *opposed* to the nation's future, and throws them into the ring in alliance with the nation's enemies.

We do not have peace and human happiness to bequeath to our posterity, but rather the *eternal struggle* for the maintenance and improvement by careful cultivation of our national character. And we should not abandon ourselves to the optimistic expectation that we have done what is necessary once we have developed economic progress to the highest possible level, and that the process of selection in the freely conducted and 'peaceful' economic struggle will thereupon automatically bring the victory to the more highly developed human type.

Our successors will not hold us responsible before history for the kind of economic organization we hand over to them, but rather for the amount of elbow-room we conquer for them in the world and leave behind us. Processes of economic development are in the final analysis also *power struggles*, and the ultimate and decisive interests at whose service economic policy must place itself are the interests of national *power*, where these interests are in question. The science of political economy is a *political* science. It is a servant of politics, not the day-to-day politics of the individuals and classes who happen to be ruling at a particular time, but the lasting power-political interests of the nation. And for us the *national state* is not, as some people believe, an indeterminate entity raised higher and higher into the clouds in proportion as one clothes its nature in mystical darkness, but the

temporal power-organization of the nation, and in this national
state the ultimate standard of value for economic policy is 'reason
of state'. There is a strange misinterpretation of this view current
to the effect that we advocate 'state assistance' instead of 'self-
help', state regulation of economic life instead of the free play of
economic forces. We do not. Rather we wish under this slogan of
'reason of state' to raise the demand that for questions of German
economic policy – including the question of whether, and how far,
the state should intervene in economic life, and when it should
rather untie the economic forces of the nation and tear down the
barriers in the way of their free development – the ultimate and
decisive voice should be that of the economic and political
interests of our nation's power, and the vehicle of that power, the
German national state.

Has it been superfluous to recall things that appear to go
without saying? Or was it unnecessary for precisely a younger
representative of economic science to recall these matters? I do not
think so, for it appears that our generation is liable very easily to
lose sight of these simple bases for judgement. We have witnessed
a hitherto unimaginable growth in the present generation's interest
in the burning issues of our field of science. Everywhere we find
an advance in the popularity of the economic method of approach.
Social policy has become the central preoccupation instead of
politics, economic relations of power instead of legal relations,
cultural and economic history instead of political history. In the
outstanding works of our historical colleagues we find that today
instead of telling us about the warlike deeds of our ancestors they
dilate at length about 'mother-right', that monstrous notion, and
force into a subordinate clause the victory of the Huns on the
Catalaunian Plain. One of our most ingenious theorists was self-
confident enough to believe he could characterize jurisprudence as
'the handmaiden of political economy'. And one thing is certainly
true: the economic form of analysis has penetrated into jurisprudence itself. Even its most intimate regions, the treatises on
the Pandects, are beginning to be quietly haunted by economic
ideas. And in the verdicts of the courts of law it is not rare to find
so-called 'economic grounds' put in where legal concepts are
unable to fill the bill. In short, to use the half-reproachful phrase
of a legal colleague: we have 'come into fashion'. A method of
analysis which is so confidently forging ahead is in danger of
falling into certain illusions and exaggerating the significance of its
own point of view. This exaggeration occurs in a quite specific
direction. Just as the extension of the material of *philosophical*
reflection – already made apparent externally through the fact that
nowadays we frequently find e.g. prominent physiologists occupy-

ing the old Chairs of Philosophy – has led laymen to the opinion that the old questions of the nature of human knowledge are no longer the ultimate and central questions of philosophy, so in the field of political economy the notion has grown in the minds of the coming generation that the work of economic science has not only immensely extended our *knowledge* of the nature of human communities, but also provided a completely new *standard* by which these phenomena can ultimately be *evaluated*, that political economy is in a position to extract from its material its own specific ideals. The notion that there exist independent economic or 'socio-political' ideals is revealed as an optical illusion as soon as one seeks to establish these 'peculiar' canons of evaluation by using the literature produced by our science. We are confronted instead with a *chaotic mass* of standards of value, partly eudaemonistic, partly ethical, and often both present together in an ambiguous identification. Value-judgments are made everywhere in a nonchalant and spontaneous manner, and if we abandon the evaluation of economic phenomena we in fact abandon the very accomplishment which is being demanded of us. But it is not the general rule, in fact it is well-nigh exceptional, for the maker of a judgment to clarify for others and *for himself* the nature of the ultimate subjective core of his judgments, to make clear the *ideals* on the basis of which he proceeds to judge the events he is observing; there is a lack of conscious self-inspection, the internal contradictions of his judgment do not come to the writer's notice, and where he seeks to give a general formulation of his specifically 'economic' principle of judgment he falls into vagueness and indeterminacy. In truth, the ideals we introduce into the substance of our science are not peculiar to it, nor have we worked them out independently: they are *old-established human ideals of a general type*. Only he who proceeds exclusively from the pure Platonic interest of the technologist, or, inversely, the actual interests of a particular class, whether a ruling or a subject class, can expect to derive his own standard of judgment from the material itself.

And is it so unnecessary for us, the younger representatives of the German historical school, to keep in sight these extremely simple truths? By no means, for we in particular are liable to fall victim to a special kind of illusion: the illusion that we can *entirely do without* conscious value-judgments of our own. The result is of course, and the evidence is quite convincing on this point, that we do not remain true to this intention but rather fall prey to uncontrolled instincts, sympathies, and antipathies. And it is still more likely to happen that the point of departure we adopt in analysing and *explaining* economic events unconsciously becomes

determinant in our *judgement* of the events. We shall perhaps have
to be on our guard lest the very qualities of the dead and living
masters of our school to which they and their science owed its
success turn in our case into weaknesses. In practice we have
essentially to consider the following two different points of
departure in economic analysis.

Either we look at economic development mainly from above: we
proceed from the heights of the administrative history of the larger
German states, pursuing to its origins the way they have
administered economic and social affairs and their attitude to these
matters. In that case we involuntarily become their apologists. If –
let us keep to our original example – the administration decides to
close the Eastern border, we are ready and inclined to view the
decision as the conclusion of a historical development, which as a
result of the gigantic reverberations of the past has posed great
tasks the present-day state must fulfil in the interest of the
maintenance of our national culture. If on the other hand that
decision is not taken it is very easy for us to believe that radical
interventions of that kind are in part unnecessary and in part do
not correspond any longer to present-day views.

Or, and this is the other starting-point, we may view economic
development more from below, we may look at the great spectacle
of the emancipatory struggles of rising classes emerging from the
chaos of conflicts of economic interest, we may observe the way in
which the balance of economic power shifts in their favour. Then
we unconsciously take sides with the rising classes, because they
are the stronger, or are beginning to be so. They seem to prove,
precisely because they are victorious, that they represent a type of
humanity that stands on a higher level 'economically': it is all too
easy for the historian to succumb to the idea that the victory of the
more highly developed element in the struggle is a matter of course,
and that defeat in the struggle for existence is a symptom of
'backwardness'. And every new sign of the shift of power gives
satisfaction to the historian, not only because it confirms his
observations, but because, half unconsciously, he senses it as a
personal triumph: history is honouring the bills he has drawn on
it. Without being aware of it, he observes the resistance that
development finds in its path with a certain animosity; it seems to
him to be not simply the natural result of the interplay of various
inevitably divergent interests, but to some extent a rebellion
against the 'judgment of history' as formulated by the historian.
But criticism must also be made of processes which appear to us to
be the unreflected result of tendencies of historical development;
and precisely here, where there is most need of it, the critical
spirit deserts us. In any case, there is a very obvious temptation on

the historian to become a part of the camp-following of the victor in the economic struggle for power, and to *forget that economic power and the vocation for political leadership of the nation do not always coincide.*

With this we now arrive at a final series of reflections belonging more to the realm of practical politics. There is only one *political standard of value* which is supreme for us economic nationalists, and it is by this standard that we also measure the classes which either have the leadership of the nation in their hands or are striving for it. What we are concerned with is their *political maturity*, i.e. their understanding of the lasting economic and political interests of the nation's *power* and their ability to place these interests above all other considerations if the occasion demands. A nation is favoured by destiny if the naive identification of the interests of one's own class with the general interest also corresponds to the interests of national power. And it is one of the delusions which arise from the modern over-estimation of the 'economic' in the usual sense of the word when people assert that feelings of political community cannot maintain themselves in face of the full weight of divergent economic interests, indeed that very possibly these feelings are *merely* the reflection of the economic basis underlying those changing interests. This is approximately accurate only in times of fundamental social transformation. One thing can certainly be said: among nations like the English, who are not confronted daily with the dependence of their economic prosperity on their situation of political power, the instinct for these specifically political interests does *not*, at least not as a rule, dwell in the broad *masses* of the people, for they are occupied in the fight to secure their daily needs. It would be unfair to expect them to possess this understanding. But in great moments, in the case of war, their souls too become conscious of the significance of national power. Then it emerges that the national state rests on deep and elemental psychological foundations within the broad economically sub-ordinate strata of the nation as well, that it is by no means a mere 'superstructure', the organization of the economically dominant classes. It is just that in normal times this political instinct sinks below the level of consciousness for the masses. In that case the specific function of the economically and politically leading strata is to be the repositories of political understanding. This is in fact the *sole* political justification for their existence.

At all times it has been the *attainment of economic power* which has led to the emergence within a given class of the notion that it has a *claim to political leadership*. It is dangerous, and in the long term incompatible with the interests of the nation when an economically declining class is politically dominant. But it is still more dangerous when classes which are beginning to achieve economic power and thereby the expectation of political domination are not yet politically mature enough to assume the direction of the state. Germany is at present under threat from both these directions, and this is in truth the key to understanding the present dangers of our situation. The changes in the social structure of eastern Germany, with which the phenomena discussed at the outset are linked, also belong within this larger context.

Right up to the present time in Prussia the dynasty has been politically based on the social stratum of the Prussian *Junkers*. The dynasty created the Prussian state against them, but only with their assistance was it possible. I know full well that the word 'Junker' resonates harshly in South German ears. It will perhaps be thought that if I now say a word in their favour, I shall be speaking a 'Prussian' language. I cannot be sure. Even today in Prussia the Junkers have open to them many paths to influence and power, many ways to the ear of the monarch, which are not available to every citizen; they have not always used this power in accordance with their responsibility before history, and there is no reason for a bourgeois scholar like myself to love them. But despite all this the strength of their political instincts is one of the most tremendous resources which could have been applied to the service of the state's power-interests. They have done their work now, and today are in the throes of an economic death-struggle, and no kind of economic policy on the part of the state could bring back their old social character. Moreover the tasks of the present are quite different from those they might be able to solve. The last and greatest of the Junkers stood at the head of Germany for a quarter of a century, and the future will very likely find the tragic element in his career as a statesman, alongside his incomparable greatness, in something which even today is hidden from view for many people: in the fact that the work of his hands, the nation to which he gave unity, gradually and irresistibly altered its economic structure even while he was in office, and became something different, a people compelled to demand other institutions than those he could grant to them, or those his autocratic nature could adapt itself to. In the final analysis it is this fate which brought about the partial failure of his life's work. For this was intended to lead not just to the external but to the inner unification of the nation, and, as every one of us knows, that has not been achieved. With his means he could not achieve it. And when, last winter, ensnared by the graciousness of his monarch, he made his way into the splendidly decorated capital of the *Reich*, there were many people who felt – I can vouch for this – as if the Kyffhäuser legend was about to come true, felt that the Sachsenwald had opened up and the long-lost hero was emerging from its depths.[6] But this feeling was not shared by everyone. For it seemed as if the cold breath of historical impermanence could be sensed in the January air. A strangely oppressive feeling overcame us, as if a ghost had stepped down from a great past epoch and were going about among a new generation, and through a world become alien to it.

The manors of the East were the points of support for the ruling class of Prussia, which was scattered over the countryside, they were the social point of contact for the bureaucracy. But with their decline, with the disappearance of the social character of the old landed nobility, the centre of gravity of the political intelligentsia is shifting irresistibly towards the towns. This displacement is the decisive *political* aspect of the agrarian development of the East.

But whose are the hands into which the political function of the Junkers is passing, and what kind of political vocation do they have?

I am a member of the bourgeois classes. I feel myself to be a bourgeois, and I have been brought up to share their views and ideals. But it is the task of precisely our science to say what people do not like to hear – to those above us, to those below us, and also to our own class – and when I ask myself whether the German bourgeoisie is at present ripe to be the leading political class of the nation, I cannot answer this question in the affirmative *today*. The German state was not created by the bourgeoisie with its own strength, and when it had been created, there stood at the head of the nation that Caesar-like figure hewn out of quite other than bourgeois timber. Great power-political tasks were not set a second time for the nation to accomplish: only much later on, timidly, and half unwillingly, did an overseas 'power policy' begin, a policy which does not deserve the name.

And after the nation's unity had thus been achieved, and its political 'satiation' was an established fact, a peculiarly 'unhistorical' and unpolitical mood came over the growing race of German bourgeois, drunk as it was with success and thirsty for peace. German history appeared to have come to an end. The present was the complete fulfilment of past millennia. Who was inclined to question whether the future might judge otherwise? Indeed it seemed as if modesty forbade world history from going over to the order of the day, from resuming its day-to-day course after these successes of the German nation. Today we are more sober, and it is seemly to make the attempt to lift the veil of illusions which has hidden the position of our generation in the historical development of the fatherland. And it seems to me that if we do this we shall judge differently. Over our cradle stood the most frightful curse history has ever handed to any race as a birthday-gift: the hard destiny of the political *epigone*.

Do we not see his miserable countenance wherever we look in the fatherland? Those of us who have retained the capacity to hate pettiness have recognized, with passionate and furious sorrow, the petty manoeuvring of political epigones in the events of the last few months, for which bourgeois politicians are responsible first and foremost, in far too much of what has been said recently *in* the German parliament, and in a certain amount of what has been said *to* it. The gigantic sun which stood at its zenith in Germany and caused the German name to shine forth in the furthest corners of the earth was too strong for us, it might almost seem, and burnt out the bourgeoisie's slowly developing sense of political judgment. For where is this to be seen at the present moment?

One section of the haute bourgeoisie longs all too shamelessly for the coming of a new Caesar, who will protect them in two directions: from beneath against the rising masses of the people, from above against the socio-political impulses they suspect the German dynasties of harbouring.

And another section has long been sunk in that political Philistinism from which broad strata of the lower middle classes have never awakened. Already when the first positive political task began to come on the nation's horizon, after the wars of unification – I mean the idea of overseas expansion – this section of the bourgeoisie lacked the simplest *economic* understanding of what it means for Germany's trade in far-off oceans when the German flag waves on the surrounding coasts.

The political immaturity of broad strata of the German bourgeoisie is not due to economic causes, nor is it due to the much-bruited 'interest politics', which is present in no less a degree in other nations than the German. The explanation lies in its unpolitical past, in the fact that one cannot make up in a decade for a missing century of political education, and that the domination of a great man is not always an appropriate instrument for such a process. And this is now the vital question for the political future of the German bourgeoisie: is it *too late* for it to catch up on its political education? No *economic* factor can make up for this loss.

Will other classes become the repositories of a politically greater future? The modern proletariat is self-confidently announcing itself as the heir of the ideals of the middle classes. What then of its claim to inherit the political leadership of the nation?

If anyone were to say of the German working class at present that it was politically mature, or on the road to political maturity, he would be a flatterer, a seeker after the dubious accolade of popularity.

The highest strata of the German working class are far more mature *economically* than the possessing classes in their egoism would like to admit, and it is with justification that the working class demands the freedom to put forward its interests in the form of the openly organised struggle for economic power. *Politically* the German working class is infinitely less mature than a clique of journalists, who would like to monopolize its leading positions, are trying to make the working class itself believe. In the circles of these *déclassé* bourgeois they like to amuse themselves with reminiscences of an epoch now one hundred years in the past. In some cases they have even succeeded in convincing other people: here and there anxious souls see in them the spiritual successors of the men of the Convention. But they are infinitely more harmless than they appear to themselves, for there lives in them not one glimmer of that Catiline energy *of the deed* which agitated the halls of the Convention. By the same token however they possess no trace of the Convention's tremendous *national* passion. Wretched political manipulators – that is what they are. They lack the grand *power* instincts of a class destined for political leadership. The workers are led to believe that only the upholders of capital's interests are at present politically opposed to giving them a share in state power. It is not so. They would find very few traces of a community of interest with capital if they investigated the study-rooms of Germany's scholars and intellectuals.

However the *workers too* must be asked about their *political maturity*. There is nothing more destructive for a great nation than to be led by politically uneducated philistines, and the German proletariat has not yet lost this character of philistinism; that is why we are politically opposed to the proletariat. Why is the proletariat of England and France constituted differently, in part? The reason is not only the longer period of *economic* education accomplished by the English workers' organized fight for their interests; we have once again what is above all a *political* element to bear in mind: *the resonance of a position of world power*. This constantly poses for the state great power-political tasks and gives the individual a political training which we might call 'chronic', whereas with us the training is only received when our borders are threatened, i.e. in 'acute' cases. The question of whether a policy on the grand scale can again place before us the significance of the great political issues of power is also decisive for *our* development. We must understand that the unification of Germany was a youthful prank committed by the nation at an advanced age, and should rather have been avoided on grounds of excessive cost if it was to form the conclusion instead of the point of departure for a policy of German world power.

The *threatening danger* in our situation is this: the bourgeois classes, as repositories of the *power*-interests of the nation, seem to be withering, and there is still no sign that the workers have begun to mature so that they can take their place.

The danger does *not* lie with the masses, as is believed by people who stare as if hypnotized at the depths of society. The final content of the *socio*-political problem is not the question of the *economic* situation of the *ruled* but of the *political* qualifications of the *ruling and rising* classes. The aim of our socio-political activity is not world happiness but the *social unification* of the nation, which has been split apart by modern economic development, for the severe struggles of the future. At present the bourgeoisie is carrying the burden of these struggles, but it is becoming too heavy. Only if we were in fact to succeed in creating a 'labour aristocracy', of the kind we now miss in the workers' movement, which would be the repository of its political sense, only then could the burden be transferred to the broader shoulders of the workers. But that moment still seems a long way away.

For the present, however, one thing is clear: there is an immense labour of *political* education to be performed, and no more serious duty exists for us than that of fulfilling *this* task, each of us in his narrow circle of activity. The ultimate goal of our science must remain that of co-operating in the political education of our nation. The economic development of periods of transition threatens the natural political instincts with decomposition; it would be a misfortune if economic science also moved towards the same objective, by breeding a weak eudaemonism, in however intellectualized a form, behind the illusion of independent 'socio-political' ideals.

Of course we do have to remember, and for that very reason, that it is the opposite of political education when one seeks to formulate a vote of no confidence, paragraph by paragraph, against the nation's future social peace, or when the secular arm reaches for the hand of the church to give support to the temporal authorities. But the opposite of political education is also proclaimed by the stereotyped yelping of the ever growing chorus of the social politicians of the woods and fields – if I may be forgiven the expression. And the same may be said of that softening of attitude which is human, amiable, and worthy of respect, but at the same time unspeakably narrowing in its effects, and leads people to think they can replace political with 'ethical' ideals, and to identify these in turn harmlessly with optimistic expectations of felicity.

In spite of the great misery of the masses, which burdens the sharpened social conscience of the new generation, we have to confess openly that one thing weighs on us even more heavily today: the sense of our responsibility *before history*. Our generation is not destined to see whether the struggle we are engaged in will bear fruit, whether posterity will recognize us as *its forerunners*. We shall not succeed in exorcising the curse that hangs over us: the curse of being posthumous to a great political epoch. Instead we shall have to learn how to be something different: the precursors of an even greater epoch. Will that be our place in history? I do not know, and all I will say is this: youth has the right to stand up for itself and for its ideals. And it is not years which make a man old. He is young as long as he is able to remain sensitive to the grand passions nature has placed within us. And so – you will allow me to conclude with this – a great nation does not age beneath the burden of a thousand years of glorious history. It remains young if it has the capacity and the courage to keep faith with itself and with the grand instincts it has been given, and when its leading strata are able to raise themselves into the hard and clear atmosphere in which the sober activity of German politics flourishes, an atmosphere which is also pervaded by the solemn splendour of national sentiment.

Notes

1. *Gemeindelexikon*, Berlin, 1887.
2. This administrative subdivision is more characteristic evidence of social stratification than a division on the basis of the size of the enterprise. In the plains manorial enterprises of less than 100 hectares are not uncommon, nor, conversely, are peasant enterprises of more than 200 hectares in the hills.
3. For example the manorial estates of the district of Stuhm experienced a decline in population of 6.7 per cent between 1871 and 1885, and the proportion of Protestants in the Christian population fell from 33.4 per cent to 31.3 per cent. The villages of the district of Konitz and Tuchel increased in population by 8 per cent and the proportion of Catholics rose from 84.7 per cent to 86.0 per cent.
4. I need hardly point out the irrelevance for the above comments of the disputes in natural science over the significance of the principles of selection, or over the general application *in natural science* of the concept of 'breeding', and all the discussions which have taken this their starting-point. This is in any case not my field. However, the *concept* of 'selection' is today common ground, just as much as is, e.g., the heliocentric hypothesis, and the idea of 'breeding' human beings is as old as the Platonic state. Both these concepts are employed e.g. by F. A. Lange in his *Arbeiterfrage* [*Die Arbeiterfrage in ihrer Bedeutung für Gegenwart und Zukunft*, (Duisburg, 1865)] and they have long been so familiar to us that a misunderstanding of their meaning is impossible for anyone who knows our literature. More difficult to answer is the question of how much lasting value should be attached to the latest attempts of anthropologists to extend Darwin's

and Weismann's selection concept to the field of economic investigation. They are ingenious, but arouse considerable reservations as to method and factual results, and are no doubt mistaken in a number of exaggerated versions. Nevertheless the writings of e.g. Otto Ammon ('Natural Selection in Man', 'The Social Order and its Natural Basis') deserve more attention than they have been given, irrespective of all the reservations that have to be made. One weakness of most of the contributions made from natural scientific quarters to the illumination of the problems of our science consists in their mistaken ambition to provide above all a 'refutation' of socialism. Their eagerness to attain this goal leads to the involuntary conversion of what was intended to be a 'natural-scientific theory' of the social order into an apology for it.

5.   The same train of thought as mine led Professor Schmoller too to pose the demand for state purchase of land in his journal (*Schmollers Jahrbuch*, 19, 1895, pp. 625ff.). In fact that part of the stratum of big landowners whose retention as agricultural managers is desirable from the state's point of view cannot in most cases be allowed to keep their land in full ownership but only as tenants of the crown demesne. I am certainly of the opinion that the purchase of land only has long-term validity if organically combined with the colonization of suitable crown lands, with the result that a part of the land in the East passes through the hands of the state and while it is in this position undergoes an energetic course of improvement with the assistance of state credits. The Settlement Commission [set up in 1886 to buy Polish estates and settle German farmers on them. Trans.] has to contend with two difficulties in this connection. One is that it is burdened with the 'after-effects of the cure', in the shape of the colonists who have been planted and who ought preferably to be handed over after a while, along with their requests to postpone repayment to the ordinary state treasury, which is somewhat more hard-hearted than the Commission. The other difficulty derives from the fact that the estates which have been purchased have been for the most part in the hands of crown tenants for over a decade. Now the improvement must be carried out at breakneck speed and with great losses by the administration itself, although certainly a large number of crown lands would be suitable for immediate colonization. The consequent dilatoriness of the procedure does not by any means justify the judgment of Hans Delbrück on the national-political impact, delivered in his many well-known articles in the *Preussische Jahrbücher*. A merely mechanical calculation, comparing the number of peasant farms founded with the number of Poles, is not conclusive proof for anyone who has observed the civilizing effect of colonization on the spot: a few villages with a dozen German farms each will eventually *Germanize* many square miles, naturally with the pre-condition that the flood of proletarian reinforcements from the East is dammed up, and that we do not cut the ground from under the feet of those who are bringing progress, by leaving the big estates to the free play of the forces which are leading to their fragmentation and ruin, and are acting with even less restraint now thanks to the laws on renting land in perpetuity.

6.   Translator's note: this is a reference by Weber to the old German legend that the Emperor Frederick Barbarossa was not dead but waiting in the heart of the Kyffhäuser mountains in Thuringia to come forth and lead the German people against their enemies. Bismarck's own estate was located in the Sachsenwald.

CHAPTER 8

Germany as an industrial state

Max Weber
translated by K. Tribe

At the eighth meeting of the *Evangelisch-soziale Kongreß* in June 1987 an address was presented by Karl Oldenberg on the future of the German economy. Taking his point of departure from the second occupational census of 1895, he drew attention to the shift of the employed population from agriculture to industry, speculating that if this trend were to continue, in seventy to eighty years Germany would be an 'industrial state'. By this he meant that the livelihood of all Germans would be based upon industrial production which was necessarily export-oriented; and his development of this idea introduced into debate a new counterconcept, that of the 'industrial' as opposed to the 'agrarian' state. For Oldenberg, the former meant a condition in which German labour power became simply a commodity sold upon the world market, that is, involved a dependency upon 'foreigners'; while the latter option was seen by him as a condition of independence through self-sufficiency. Oldenberg's presentation was very long, and he was forced to leave to one side a projected second half in which he was to outline some positive proposals. However, a version of the address which was published shortly afterwards limited itself to some minor additions to the text as presented, and so the projected remainder never materialized.

In 1901 Adolf Wagner published a collection of his newspaper articles upon this theme under the title *Agrar-und Industriestaat*. The substance of his arguments went no further here than Oldenberg's original presentation, and it is noteworthy that neither he nor Oldenberg seriously considered the nature and consequences of the 'agrarian state' as a self-sufficient, autarchic economy. Nevertheless, the emergence of this debate in Germany at the turn of the century is significant since the blockade by the Allies during the First World War forced Germany into a degree of autarchy, and the whole conception of an autarchic economy persisted in German and Russian conceptions of economic strategy until mid-century.

The meeting of the *Kongreß* took place in Leipzig on 10–11 June 1897. In January that year Weber had been appointed the successor of Knies as Professor of Economics and Financial Science at Heidelberg, and it was only shortly after Weber delivered this speech in Leipzig that he had the altercation with his father that is widely held to have prompted his illness of the following years. Max Weber senior died on 10 August of that year without being reconciled with his son; Marianne Weber's biography mentions that the funeral rites for the father took place some seven weeks after the family row. Weber's active participation in the Leipzig meeting therefore brings to a close the public political engagement that had marked his work since 1893; although no year was to go by without some kind of publication, the next significant publication of Weber's (the first part of the essay on Roscher and Knies) is six years later, in 1903. This opens a new phase in his work.

Ladies and Gentlemen! For my part I did not share the dread which seized our chairman on hearing the presentation of my friend Oldenberg, and moreover I cannot say that I am as curious as he is with respect to the positive side of the remarks made by the previous speaker. For *there is no* positive side to these remarks. This is clear from his own words – positive future ideals are lacking to the same extent that his strength lies in criticism. And it is my opinion that a sharp and aggressive critique of the kind presented here of the actual or alleged course taken by our economic policy is only justifiable when positive ideals lie behind this critique, and when the critic seeks to outline a more preferable path or at least believes that he recognizes some such path. But here even the critique itself seems to me to be unhappy in nearly every respect. I am able to deal with only a few of these points.

Ladies and Gentlemen! When my colleague Oldenberg began his philippic against the promotion of export I thought that he would eventually refer to the premiums on sugar, the legislation relating to the taxation on spirits – those export premiums by which we endow *agricultural* exports with a special status equivalent to the form lent to duties on corn. For here – in the subsidizing of *agriculture* – is where we find the *sole* examples of genuine export premiums known to us in Germany. I know of nothing similar in the domain of industry, nor of any country based upon exports; but the talk here was all the same of an *export-industry-state*.

Of course my colleague touched upon certain relations in the area of the iron industry as an example of 'latent' export premiums in manufacture: the practice, which can be observed in certain industrial cartels, by which cheap prices are set abroad to undercut foreign competitors, the dearer prices charged at home making this possible. If one asks oneself however where there is here a real premium upon exports – in so far as *state* measures are involved which are comparable with the preferential treatment of agriculture – then we find it in the duties on iron; and from that the *positive* conclusion of my colleague should be for *free trade* in

iron, hence the breaching of that same national economic policy
which he seeks to intensify. This is proof enough of the
arbitrariness of his criticism. I for my part do not at present
advocate such a measure, but what other positive means for the
removal of this *sole* instance of 'export promotion' in the industrial
domain my colleague Oldenberg might have in mind he did not
say, nor do I know of any. Having made this correction let us now
come to the real heart of his critique.

In a certain respect Oldenberg's lecture, in many ways excellent
and logically sharp, deserves to become a monument. Nothing
illustrates so clearly the massive shift in opinion on economic
policy in Germany which we have experienced in the last quarter-
century. Then it was taken for granted that increasing exports
were a quite natural expression of an increasing international
division of labour and production, conditioned by variations in
climate and location of production, hence something quite as
natural and healthy as the exchange of goods *within* geographical
areas united politically by the accident of history. But today we
have experienced a prominent German economist who, before an
assembly of economists who regard this international exchange of
goods not as something to be artificially promoted but rather as
something which has to some extent become something *unavoidable*, stands up and believes himself able to accuse them of 'idiotic
money-economy prejudice'.

Now we no longer have that technological optimism and belief
in free-trade dogmas that we shared twenty-five years ago; that has
gone for good. But this does not alter the fact that this view did
have a core of truth, and it is this core that my colleague
Oldenberg has ignored in a hardly believable fashion.

If, ladies and gentlemen, you followed closely the lecture of
Oldenberg so you must have gained the impression – those of you
at any rate who have never had in their hands a statistical
summary of Germany's external trade – that the customers for our
exports are nine-tenths the savages of Africa, East Asia and South
America along with similar specifically *backward* peoples with
respect to capitalist and industrial development; that the 'pillars'
supporting the export 'verandas and balconies' of our industry are
planted in the unfamiliar land of sombre barbarian countries and
strive to extend themselves there further, so that when others
come along and knock away these pillars then the building,
according to Oldenberg, will collapse; and that further in the
course of development these lands will in turn *dwindle* to an
'industrial state' or to a condition of export capitalism. Those
among you who gained this impression will after this lecture be
astonished to learn from export surveys that our greatest customer

for exported goods is *England*. That it is the economically most
developed, the great capitalistically-developed nations and
especially the industrial states among them who are our greatest
customers, and particularly of our *industrial* products – Oldenberg's
presentation was silent on this point. With that the whole terrible
image of horror drawn for the problematic future of those distant
peoples now in the beginnings of capitalist development collapses.
I do not belong to those optimists of capitalism and of the
integration of the international division of labour whom my
colleague Oldenberg was primarily criticizing. But I find it
impossible to share with him the attempt to characterize as 'export
promotion' those barriers to be placed in the way of the natural
development of the markets for German industry through
measures imposed by the economic policy of our competitors –
barriers which should be removed by commercial treaties. He
indicated that export involves a dependence upon the policies of
foreign powers, and argued from there that the resulting
fluctuations in certainty concerning the prospects of commerce
become greater in step with the increase of exports. On the
contrary, it is my opinion that the rising significance of fixed
capital will gradually bring about a situation in leading nations
whereby interest in a *stabilization* of mutual trade relations will
gain a constantly increasing force. *Absolute uncertainty* with respect
to the conditions of existence of domestic industry will become
rather a characteristic of those nations which pursue an 'autonomous' policy on tariffs of the kind which Oldenberg obviously
regards as ideal. Despite this, I go along with my colleague
Oldenberg in regarding as a massive *risk* the progressive shift of a
portion of the economic activity of our domestic population onto
the market-opportunities presented by exports, a risk that the
nation in economic terms takes upon itself. But this is the same
risk that all great trading and industrial peoples of the past, all
leading peoples in cultural development in the past, all great
nations of the past at the time of their greatness have taken upon
themselves; and it is my opinion that we are not pursuing a policy
of national *comfort* but rather one of *greatness*, hence we must take
this burden upon our shoulders if we wish to have a national
existence other than that of Switzerland, for example. I am further
of the opinion that historical development *will not ask us* whether
we want it. If we seek to refuse our imposed fate then something
quite different to the rural idyll of Oldenberg will develop here. If
one accepts that, consequent upon the immobilization of commercial development in the way that Oldenberg wishes, there follows
a mass emigration of our psychically and physically strongest men,
then there will be for the remainder, or residuum, some form of

'rural' existence; but it has to be made plain that this self-satisfied policy of Oldenberg practically means that Germany calls out to its best children: 'Find another home, for I want peace and quiet.' How it is with 'inner impoverishment' in the one and the other case – that is ultimately a matter of taste. I would like to stand Oldenberg before the real representative of the 'independent economy' (*Eigenwirtschaft*) which he presents to us in the mode of 'village stories'; to present him to a Kassubian peasant and, placing alongside this peasant a worker chosen from our entire export industry, seeing where Oldenberg can find 'inner wealth'. Those who would be most astonished at the idyllic pictures that he unfurls would certainly be those who have to exist in these 'independent economies'.

But I do not see why I should devote so much attention to the question of *exports*. Oldenberg himself in his essay on unemployment made the (in my opinion erroneous) claim that our exports were not increasing. But here today we are dealing with the 'industrial state', and the whole of the first half of Oldenberg's presentation was an angry thrust against industrialism and capitalism, against the domination and leading role of capital. Of course the international division of labour is a normal corollary of expanding capitalism; but if one so to say strikes it dead that does not mean today that capitalism is dead. Instead of Oldenberg's wrath at capitalism a more fitting question from the scientific point of view would be: *can* this capitalistic development for Germany be prevented, and so long as Oldenberg merely asserts the opposite, then I say: *no, it cannot be prevented*, for us it is unavoidable and it is only possible to economically influence the course which it takes. Whether the economic policy which Oldenberg seems to want would direct capitalist development into a more *agreeable* course is more than doubtful. Restriction to domestic industrial development means that German capital would to an ever increasing extent seek investments *abroad* and the most capable elements of our industrial population would drain away; remaining behind we would have lazy rentiers and a dull traditionalistic mass; in the place of the industrialism that a healthy mercantile policy seeks to create there would develop a *rentier* capitalism. The German capitalist draws his profit from *foreign* enterprises. Is this the ideal of my colleague Oldenberg?

Let us however consider the rural side of the course of development which he presents to us. If one were to accept Oldenberg's critique, one would have to ask: what is to take the place of this capitalist organization of the economy? On this Oldenberg is silent; he doesn't say a word. But according to the indications that he has given he clearly seeks an intensification of the so-called 'national economic policy' of the kind that Bismarck inaugurated in 1879. For my part I regard this policy as a necessary phase of our development, but let us consider what its continuation and intensification would mean. Nothing other than the maintenance and extension of capitalism in *agriculture* alongside capitalism in industry. The *market-oriented production of corn in a money economy* favours, and is intended to favour, that coalition of interests which is created by this particular economic policy. This 'company business', this association of *large-landowning* capitalist interests and the capital of *large industrial* concerns is something which we can now become thoroughly acquainted with as a consequence of isolationist policy, the policy of the 'internal market'.

It is this coalition of interests that has produced all those phenomena and which has met with united opposition, and which my colleague Oldenberg here opposed without directly naming it as such and to which opposition I have also I think to add myself, no matter how little I do for example agree in every detail with Brentano or my friend Schulze-Gävernitz. This coalition came into being in the 1860s, and brought about the linking of the large industrial bourgeoisie with the interests of large landownership – one could say that it involved the feudalization of bourgeois capital. That was its great success, and this success implied politically the preservation of domination on the part of the eastern Junkers whose economic base had become uncertain, and whose interest previous economic policy had served virtually exclusively. For in contrast to Miquel's repeated claims, in contrast to the conclusions one would have to draw on the basis of Oldenberg's speech, I believe that we have *never* pursued any other policy than that which was acceptable to the interests of landed property, to agricultural interests and *not* industrial interests. This does not mean of course that this objectively corresponded to their economic interests, since the given interested parties are not always the most objective judges of that which is in the *lasting* interest of their *Stand*. We were freetraders so long as large landowners in Prussia were, for as long as the saying held: 'I am conservative and therefore a freetrader'; and we became Protectionists the moment that particular events caused large landowners to turn to protection. During the period that industry could have had absolute need of protective duties we gave in to the interest of agriculture and abolished such duties; only when agriculture become Protectionist, when the coalition of which I spoke came into being, did we gain a 'national economic policy'. And just as soon this coalition brought forth its peculiar fruits.

We experienced that curious welling up of that purely

superficial and formal bureaucratic religiosity peculiar to feudalism and conservatism, to the officer estate and feudalized officialdom, the penetration of this bureaucratically formal ecclesiastic spirit (*Kirchlichkeit*) into our bourgeoisie. We experienced the turn to the feudal aspects of the moral attitudes of our ruling strata. I myself clearly remember from my younger years how the perhaps 'petty-bourgeois' views of bourgeois circles became feudalized, passing on to their offspring for example views concerning what is honourable and dishonourable in the sexual domain, i.e. were altered in favour of other views which derived not from the bourgeoisie but from those circles with which they then identified themselves. More recently we have endured the disagreeable sight of the ennobled industrialist making a public show of duelling, truly a disgusting spectacle for adherents of the sport; duellists who are not representatives of the old aristocracy but rather blustering parvenus before whom the Prussian Minister of Culture must tremble – so much so that he has to make recourse to a clever misunderstanding of the expression 'practitioner'. They are the very same persons who yearn for the moment when social policy will be conducted with cannons. The further proliferation of this *feudalization of bourgeois capital* will be the 'rural' idyll which will be delivered by an economic policy shaped in the manner that Oldenberg wishes. For this coalition is based upon that economic conception which constitutes the *sole possible* positive reverse of Oldenberg's critique: the theory of the fostering of the '*internal market*' in place of the international division of labour, that is to say, a situation in which: 1. German industry is offered a substitute for the limitation of exports by the artificially increased purchasing power of agriculture; and 2. Germany is supposed to meet its entire requirement for grain out of its domestic production. Here, in this theory, and especially in the second point, lies the decisive problem. For what my colleague finds odious is not that goods are exported, but that grain is and must be imported.

In this Oldenberg has assumed that Germany is an economic unit, believing that he could pose the question of whether Germany, that is, this *unit*, should proceed further along this path to the 'industrial state'. *Germany is not however an economic unit*, Germany is welded together out of two quite distinct economic regions in which one looks to the West and the other to the East; in which the former has for some time been an 'industrial state' and the latter has until now remained an 'agrarian state'; and the fundamental problem of our entire national economic policy rests in the unstable relation of these two halves, parting as they do roughly speaking along the Elbe and the lower Weser and which while belonging together politically, diverge economically.

The practical side of this problem is in the question: can we create an 'internal market' for our industry in this agrarian half through protective tariffs for agriculture, thereby replacing the market for industrial exports – and in addition, can we so arrange our economic policy that it will be possible to feed our entire population from our own land, that is, from the surplus of that agrarian half meet the requirements of the industrial half? Should we or should we not pursue an economic policy which concentrates upon *this* problem, *can* we above all pursue such a policy?

Today I wish to say only a few words on this decisive question. Since the population of Germany is rapidly growing, the surplus of the agrarian half which appears in the market also has to be constantly *increased*. If this is to happen a constant *reduction* of the rural population of the agrarian half is necessary. Seen from the perspective of providing the highest possible marketed share for feeding the German population the countryside of Germany is today still overpopulated – our peasants and the products of our policy of inner colonization *are harmful*. Two things that are often confused are all the same not identical, but rather the *opposite*: a strong *i.e. numerous rural population* on the one hand, and on the other large *surpluses* of corn over that required for *needs* of that population. The more thickly settled the countryside, the *less* the surplus that is available for the towns, the food supply of which therefore *increasingly depends upon the import of grain, which becomes progressively more indispensable* and thus even more reliant on the *export* of the industrial goods so detested by Oldenberg. Whoever wishes to produce the maximum grain yield on German soil in the interest of subsisting a maximum number of people with domestic corn must needs carve the land up into rationally-managed *large enterprises*, and thereby depopulate the countryside for the benefit of the towns – and thereby also favouring the increase of the industrial proletariat. So that as much corn as possible might be gained in the most economical manner the rural population will henceforth drain into the towns and thus provide industrial entrepreneurs with a cheap pool of poorly-paid labour power, thereby enabling continued capitalist development and also *cheap exports*. This is the curious circle within which the economic policy proposed by my colleague Oldenberg would travel. I will soon show that this is not mere theory by using the results of the population census for specific periods to show how the movement of the rural population does *in fact* follow these regularities. Production for the agricultural *market* drives the population off the land. A numerous German rural population and the feeding of Germany solely from domestic grain is an irreconcilable contradiction.

How then do things stand with the 'internal market' which is to be offered to our industry by this policy of 'self-sufficiency'? The idea behind this 'internal market' can be summarized as follows: so that German entrepreneurs might secure ready purchasers among German agriculturalists the latter are granted yet more corn duties, that means a contribution paid out of the pockets of the industrial workers – not *only* from their pockets, but *also* out of ours, but so long as we are considering the relation between industry and agriculture, then from the pocket of the industrial worker. This contribution from the pocket of the worker flows into that of the agriculturalist and from there into that of the industrial entrepreneur, whose products the 'moneyed' agriculturalist purchases. It is our own workers who, via agriculture, have to pay for the 'internal market' of the industrialist, for the burdening of the remaining part of the population *reduces* their purchasing power with respect to industrial products by the same amount that the purchasing power of agriculture is correspondingly increased. Put theoretically, that is the curious circle that is called the 'extension of the internal market'. The intensification of this economic system does not mean the *diminution* of capitalism, but rather its *enhancement* – an enhanced differentiation of incomes, an enhanced proletarianization of the workforce that pays for the 'internal market'. Out of this there develops that peculiarly conservative *domestic capitalism* which seeks its gain not in the opening up of new markets but rather in the economic suppression of the workforce, in economic terms promotes class struggle *from above* and in political terms sees its deadly enemy to be the rise of the working class and free institutions in the land. This is the *social policy* associated with Oldenberg's programme – a programme from which he with good reason is shy of presenting positively, but which is all the same the *sole positive* side of his critique. He will have spoken from the heart to those interested in *this* capitalism.

All those whom today my colleague Oldenberg has attacked are opposed to the artificial creation of such circumstances. They want a civil politics, they wish for the disengagement of a self-centred bourgeoisie, perpetually caught up in a self-conscious nursing of its own ideals, from its unnatural association, in the interest of progressive social development and in that of the development of political freedom in the land.

While Oldenberg threatened us with a time when land and bread would be short, we on the other hand think that it is not the alleged export policy but rather the *increase of population* – whatever may be the economic organization of the earth – which will in the future intensify the struggle for existence, the struggle of man against man; we conclude therefore that the gospel of *struggle* is a national duty, an unavoidable economic task for individual and for the collectivity of which we are not 'ashamed' and represents for us the sole path to greatness. We know well enough that the further development of the nation has to lead to the constitution of its future. We regard that however as an unavoidable consequence of historical development, and we believe that those nations which today fail to mobilize their economic future for national greatness do not in fact have a future. (Vigorous applause and hissing)

[Two further contributions followed that of Weber, one from Max Lorenz and one from the prominent conservative economist Adolf Wagner. While Lorenz warmly supported Weber's criticisms of Oldenberg and added his own, Wagner confined himself to supporting some of the points made in the original presentation and in general associating himself with the arguments that Oldenberg had advanced. In so doing he adopted a position with respect to Weber similar to that which had emerged at the 1894 meeting when, following Weber's presentation, Wagner sought to blur the choices which were identified by Weber rather than reject Weber's line of argument. Weber must have felt this at the time, for he made some additional remarks before Oldenberg made his concluding observations.]

Two words in reply to some remarks of Professor Wagner. He asked why it should be that not only the East Elbian Junker but also the French and Rhenish peasant are supporters of grain duties? Might I reply to that: that is because every person takes what he can. From the fact that the offer of increased grain prices is quietly pocketed by those peasants it does not follow that they have *need* of it. If they were presented with the question of whether they would prefer to do without protective grain tariffs *or* do without the development of the industry along the Rhine which represents the only ready consumer for their products, then they would after a brief trial adopt a position on Germany's development towards an 'industrial state' that would diverge radically from that of Oldenberg.

Permit me with my second remark to repeat once more a point that I believe has escaped Professor Wagner, since he otherwise would not have been able to make many of his own comments. My colleague Oldenberg and it appears Professor Wagner seem to share the prevailing illusion that two things are identical: on the one hand the presence of a quantum of domestic grain at the disposal of the population's requirements and adequate to them, and on the other a numerous German rural population. These two things are not however the same; they are opposites. The thinner the rural population (and it is at its thinnest where large enterprises predominate) the greater the grain surplus available for urban consumption; whereas a more densely-settled rural area has correspondingly less grain available for the towns. Every augmentation of Germany's peasant population renders the import of grain for Germany's industrial population ever more indispensable. The more the rural population increases, the more grain that has to be imported, and the more the industrial portion of the population edges out on to the 'balcony' of which Oldenberg spoke.

Finally another remark. Professor Wagner was surprised that I became so heated in my comments on my friend Oldenberg. He himself will be least able to understand this. We do not mince words, just as little as Professor Wagner. I was struck by the mischievous expression concerning 'a national greatness of which one should be ashamed'. There is no such national greatness of this sort for me. In conclusion I can only recapitulate: with respect to the future of German development there are optimists and pessimists. Now I do not belong among the optimists. I also recognize the enormous risk which the inevitable outward economic expansion of Germany places upon us. But I regard this risk as unavoidable and therefore say: 'So must you be, you will not escape from yourself.' (Applause)

[In replying to the discussion, Oldenberg expressed puzzlement at the point Weber makes here relating to the density of the rural population, and argues that it is not a matter of gross, but of net product. Oldenberg's confusion on this point turns on the fact that an increase in the density of peasant settlement means that the size of holding declines while the number of 'mouths' to be subsisted from each holding increases, reducing the marketable surplus. Oldenberg's reference to the decline of the density of English rural settlement and the absolute decline of English agriculture further underscores his failure to grasp the basic principles at stake. Winding up, the chairman suggested that, if the participants agreed, the meeting might pass a resolution on the social and ethical dangers confronting the German people if national capital was ever more placed in the one-sided service of export-oriented industry. This indicates that he also had not properly understood Weber's argument; and when Weber objected to such a resolution from the floor, the idea was dropped.]

Index